P9-BAV-281

The BOOK of BOOKS

**The Continuously Updated Book Guide
To Recommended Reading, Including
The Best Novels And Nonfiction From
The Classics And Best Sellers
To The Newest Top Authors**

Second Edition

TheBookofBooks.org

Contact information: Info@TheBookofBooks.org

VISIT OUR WEBSITE:
TheBookofBooks.org

This volume is the main title in
The Book of Books Series

Best Fiction, A Companion to The Book of Books
Books for Children, A Companion Title to The Book of Books

Copyright 2013 ©The Book of Books.org

Publisher: Les Krantz
Editor-in-chief: Timothy Knight

Managing Editor: Marjorie Krantz
Associate Editor: Saxon Burns
Manuscript Editor: Chris Smith
Assistant Editor: Ellen Krolow

Contributing Writers:
Paul Adomites, Ken DuBois, Sharon Exley,
Elizabeth Foz, Pam Grady, Ross Levine, Debra Ott

TABLE OF CONTENTS

INTRODUCTION

The days when we asked our local bookseller for reading recommendations are sadly fading from memory. How fondly some of us recall the great booksellers who are now gone: Scribner's of New York, Stewart Brent of Chicago, Dutton's Brentwood Books of Los Angeles and myriad other bookstores across America where we loved to "talk books." Booksellers catered to our literary tastes and helped us buy new titles that they just *knew* were right for us. Those treasured recommendations came from pros who read for a living and got to know our literary tastes, too. How can we forget the relationship!

Not long after we bid farewell to many of our trusted booksellers, Borders Books and Music closed too, amid an explosion of self-published eBooks — some great ones, some awful. Indeed the book world is vastly different now as we launch our second edition of *The Book of Books,* originally published in 2007.

These changes in the book world have made this new edition of *The Book of Books* all the more relevant. Instead of well-read booksellers to guide us through the *millions* of titles in print, this volume offers recommendations from our staff of literary professionals, including publishers, editors, critics, scholars and authors whose names you will find on the copyright page. Who better to turn to for a book recommendation? And since we've embedded Amazon.com links in every title of the eBook version, you can not only read more about these books online, but you can purchase them too, with just one click or tap on your eReader.

We have also expanded our coverage to a wider range of literary genres: 116 to be exact, encompassing over 1,000 book titles. And while there's no shortage of books by the usual suspects, i.e., "dead white men," we also feature notable books by African-American, Asian-American and Latino novelists, among others. In the pages that follow, Russian classics are found with illustrated children's books, political memoirs, Christian self-help titles, Civil War histories, romance novels, zombie books and more. Our recommendations encompass *both* the sure-fire classics and exciting finds from the hottest new authors.

In sum, this new edition of *The Book of Books* is an amalgam of the best of yesterday and today: recommendations for books and eBooks that you can easily purchase online. It's also an entertaining and essential must-read for people whose passion for books is best summed up by the following quote from the ancient Roman philosopher/politician Cicero: "A room without books is like a body without a soul."

We couldn't agree more. Enjoy!

AFRICAN-AMERICAN NOVELS
Stories of African-American Life, 1900 to Present

When Ralph Ellison died at the age of eighty in 1994, the *New York Times* eulogized him as "one of the major American writers of the 20th century." That Ellison merited such a glowing tribute is remarkable, when you consider the fact that he published only *one* novel in his lifetime. Then again, *Invisible Man* is a novel like no other — a magnificently realized portrait of a young African-American man confronting racism as he struggles to find his identity in a country that can't see past the color of his skin. Praised by Irving Howe as "a soaring and exalted record of a Negro's journey through contemporary America" in *The Nation*, Ellison's first novel won the 1953 National Book Award. His long-awaited and long-delayed follow-up, **Juneteenth**, would appear five years after his death, but despite mostly favorable reviews, it probably won't have the shelf life of *Invisible Man* — one of twelve books by African-American writers, listed alphabetically, that evoke African-American life from 1900 to today in all its complexity and diversity.

1. **Another Country** by James Baldwin, 1962 – Sensual, passionate novel about a group of Greenwich Village friends crossing sexual and racial boundaries as they search for meaning following a friend's suicide. Baldwin's matter-of-fact depiction of homosexuality and bisexuality shocked readers and critics in 1962. Today, *Another Country* is recognized as a brave and groundbreaking classic, championed by authors ranging from Toni Morrison to Anthony Burgess (***A Clockwork Orange***), who included in his 1984 book, ***Ninety-Nine Novels: The Best in English Since 1939 – A Personal Choice***.

2. **A Gathering of Old Men** by Ernest J. Gaines, 1983 – In rural, seventies-era Louisiana, a group of elderly African-American men tempt violent retribution when they stand up to racist locals, out to avenge the murder of a Cajun farmer. A finely-etched and riveting novel from the author of the National Book Critics Circle Award-winning ***A Lesson Before Dying***. A Louisiana native, Gaines burst into literary prominence with ***The Autobiography of Miss Jane Pittman***. In honor of his contributions to literature, the University of Louisiana at Lafayette established the Ernest J. Gaines Center in 2008.

3. **The Healing** by Gayl Jones, 1998 – An itinerant faith healer reflects on her rough-and-tumble, often bizarre life as she travels through the rural South. A finalist for the National Book Award, *The Healing* is a virtuoso, stream-of-consciousness novel from the author of ***Corregidora***. Reviewing *The Healing* in the *New York Times*, novelist Valerie Martin hailed it as "a rich, complicated narrative."

4. **The Intuitionist** by Colson Whitehead, 1998 – An ingenious and wildly original, genre-spanning novel that succeeds as both a futuristic mystery and racial

allegory. In the world's tallest city, the only black female elevator inspector must clear her name when she's blamed for the "total free fall" of an elevator. A finalist for the Hemingway/PEN Award, *The Intuitionist* has drawn comparisons to Thomas Pynchon's satirical novel ***The Crying of Lot 49***.

5. **Invisible Man** by Ralph Ellison, 1952 – Ellison's masterpiece was chosen one of *Time* magazine's one hundred best English-language novels published since 1923. Sixty years after its publication, *Invisible Man* has lost none of its visceral power. In a 2012 essay for *The Daily Beast*, novelist Nathaniel Rich wrote that readers "experience American history as a nightmare" in the pages of Ellison's novel.

EXCERPT: INVISIBLE MAN:

There was a rush against me and I fell, hearing a single explosion, backward into a whirl of milling legs, overshoes, the trampled snow cold on my hands. Another shot sounded above like a bursting bag. Managing to stand, I saw atop the steps the fist with the gun being forced into the air above the crowd's bobbing heads and the next instant they were dragging him down into the snow; punching him left and right, uttering a low tense swelling sound of
desperate effort; a grunt that exploded into a thousand softly spat, hate-sizzling curses.

6. **Kindred** by Octavia Butler, 1979 – The first science fiction writer awarded a MacArthur Fellowship (also known as a "genius" grant), Butler received the prestigious Hugo and Nebula Awards for her novels and short stories. *Kindred*, which she described as a "grim fantasy," is a provocative and unsettling time-travel novel about Dana, a black woman in modern day California, who is transported back to the antebellum South, where she saves the life of Rufus, the young son of a plantation owner. It's a selfless act that has profound repercussions — Rufus will grow up to be the owner of Dana's slave ancestors.

7. **Little Scarlet: An Easy Rawlins Novel** by Walter E. Mosley, 2004 – Set against the backdrop of the Watts riots of 1965, Mosley's ninth book in his Easy Rawlins mystery series finds the world-weary private eye investigating the murder of a young woman known as Little Scarlet. What he ultimately learns will force Rawlins to examine his conflicted feelings about the riots. Another outstanding book from Mosley, whom former President Clinton named as one of his favorite writers.

8. **Meridian** by Alice Walker, 1976 – Walker's excellent second novel follows an educated young black woman whose unwavering commitment to the civil rights movement ultimately takes a toll on her health. Walker reportedly drew on her own experiences as a sixties-era civil rights activist to write *Meridian*, which the

New York Times hailed as "a fine, taut novel that accomplishes a remarkable amount."

9. **Native Son** by Richard Wright, 1940 – After he accidentally kills the daughter of his wealthy white boss, a young black man finds himself trapped in a downward spiral that climaxes with his arrest and trial. More than seventy years after Wright's debut novel ignited a firestorm of controversy, this classic hasn't lost its power to shock. Wright later earned widespread acclaim for his autobiography ***Black Boy: A Record of Childhood and Youth.***

10. **Open City** by Teju Cole, 2011 – Julius, a young Nigerian doctor, wanders the streets of Manhattan, grappling with his past and the notions of home, in Cole's acclaimed debut novel, the winner of the Hemingway Foundation/PEN Award for a distinguished first book of fiction. Poetic and subtle, Cole's luminous prose draws readers into Julius' existential journey, which ultimately takes him to three cities on three continents. A writer, photographer and art historian of Nigerian descent, Cole has drawn frequent and favorable comparisons to W. G. Sebald (***Austerlitz***) for what *The New Statesman* called his "dreamlike and meandering" approach to narrative.

11. **Salvage the Bones** by Jesmyn Ward, 2011 – Ward's compelling novel depicts the struggles of four motherless children, abandoned by their drunken father as a hurricane threatens to strike their rural community on Mississippi's Gulf Coast. The *New York Times* hailed *Salvage the Bones* as "smartly plotted and voluptuously written," particularly with regard to the heroine Esch, a pregnant fifteen-year-old "who breaks the mold of the typical teenage female protagonist. Esch isn't plucky or tomboyish. She's squat, sulky and sexual. But she is beloved." The winner of the 2011 National Book Award.

12. **Song of Solomon** by Toni Morrison, 1977 – Oprah Winfrey's favorite novelist won the National Book Critics Circle Award for her third novel, a masterful and poetic saga about a black Michigan family with the unfortunate last name of Dead. Although it's revered as a classic — and President Barack Obama named it one of his all-time favorite books— *Song of Solomon* has frequently been challenged by school boards for its frank depiction of sexuality.

ALLEGORICAL LITERATURE
More Than Meets the Eye

For all the pure entertainment that reading brings us, one of its most intellectually satisfying pleasures is discovering the metaphorical and symbolic meanings of a literary work. Allegories give vivid form to beliefs, political arguments, and any number of ideas and experiences through the use of symbolic characters, settings and events. Here are five classic allegories, listed in chronological order of publication.

1. **The Faerie Queene** by Edmund Spenser, 1596 – Written in Elizabethan England, this fantastical epic poem is full of characters who represent various virtues, vices, and political figures, especially the Catholic enemies of the Queen. Then there is Gloriana, the Faerie Queene, who represents Queen Elizabeth herself.

2. **The Pilgrim's Progress** by John Bunyan, 1678 – The pilgrim is a man named Christian, who's warned by Evangelist to abandon the City of Destruction and go instead to the Celestial City. On his journey, Christian encounters all kinds of challenges, arguments, and temptations to waver from the right path. He manages to find his way out of the Slough of Despond, Vanity Fair, and all the other troubles along his way in this an inspiring religious adventure story.

3. **The Tale of a Tub** by Jonathan Swift, 1704 – Swift makes fun of religious extremists in the story of three brothers — Peter, Jack, and Martin — who represent the Roman Catholic Church, English Protestant dissenters, and Lutherans or Anglicans, respectively. When their father dies they receive coats (representing pure Christianity) with instructions not to alter them, but Peter's instinct for ornamentation and Jack's opposing impulse to rip his coat to tatters keep them from living peacefully.

4. **The Metamorphosis** by Franz Kafka, 1915 – The dehumanization of modern life becomes literal in this story of an earnest fellow named Gregor Samsa. He works hard as a traveling salesman, laboring to pay off a large debt his parents owe his employer, but is forced to miss work for the first time in five years when he wakes up one morning "transformed in his bed into a gigantic insect." He injures himself trying to maneuver his body around, and when he ventures out of his room his family drives him right back in — in all, one of the grimmest and most affecting short stories you'll ever read.

5. **Animal Farm** by George Orwell, 1945 – Oppressed by their human masters, the animals of a farm decide to revolt and reorganize it along the lines of justice and equality. Over time their ideals become corrupted as their leaders, the pigs, begin to abuse their power. Even the early slogans of the movement are changed — from "All animals are equal," for example, to "All animals are equal, but some animals are more equal than others." Orwell's depiction of liberators turning into oppressors mirrors the course of the Soviet Union under Stalin.

EXCERPT: ANIMAL FARM:

At this moment there was a tremendous uproar. While Major was speaking four large rats had crept out of their holes and were sitting on their hindquarters, listening to him. The dogs had suddenly caught sight of them, and it was only by a swift dash for their holes that the rats saved their lives. Major raised his trotter for silence.

"Comrades," he said, "here is a point that must be settled. The wild creatures, such as rats and rabbits-are they our friends or our enemies? Let us put it to the vote. I propose this question to the meeting: Are rats comrades?"

The vote was taken at once, and it was agreed by an overwhelming majority that rats were comrades. There were only four dissentients, the three dogs and the cat, who was afterwards discovered to have voted on both sides.

AMERICAN NOVELS
Top Ten Favorites of 125 Authors

Universally acknowledged as Mark Twain's masterpiece, *The Adventures of Huckleberry Finn* holds an exalted place in the American literary canon. The normally vitriolic critic H. L. Mencken hailed it as "the full equal of ___**Don Quixote**___." And Ernest Hemingway called Twain's picaresque classic "the best book we've had … There was nothing before. There has been nothing as good since."

Although Hemingway made that bold proclamation in his 1934 book ___**The Green Hills of Africa,**___ his opinion is apparently shared by many contemporary authors. In the 2007 book ___**The Top Ten: Writers Pick Their Favorite Books**___, editor J. Peter Zane asked 125 writers, including such literary heavyweights as Stephen King, Norman Mailer and Annie Proulx, to list their ten favorite novels. When the responses were tallied for American fiction, *The Adventures of Huckleberry Finn* topped the following list of the top ten novels by American authors.

1. **The Adventures of Huckleberry Finn** by Mark Twain, 1885 – Twain's account of the title character's raft journey down the Mississippi River with a runaway slave is a magnificent, multi-layered achievement. Through their encounters with unsavory and colorful characters, Huck comes to regard his companion Jim, a runaway slave, as the one honorable and trustworthy man he knows. One of the most frequently challenged and banned books in the United States, primarily because of Twain's use of racial epithets, *The Adventures of Huckleberry Finn* continues to promote debate, 127 years after its publication.

EXCERPT: THE ADVENTURES OF HUCKLEBERRY FINN:

I set down again, a shaking all over, and got out my pipe for a smoke; for the house was all as still as death, now, and so the widow wouldn't know. Well, after a long time I heard the clock away off in the town go boom—boom—boom— twelve licks—and all still again—stiller than ever. Pretty soon I heard a twig snap, down in the dark amongst the trees—something was a stirring. I set still and listened. Directly I could just barely hear a 'me-yow! me-yow!' down there. That was good! Says I, 'me-yow! me-yow!' as soft as I could, and then I put out the light and scrambled out of the window onto the shed. Then I slipped down to the ground and crawled in amongst the trees, and sure enough there was Tom Sawyer waiting for me.

2. **The Great Gatsby** by F. Scott Fitzgerald, 1925 - This dazzling portrait of the excess, extravagance and decadence of socialites in West Egg, New York during the Jazz Age depicts the superficiality of life in the fast lane. The story of Jay Gatsby, a poor boy turned millionaire who falls in love with Southern belle Daisy Buchanan, gradually unfolds as Gatsby's neighbor Nick Carraway learns of Gatsby's humble origins and his simmering passion for the married Daisy. Extravagant parties, greed and ambition are the backdrop of Fitzgerald's cautionary tale about the risks and rewards of the American Dream.

3. **Moby Dick** by Herman Melville, 1851 – While contemporary readers may find Melville's huge, sprawling allegorical novel a bit unwieldy, Moby Dick is nonetheless a stunning, one-of-a kind novel that depicts Captain Ahab's obsessive quest for the legendary white whale. Overlooked when it was first published, *Moby Dick* didn't become a literary sensation until after World War I. In his 2011 book ***Why Read Moby Dick?***, historian Nathaniel Philbrick (***In the Heart of the Sea: The Tragedy of the Whaleship Essex***) calls Melville's novel " a metaphysical survival manual — the best guidebook there is for a literate man or woman facing an impenetrable unknown: the future of civilization in this storm-tossed 21st century."

4. **The Sound and the Fury** by William Faulkner, 1929 - Faulkner's fourth novel is a challenging read, due to his stream-of-consciousness style and interior monologues. It is also an unforgettable story charting the decline of the Compsons, a once-prominent Mississippi family. The changing social order of the South is revealed from four points of view, representing the perspectives of very different personalities: Compson son Benjy, an "idiot;" Quentin, a Harvard student; the oldest son Jason; and the family's black servants.

5. **The Complete Stories,** by Flannery O'Connor, 1971 - The ailing young woman from Georgia who kept peacocks on her lawn wrote some of American literature's most haunting short fiction. There are always unexpected moral dimensions to the portraits she drew of Southerners in such classics as "Good Country People," "A Good Man is Hard to Find" and "Everything That Rises Must Converge." Winner of the National Book Award.

6. **Absalom, Absalom!** by William Faulkner, 1936 – Peripherally connected to *The Sound and the Fury*, *Absalom, Absalom!* is a quintessentially Southern Gothic saga of three Mississippi families before, during and after the Civil War. Told in flashback form, Faulkner's mesmerizing novel paints a disturbing portrait of the American South at its most degenerate. In 2009, *Absalom, Absalom!* was named the best Southern novel of all time in a poll of 134 writers conducted by *The Oxford American*.

7. **To Kill a Mockingbird** by Harper Lee, 1960 – A perennial favorite that's brought generations of readers to tears, Lee's elegiac, sensitively written coming-of-age novel is set against the backdrop of a racially-charged rape trial in Depression-era Alabama. The six-year-old tomboy heroine Jean Louise "Scout" Finch is one of the most appealing characters in all American literature; the story unfolds through her eyes in Lee's only novel, which won the Pulitzer Prize and inspired a classic film. In 1999, *To Kill a Mockingbird* voted "Best Novel of the Century" in a *Library Journal* poll.

8. **Invisible Man** by Ralph Ellison, 1953 – Winner of the National Book Award, Ellison's magisterial novel follows the unnamed African-American narrator on his journey of self-discovery from the South to Harlem, where he becomes involved with a black nationalist group called The Brotherhood. A startling, provocative novel that burns itself in your memory.

9. **Beloved** by Toni Morrison, 1987 – An extraordinary work by the Nobel Prize winner, *Beloved* is a lyrical, emotionally shattering story of Sethe, an escaped slave literally haunted by an unspeakable crime in post-Civil War Ohio. And while it's not an easy read by any stretch of the imagination, *Beloved* grips your attention from the first page, thanks to the power and beauty of Morrison's prose. Based on a true story, *Beloved* won the Pulitzer Prize in 1988. In a 2006 *New York Times* survey of writers and critics, it was named the best work of American fiction published between 1980 and 2005.

10. **The Portrait of a Lady** by Henry James, 1881 – Revered as one of the finest writers of "trans-Atlantic" literature, James writes perceptively of the cultural collision of the Old and New Worlds in such classics as ***Daisy Miller***, ***The Ambassadors*** and *The Portrait of a Lady*, which is generally regarded as his best novel. When Isabel Archer inherits a fortune, the spirited young woman from Albany, New York goes to Europe, where she ultimately falls prey to scheming expatriates.

AMERICAN WEST NOVELS
Best of the Twentieth Century

Although he never achieved the international renown of John Steinbeck, the late Wallace Stegner was often referred to as the "dean of Western writers." An ardent environmentalist and creative writing teacher whose students included Larry McMurtry, Ken Kesey and Edward Abbey, Stegner depicts life in the American West with a singular mixture of unsparing honesty and heartfelt reverence for the landscape. His masterpiece is generally conceded to be *Angle of Repose*, a family saga that won Stegner the Pulitzer Prize in 1972.

Twenty-seven years later, this generation-spanning novel based loosely on the life of nineteenth century author/illustrator Mary Hallock Foote would bring Stegner another (posthumous) honor. In a 1999 readers' poll conducted by the *San Francisco Chronicle*, *Angle of Repose* was chosen the best twentieth century novel about the American West, just ahead of Steinbeck's *The Grapes of Wrath*, which came in second.

According to the poll's guidelines, readers could only vote for novels that met one of the following three criteria. Its subject matter pertains to the American West. The novel was written in the American West — or the writer hails from the region, which the *Chronicle* editors designated as the land west of the Rockies.

Of the 600-odd readers who voted in the poll, nearly one hundred voted for *Angle of Repose*. Here are the top ten vote-getters, listed in descending order:

1. **Angle of Repose** by Wallace Stegner, 1971 – Estranged from his immediate family, a retired, wheelchair-bound historian assuages his loneliness by researching the life of his deceased grandmother in the nineteenth century American West. Through her journals and letters, he gains a keen understanding of his family's emotional dynamic over the years.

   EXCERPT: ANGLE OF REPOSE:

   A Quaker lady of high principles, the wife of a not-very-successful engineer whom you supported through years of delayed hope, you lived in exile, wrote it, drew it — New Almadén, Santa Cruz, Leadville, Michoacán, the Snake River Valley, the deep quartz mines right under this house — and you stayed a cultural snob through it all. Even when you lived in a field camp in a canyon, your children had a governess, no less, unquestionably the only one in Idaho. The dream you had for your children was a dream of Eastern cultivation.

2. **The Grapes of Wrath** by John Steinbeck, 1939 – One of the authentic literary giants of twentieth century American literature, Steinbeck won the Pulitzer Prize for this magnificent account of the sharecropping Joad family, devastated by the Great Depression and the Dust Bowl. Unquestionably Steinbeck's greatest novel, *The Grapes of Wrath* was subsequently adapted for the screen by John Ford in 1940.

3. **Sometimes a Great Notion** by Ken Kesey, 1964 – Kesey's follow-up to **_One Flew Over the Cuckoo's Nest_** is a richly compelling family drama set in an Oregon logging community. When the local logging union calls for a strike, the Stamper family patriarch and his equally stubborn son ignore the union's call — and suffer grave consequences as a result.

4. **The Call of the Wild** by Jack London, 1903 – Praised by E. L. Doctorow as a "mordant parable," London's novella is a Darwinian-themed survival tale about Buck, a sled dog who escapes into the frozen Yukon, where he battles for a place in a wolf pack.

5. **The Big Sleep** by Raymond Chandler, 1939 – So complicated that even Chandler himself reportedly wasn't sure *whodunit*, *The Big Sleep* spins a labyrinthine web of murder and blackmail in sunny Los Angeles, the home turf of cynical, hard-boiled private detective Philip Marlowe.

6. **Animal Dreams** by Barbara Kingsolver, 1990 – Told in alternating voices, Kingsolver's second novel is a beautifully written story of a woman returning to her rural Arizona hometown to care for her Alzheimer's-afflicted father. Native-American imagery and cultural motifs play a prominent role in *American Dreams*, which also won raves for its vivid evocation of the Arizona landscape.

7. **Death Comes for the Archbishop** by Willa Cather, 1927 – With her customary plain-spoken eloquence, Cather trades the Nebraska prairie setting of *My Antonia* for the New Mexico territory, where this unforgettable novel takes place. Based on a true story, *Death Comes for the Archbishop* portrays the struggles of a French Catholic bishop and a priest to establish a church among the Arapaho and Hopi Indians.

8. **The Day of the Locust** by Nathanael West, 1939 – Barely scraping by as a writer-for-hire at one of Hollywood's infamous "Poverty Row" film studios, West wrote this despairing portrait of the has-beens and wannabes seeking fame and fortune in Tinsel Town.

9. **Blood Meridian** by Cormac McCarthy, 1985 – McCarthy's virtuoso depiction of a nineteenth century scalping expedition in Mexico is a graphically violent novel, written in a baroque prose style that's earned McCarthy favorable comparisons with William Faulkner. Rapturous in his praise of McCarthy, influential literary critic Harold Bloom hailed *Blood Meridian* as the reclusive novelist's masterpiece.

10. **The Maltese Falcon** by Dashiell Hammett, 1930 – Hammett's cynical private eye, Sam Spade, reportedly served as the model for Raymond Chandler's Philip Marlowe. In lean, staccato prose, the former Pinkerton detective-turned writer draws you into Spade's twist-laden search for his partner's killer.

ANCIENT GREEK DRAMA
Classics of Antiquity

The ancient Greeks didn't spend all their time building temples, debating the nature of reality, and battling Persians or fellow Greeks. In their spare time, they were great theatergoers. And who wouldn't be, with such talented writers? Or perhaps it was the other way around — enthusiastic audiences spurred the playwrights to write the most biting satires or the most heartrending tragedies. However it happened, the works that have come down to us have endured for centuries. And while we may no longer believe that competitive gods are interfering in our domestic affairs, almost everyone can relate to the feeling of being at the mercy of forces beyond our control. Here are five classics of ancient Greek drama, listed alphabetically.

1. **The Clouds** by Aristophanes, 423 BC – This comedy takes aim at the revered philosopher Socrates. An old farmer named Strepsiades is having trouble with his son, Pheidippides, and sends the young man to learn from Socrates how to argue his way out of debts. But at Socrates' "Thinkery," Pheidippides becomes an even more pretentious and formidable scoundrel than his father had bargained for, and it all ends with Strepsiades burning down the establishment.

EXCERPT: THE CLOUDS:

Strepsiades:
Damn! Lord Zeus, how this night drags on and on!
It's endless. Won't daylight ever come?
I heard a cock crowing a while ago,
but my slaves kept snoring. In the old days,
they wouldn't have dared. Damn and blast this war—
so many problems. Now I'm not allowed
to punish my own slaves. And then there's him—
this fine young man, who never once wakes up,
but farts the night away, all snug in bed,
wrapped up in five wool coverlets.

2. **The Grouch** by Menander, 316 BC – The grouch in question is a poor old man named Knemon who despises his fellow men. When the god Pan arranges a love match between his daughter and the wealthy young Sostratos, Knemon's life is turned upside down. Lucky for all the characters, this is a comedy, so the divine matchmaking ends on a happier note than does another ancient play, *Hippolytus.*

3. **Hippolytus** by Euripides, 428 BC – Hippolytus, a son of the hero Theseus, is devoted to the virgin goddess Artemis (later known to the Romans as Diana the huntress) but will have nothing to do with earthly women. Aphrodite, the goddess of love, is offended by his chastity, and decides to interfere. She causes his stepmother, Phaedra, to fall violently in love with him. When the virtuous young man rejects her advances, love turns to hatred. Phaedra commits suicide, leaving a note for Theseus in which she accuses Hippolytus of raping her. Theseus curses his son — his curses carry special weight because his own father, the sea god Poseidon, has granted them to him — and Hippolytus is gravely wounded on his way into exile.

4. **Oedipus Rex** by Sophocles, late fifth century BC – The Freudian theory of the "Oedipus Complex," in which young children are hostile to the parent of their own sex and attracted to the parent of the opposite sex, may be named after the

hero of this tale, but it isn't that poor Oedipus *meant* to kill his father and marry his mother. It was fate and a case of mistaken identity that led him to these abhorrent deeds. If you only read one Greek tragedy, this is perhaps the most brilliant.

5. **Prometheus Bound** by Aeschylus, fifth century BC – Aeschylus is considered the father of tragedy. This tale of power politics in the heavens is indeed tragic. Prometheus once helped Zeus overthrow his rival Titans and attain the supreme position among gods he now holds, but Zeus became enraged when Prometheus stole fire and made a gift of it to mankind. Now Zeus is punishing Prometheus by sending another god, Hephaestus, to fasten him to a mountaintop. Prometheus has the sympathy of the other immortals, but none will oppose Zeus in order to help him. Still, Prometheus retains a measure of power because he can see into the future of Zeus — but he isn't telling.

ANIMAL BEHAVIOR STUDIES
Heeding the Call of the Wild

Some of the world's most dedicated scientists don't work in labs. Instead, they leave the comforts of city life and set up camp in remote parts of the globe, where they study wild animals. They learn about their subjects' means of survival, how their societies are ordered, and, in many cases, their individual personalities, all while managing to survive themselves in the animals' beautiful but often harsh environments. Here are twelve informative, entertaining, and passionate books written by naturalists who dedicated many years to studying our wild fellow creatures.

1. **Animal Tool Behavior: The Use and Manufacture of Tools by Animals** by Robert W. Shumaker, Kristina R. Walkup, and Benjamin B. Beck, updated 2011 – As the first book to catalog studies on animal tool use and construction, *Animal Tool Behavior* was groundbreaking when first published in 1980, and continues to evolve with this revised and expanded edition. By synthesizing the latest research in this area, the authors have created a comprehensive volume showing the creation and use of tools by invertebrates, birds, fish, and mammals.

2. **Bonobo Handshake: A Memoir of Love and Adventure in the Congo** by Vanessa Woods, 2010 – Vanessa Wood's memoir is part adventure story and part romance, as she follows her fiancé on a research trip to a bonobo ape sanctuary in war-torn Congo. What she learns about these rare apes, who share 98.7 percent of their DNA with humans, informs her ideas about society, love, friendship, and other traits she previously associated only with homo sapiens.

3. **Cry of the Kalahari** by Mark and Delia Owens, 1984 – The authors, a husband-and-wife team of naturalists, spent seven years in the Kalahari Desert on a

shoestring budget, studying jackals, hyenas, lions, and other wild animals. In this book they share the drama of learning about the animals around them — getting to know their individual personalities, and witnessing the shifting balance of interdependence and rivalry within and between the different species. Who knew that hyenas (which can crush bones as thick as baseball bats with their teeth and make a meal of the shards) could be so intriguing? There is violence and hardship in their account, but also much that is touching and inspiring.

EXCERPT: CRY OF THE KALAHARI:

In the early evening I was stirring my supper over the fire when seven lions came padding directly toward camp. My heart began doing flip-flops, and I quickly put the pot of stew on top of the hyena table and hurried deeper into the tree island. Peering through the branches, I could see the long, low forms gliding silently toward me, just 100 yards away. It was the same lionesses and their adolescent young had often seen. But on the other occasions when they had visited camp, the truck had always been nearby; now I felt as vulnerable as a turtle without a shell.

4. **Elephant Memories: Thirteen Years in the Life of an Elephant Family** by Cynthia Moss, 1988 – This is the story of one family of elephants in Kenya's Amboseli National Park. In a vivid and poetic style, Moss describes all the phases of their lives, from birth to adolescence, maturity, and death. You'll come away from the book with an intimate understanding of these complex and playful creatures' daily experiences.

5. **Gifts of the Crow: How Perception, Emotion, and Thought Allow Smart Birds to Behave Like Humans b**y John Marzluff and Tony Angell, 2012 – Once regarded as the harbinger of death, the crow is now known to be one of the world's most intelligent and complex animals. The crow's uncanny ability to reason, use tools and assess situations is documented in Marzluff's wonderfully engaging study of this remarkable bird species. Illustrated with diagrams and beautiful line-drawings, *Gifts of the Crow: How Perception, Emotion, and Thought Allow Smart Birds to Behave Like Humans* will entertain and enlighten you with its stories of crows who play, grieve and swill beer (!). One of Amazon.com's best books of 2012.

6. **Gorillas in the Mist** by Dian Fossey, 1983 – Before Fossey went to central Africa to study mountain gorillas in the wild, not much was known about these animals. She fell in love with them and devoted her life to researching them and trying to protect them from poachers, who may have been responsible for her murder in 1985. Her book describes the gorillas' surprisingly peaceful societies and communicates why she was willing to risk her life for them.

7. **Hunting With the Moon: The Lions of Savuti** by Dereck and Beverly Joubert, 1997 – Another husband-and-wife team, the Jouberts spent more than two decades living in a national park in Botswana, observing and photographing the lions that live there. They followed the lions at night, and include more than a hundred color photos in the book. In words and pictures, the couple documents in loving detail the relationships of pride members, the lions' conflicts with hyenas and elephants, and much more.

8. **In the Shadow of Man** by Jane Goodall, 1971 – One of the world's most famous naturalists, Jane Goodall shares her pioneering research on a group of chimpanzees, mankind's closest relative. She focuses in particular on one matriarch, "Flo," and her family. If you fall in love with this chimp family (which is likely), you can find out about its next generation in Goodall's ***Through a Window***.

9. **Listening to Whales: What the Orcas Have Taught Us** by Alexandra Morton, 2002 – Inspired by John Lilly's work on dolphin communication, the author decided to record and analyze the noises made by orcas (also known as killer whales, although orcas are actually a species of dolphin). She began with a pair in captivity but then set out to listen to wild orcas off the coast of British Columbia, learning their ways of life and how they "talk" to each other using different frequencies. It's an impressive story of the joys and sacrifices of doing research in a rugged environment.

10. **Never Cry Wolf: The Amazing True Story of Life Among Arctic Wolves** by Farley Mowat, 1963 – Originally, the author was sent to the tundra of northern Canada to study wolves that were thought to be menacing the caribou population. When he observed them firsthand, though, he realized that they were much less a threat than had been thought. His account describes how he not only documented the wolves' behavior but also, amusingly, participated in some of it.

11. **The Shark Chronicles: A Scientist Tracks the Consummate Predator** by John Musick and Beverly McMillan, 2002 – Sharks are frightening, but also awe-inspiring. This book takes readers across the globe, sharing the drama of shark research. Along with sharks' evolution and ecological challenges, the authors cover sharks' special physiology, their reproductive lives, and some of the remarkable things that have been found in their stomachs.

12. **To Touch a Wild Dolphin: A Journey of Discovery with the Sea's Most Intelligent Creatures** by Rachel Smolker, 2001 – This is a delightful account of fifteen years with the wild dolphins off the coast of western Australia. Playful, clever, and friendly (though not always peaceable), the dolphins communicate using whistles and clicks. In the course of her research the author even discovered them using tools.

APHORISTS
Brevity is the Soul of Wit — and Wisdom

The literary expression of great insights into human nature can take many different forms, from epic poems to fables to complex psychological novels. A few writers, philosophers, and conversationalists have a gift for putting their most perceptive thoughts into just one or two sentences — brief sayings that surprise by their bite, wit, or expansiveness. Unpleasant and seldom acknowledged truths, upendings of conventional wisdom, paradoxes that actually make sense — the great aphorists provide food for thought in a most concentrated form. This list, ordered chronologically, introduces a few of the best.

1. **Lao Tzu, probably sixth or fifth century BC** - One of the sages of ancient China, Lao Tzu had an outlook that was anything but cynical. Some of his sayings are mystifying at first, which he freely acknowledged — "Indeed," he says, "truth sounds like its opposite!" — but he wasn't talking nonsense. One way to understand his writings is to see them as contrasting two different states of mind: on one hand, a fragmented, grasping state in which we are so obsessed with controlling things that we defeat our own purposes; and on the other hand, an open, tranquil, perceptive state much like what some modern psychologists call "flow." From the collection of his teachings, the ***Tao Te Ching***:

   EXCERPT: TAO TE CHING:
   To be empty is to be full.
   He who conquers men has force; he who conquers himself is truly strong.
   He who knows does not speak. He who speaks does not know.
   A journey of a thousand miles must begin with a single step.
   Only when we are sick of our sickness shall we cease to be sick.

2. **François, Duc de la Rochefoucauld, 1613–1680** - The French nobleman sought to expose the pettiness and vanity that he believed to lie beneath the surface of polite society and, in fact, of most human interactions. For all his despair of finding true virtue, humility, and selflessness, one senses that he still valued them. Perhaps he even viewed his unsparing attempts at honesty as a tonic (albeit one of very limited power) against vanity and self-deception. Judge for yourself. From his ***Maxims***:

   EXCERPT: MAXIMS:
   We all have strength enough to endure the misfortunes of others.
   If we had no faults of our own, we would not take so much pleasure in noticing those of others.
   We always like those who admire us; we do not always like those whom we admire.

When modesty appears to be refusing praise, it is in reality seeking it in a more delicate form.

3. **Benjamin Franklin, 1706–1790** - Apart from being a printer, reformer, diplomat, political writer, and scientist, Ben Franklin was also quite a wit. Here are some of his gems from ***Poor Richard's Almanack***, which was published each year between 1732 and 1757:

EXCERPT: POOR RICHARD'S ALMANACK:

Three may keep a secret, if two of them are dead.
Keep your eyes wide open before marriage, half shut afterwards.
Experience keeps a dear school, but fools will learn in no other.

4. **Friedrich Wilhelm Nietzsche, 1844–1900** - Many aphorists criticize egoism, viewing it as silly, immoral, or limiting. But this controversial German philosopher believed that superior men were entitled to a just and noble egoism; it was the ordinary mass of humanity he held in contempt. He exalted strength and "high spirits," and took delight in the spirit of malice with which he attacked conventional values. Despite the sinister streak, Nietzsche seems to have been a sincere lover of beauty and was certainly an original thinker. From his ***Beyond Good and Evil***:

EXCERPT: BEYOND GOOD AND EVIL:

No one is such a liar as the indignant man.
Even when the mouth lies, the way it looks still tells the truth.
Whoever fights monsters should see to it that in the process he does not become a monster. And when you look long into an abyss, the abyss also looks into you.

5. **Ambrose Bierce, 1842–1914** - Bierce had an adventurous and difficult life. He was an officer in the Civil War and a newspaperman as well as an author of fiction, poetry, and sarcastic, world-weary aphorisms. Here are some definitions from his ***The Devil's Dictionary***:

EXCERPT: THE DEVIL'S DICTIONARY:

BORE, n. A person who talks when you wish him to listen.
CONSERVATIVE, n. A statesman who is enamored of existing evils, as distinguished from the Liberal, who wishes to replace them with others.
POSITIVE, adj. Mistaken at the top of one's voice.

6. **Oscar Wilde, 1854–1900** - Like Nietzsche, the author of ***The Picture of Dorian Gray*** and ***The Importance of Being Earnest*** enjoyed skewering convention, but Wilde did it with a comparatively light and sympathetic touch. He loved art for

art's sake (and wit for wit's sake), but, it seems, humanity too. Some of his choice aphorisms:

EXCERPTS: VARIOUS OSCAR WILDE WORKS:

I can resist everything except temptation. (From ***Lady Windermere's Fan***)
When the gods wish to punish us they answer our prayers. (From ***An Ideal Husband***)
A man cannot be too careful in the choice of his enemies. (From *The Picture of Dorian Gray*)

7. **Dorothy Parker, 1893–1967** - One of the early contributors to *The New Yorker* magazine, the petite poet, critic, and fiction writer had a sharp tongue and pen that gave her what she called her "reputation for homicidal humor." But she also had a strong instinct for self-deprecation (and melancholy). Some of her astute thoughts, which can be found in ***The Portable Dorothy Parker***:

EXCERPTS: VARIOUS DORTHY PARKER WORKS:

Excuse My Dust (Her *suggestion* for her epigraph)
Scratch a lover, and find a foe. (From *Ballade of a Great Weariness*)
Brevity is the soul of lingerie. (Attributed advertising motto)
Men seldom make passes / At girls who wear glasses (*News Item*)

ART HISTORY OVERVIEWS
Masterpieces on Your Bookshelf

Most books are repositories of words, but let's not forget that they can also be repositories of images. Modern technology has allowed the best-produced recent art books — including new editions of the classics — to be extraordinarily beautiful as well as informative. There's no real substitute for experiencing art in the original, but a good art book has a lot to offer. It's a fascinating way to learn about history and culture — art can give us a more visceral understanding of long-gone people's concerns, beliefs, and sensibilities than any number of facts alone. It's wonderful to have a collection of masterpieces right on your bookshelf. And when you visit a museum after reading a good art book, you might find that not only can you put the works into context with ease, but also see more in familiar paintings and sculptures. Sharpen your senses and your mind with these fourteen recommended overviews of art history — seven that cover the entire history of Western or world art, and seven more that focus on particular periods, regions, or groups of artists.

GENERAL OVERVIEWS

1. <u>**The Annotated Mona Lisa: A Crash Course in Art History from Prehistoric to Post-Modern**</u> by Carol Strickland and John Boswell, 1992 – An entertaining history of art that delves into the concerns and methods of the most important periods, movements, and artists, using devices like a "Velázquez artistic tree" (whose branches are the later painters inspired by Velázquez) to show how they relate to each other.

2. <u>**Art: A New History**</u> by Paul Johnson, 2003 – Johnson brings his experience as a historian and an artist to this survey of the competing forces (tradition vs. innovation, religion vs. secular life, and so on) that have given Western art much of its dynamism.

3. <u>**Art: From Cave Painting to Street Art – 40,000 Years of Creativity**</u> by Stephen Farthing, 2010 – The prominent British painter, writer and teacher does not merely offer an exhaustive history of art from prehistoric days through the first decade of the twenty-first century, he also puts that history into context in this fascinating survey. Farthing relates the story of art movement by movement, spotlighting important artists and significant works, illuminating how artistic trends, other masters and even events of the day influenced artists and their oeuvre through a timeline that runs across every page. Illustrated with more than 1,100 color reproductions, this is a book that *The Bookseller* calls, "An informative future classic."

4. <u>**Gardner's Art Through the Ages**</u> by Richard Tansey, Fred S. Kleiner, and Horst De La Croix, 1926, periodically revised – This time-tested overview of the most important periods in art all around the world provides you with your own art-history survey class, expertly taught. It's so thorough, in fact, that it almost amounts to a history of humanity.

5. <u>**History of Art**</u> by H.W. Janson, 1962, periodically revised – This enormous book offers an expansive view of Western art and architecture, focusing on four great periods — the ancient world; the Middle Ages; the Renaissance, Mannerism, and the Baroque; and the modern world. Hundreds of reproductions and lively text make it great for browsing or for reading straight through.

6. <u>**Sister Wendy's Story of Painting**</u> by Sister Wendy Beckett, enhanced and expanded edition 2000 – Sister Wendy offers a friendly and illuminating tour of Western painting, helping us understand the artists' aims, their feelings, and (with close-ups of many paintings) their ways of working.

EXCERPT: SISTER WENDY'S STORY OF PAINTING:

Like Shakespeare, Leonardo [da Vinci] came from an insignificant background and rose to universal acclaim. Leonardo was the illegitimate son of a local lawyer in the small town of Vinci in the Tuscan region. His father acknowledged him and paid for his training, but we may wonder whether the strangely self-sufficient tone of Leonardo's mind was not perhaps affected by his early ambiguity of status. The definitive polymath, he had almost too many gifts, including superlative male beauty, a splendid singing voice, magnificent physique, mathematical excellence, scientific daring ... the list is endless. This overabundance of talents caused him to treat his artistry lightly, seldom finishing a picture, and sometimes making rash technical experiments.

7. **The Story of Art** by E.H. Gombrich, 1950, periodically revised – Gombrich's book is a wonderfully clear — and impassioned — introduction to Western art. Especially compelling are his observations about the evolution of painters' techniques and modes of seeing from the Renaissance to the nineteenth century.

PERIODS, REGIONS & GROUPS

8. **Art in China** by Craig Clunas, 1997 – The oldest continuous civilization in the world has produced a wealth of marvelous calligraphy, landscape painting, ceramics, and other art forms. This carefully illustrated book seeks to put Chinese art in the proper context of Chinese life, from the court to the tomb, and from ancient times to the Cultural Revolution and beyond.

9. **Greek Art** by John Boardman, 1964 – The clarity, vitality, harmony, and searching vision of ancient Greek art inspired countless artists in later times, from Buddhist sculptors to Renaissance painters. This is a classic introduction to the seminal art of Greece and how it arose and developed.

10. **The Painting of Modern Life: Paris in the Art of Manet and His Followers** by Timothy J. Clark, 1984 – You may disagree with Clark's critique of capitalism, but his engaging argument sheds light on Manet's once-scandalous *Olympia* and other masterpieces of the Impressionist movement, as well as on cultural life in nineteenth-century Paris.

11. **The Shock of the New: The Hundred-Year History of Modern Art—Its Rise, Its Dazzling Achievement, Its Fall** by Robert Hughes, 1980 – This is one of the most passionate, witty, and opinionated narratives of modern art you're likely to find. It groups the works of the modern era (which has produced visions as disparate as Monet's serene lily ponds and Guston's disturbing cartoon world) into overarching philosophical themes, giving new insight into the works reproduced.

12. **Since '45: America and the Making of Contemporary Art** by Katy Siegel, 2011 – Part survey, part history lesson, this provocative work makes a case for American dominance of the modern art world after World War II. Siegel examines how New York became the center of the artistic universe and how themes and issues that seized the American imagination after the war's end — the threat of nuclear annihilation, the rise of suburbia, race, the self, populist culture — inspired artists as diverse as Mark Rothko, Andy Warhol, Matthew Barney, and many more.

13. **The Tribal Arts of Africa** by Jean-Baptiste Bacquart, 2002 – All the major tribes in sub-Saharan Africa are represented in this richly illustrated book. It includes sculptures, masks, jewelry, and furniture from the distant past to the beginning of the twentieth century.

14. **Women Artists: An Illustrated History** by Nancy G. Heller, 1987 – Learn about Sofonisba Anguissola, an intriguing painter of the late Renaissance; Mary Cassatt, an innovative painter and printmaker of the Impressionist movement; and more than a hundred other artists worth knowing in this beautifully illustrated survey of women artists of the Western world.

ARTHURIAN LITERATURE
The Legend of Camelot in Prose and Verse

The legend of King Arthur and his knights of the round table has spellbound readers since at least 1138 AD, when Welsh clergyman/historian Geoffrey of Monmouth published his highly romanticized ***The History of the Kings of Britain***. While most contemporary historians discount the accuracy of Geoffrey of Monmouth's book as questionable at best, he nonetheless succeeded in popularizing the story of the "once and future king" — as Arthur's grave marker on the isle of Avalon identifies him, according to T. H. White's book of the same name.

Whether or not such a figure existed in Great Britain's fog-shrouded distant past, King Arthur remains a potent symbol of the Age of Chivalry — when loyal and virtuous knights defended ladies fair, ancient wizards advised kings, and magic was an everyday reality. In the centuries since Geoffrey of Monmouth's book, the Arthurian Romance has been told in virtually every artistic medium: verse, prose, cinema, and Broadway musical. Here are ten Arthurian Romances, listed alphabetically, that evoke the swirling pageantry and mysticism of Camelot.

1. **The Acts of King Arthur and His Noble Knights** by John Steinbeck, 1976 – Unfinished at the time of his death in 1968, Steinbeck's neglected gem was published eight years later, with the author's letters to his agent outlining his plans for finishing it. Except for the novel's rather contemporary dialogue, Steinbeck's version of the King Arthur legend is remarkably faithful in spirit and tone to Malory's *Le Morte d'Arthur*.

2. **Arthur Rex: A Legendary Novel** by Thomas Berger, 1978 – The author of *Little Big Man* performs literary magic with this grand retelling of the *Le Morte d'Arthur*, which Berger gently tweaks with cheeky good humor.

3. **A Connecticut Yankee in King Arthur's Court** by Mark Twain, 1889 – Twain's whimsical blend of time-traveling fantasy and social satire sends a nineteenth-century shop foreman back to Camelot, where the know-it-all New Englander uses modern-age technology to rise in King Arthur's court.

4. **The Hollow Hills** by Mary Stewart, 1970 – The second volume in Stewart's enthralling *Arthurian Saga*, which places the wizard Merlin at the narrative center. In *The Hollow Hills*, King Uther Pendragon entrusts Merlin with the education of his son Arthur, who must pull the magical sword Caliburn to realize his destiny. The other books in Stewart's Arthurian Saga are *The Crystal Cave*, *The Last Enchantment* and *The Wicked Day*.

5. **Idylls of the King** by Alfred, Lord Tennyson, 1885 – England's Poet Laureate from 1850-1892, Tennyson dedicated this sequence of twelve transcendently beautiful poems based on *Le Morte d'Arthur* to the memory of Prince Albert, who died in 1861.

6. **Le Morte d'Arthur** by Sir Thomas Malory, 1485 – The primary source for most of the novels and films about King Arthur, Malory's epic is regarded as the first English-language novel.

7. **The Mists of Avalon** by Marion Zimmer Bradley, 1983 – King Arthur and Guinevere are supporting characters in Bradley's female-centric revisionist take on the legend. The main character is Arthur's half-sister Morgaine, a.k.a. Morgan Le Fay, who's waging a lonely battle to preserve ancient Celtic traditions in the face of Christianity. Ambitious and imaginative, Bradley's novel is a perennial bestseller.

EXCERPT: THE MISTS OF AVALON:

A few days later Morgaine went forth, with a few of the people of Avalon, to the crowning of Arthur. Never, in all her years upon Avalon — except for the few moments when she had opened the mists to allow Gwenhwyfar to find her convent again—had she set foot on the earth of the Isle of the Priests, Ynis Witrin, the Isle of Glass. It seemed to her that the sun shone with a curious harshness, unlike the soft and misty sunlight of Avalon. She had to remind herself that to almost all the people of Britain, this was the real world, and the land of Avalon only an enchanted dream, as if were the very kingdom of fairy.

8. **The Once and Future King** by T. H. White, 1958 – An ugly, self-centered Lancelot? Merlin growing younger, not older? Those are just two of the striking revisions in White's classic quartet of novels, which some critics interpret as a World War II allegory. *The Once and Future King* was subsequently adapted for the screen (Disney's *The Sword in the Stone*) and stage (*Camelot*).

9. **The Serpent and the Grail** by A. A. Attanasio, 1999 – When the Holy Grail is stolen, ancient Britain becomes a veritable wasteland. To save his kingdom, Arthur must battle his arch-nemesis, the Serpent, in Attanasio's intriguing and dark novel, the fourth and last in the science fiction writer's Arthur series.

10. **The Winter King** by Bernard Cowell, 1995 – The first novel in Cowell's *Warlord Chronicles* trilogy, *The Winter King* is narrated by Derfel Cadarn, a Saxon-born

monk and faithful warrior to King Arthur, whose reign over Britain is marred by savage fighting between Christians and Druids. Punctuated by epic battles and royal intrigue, *The Winter King* is a splendid addition to the Arthurian literary canon. The other books in Cornwell's trilogy are ***Enemy of God*** and ***Excalibur, A Novel of Arthur***.

ARTIST BIOGRAPHIES
Lives of the Masters

The history of art is the history of many traditions and many individuals, a great number of whom are anonymous. Luckily, we know enough about the art of the last few hundred years (thanks in part to records such as Giorgio Vasari's sixteenth-century lives of the Renaissance masters) to be able to explore the lives and work of key individuals in depth. There are far too many great artists — and good books about them — for an exhaustive list of volumes, but here is a sampling of some of the best. Their pages are filled with beautiful images and remarkable stories of human accomplishment. Enjoy!

1. **Caravaggio: A Life Sacred and Profane** by Andrew Graham-Dixon, 2011 – Exhaustively researched for ten years and elegantly written in novelistic style, this book takes the full measure of a towering figure in the history of art, touching upon everything from his often troubled personal life and brushes with the law (i.e., murder charges) to his place in the context of the world in which he lived. *Caravaggio* also includes color plates of many of his works, making it easy to appreciate the artist's genius. A *New York Times* Notable Selection, this book is a rare achievement by a gifted art critic.

EXCERPT: CARAVAGGIO:
The truth is that Caravaggio was as uneasy in his relationships as he was in most other aspects of life. He likely slept with men. He did sleep with women. But he settled with no one.

2. **Degas** by Robert Gordon and Andrew Forge, 1988 – The composition, palette, and psychology of Degas's work were boldly experimental, yet he never lost his exquisite sense of draftsmanship or his connection to the classical art of the past. This volume showcases his early figure studies, portraits, dancers, and bathers — plus his poetry, working methods, and prickly personality.

3. **El Greco** edited by David Davies and John H. Elliott, 2003 – The sixteenth-century artist El Greco (Spanish for "the Greek"; his real name was Domenikos Theotokopoulos) is famous for his paintings of elongated figures in dark atmospheres, illuminated with flashes of spiritual light. This volume discusses his

life and times, as well as his little-known work as a sculptor, and reproduces his strange and beautiful creations.

4. **Frida Kahlo, 1907–1954: Pain and Passion** by Andrea Kettenmann, 2002 – The author discusses the most salient aspects of Kahlo's life and work — how she used her self-portraits to explore her identity; her experience of physical suffering; and her relationship with the controversial, larger-than-life muralist Diego Rivera.

5. **Hiroshige: Prints and Drawings** by Matthi Forrer, 1997 – Ando Hiroshige (1797–1858) was one of the masters of the Japanese woodblock print. His depictions of Mount Edo, birds and flowers, and other subject matter seem spare and lush at the same time, with a lovely sense of atmosphere.

6. **Leonardo da Vinci** by Kenneth Clark, 1939 – See the *Mona Lisa* with fresh eyes! Curiosity, inventiveness, subtlety, and grace were just a few of the many qualities of Leonardo da Vinci, the exemplary "Renaissance man." Clark's text is still wonderfully readable, and the current edition has good reproductions.

7. **Lucian Freud: Paintings** by Robert Hughes, 1987 – Freud's startlingly honest nudes and portraits have a conviction and pathos achieve by few other painters of the mid-to-late twentieth century (arguably a period of decline in art based on the human figure). Hughes makes a convincing case for his importance in the history of art.

8. **Michelangelo** by Howard Hibbard, 1974 – A versatile and profound Renaissance genius, the creator of *David* and the Sistine Chapel frescoes deserves monumental appreciation. This book goes into detail about the artist's life and his work as a sculptor, painter, architect, and even poet.

9. **Monet: Nature into Art** by John House, 1988 – This book reveals how hard work and careful thought went into the Impressionist painter Claude Monet's landscapes, which were often developed in the studio as well as in the open air. The end result, of course, was a feeling of spontaneity and naturalness that has appealed to generations since.

13. **Rembrandt's Eyes** by Simon Schama, 1999 – Centuries after they were painted, Rembrandt's portraits and other works are still amazingly touching. Schama's lively book portrays the artist's life of intense joys and troubles in a fascinating time and place — the Dutch Golden Age.

10. **The Ultimate Picasso** by Brigitte Léal, et al, 2000 – Picasso was an extraordinarily prolific and influential artist. This book reproduces huge numbers of work from all his different phases and discusses his traditional academic training, his muses, and much more.

11. **Van Gogh** by Rainer Metzger and Ingo F. Walther, 1996 – Vincent Van Gogh was a much more complex person than simply a madman who cut off his ear. This book details his early life, his stunning artistic achievements, his important

relationships with his brother Theo and his fellow painter Paul Gaugin, and his tragic death.

12. **Velázquez: Painter and Courtier** by Jonathan Brown, 1986 – Diego Velázquez's paintings are known for their somber elegance (with elements of whimsy) and some of the most virtuosic illusionism of the seventeenth century (which is saying a lot). Learn about the cultural and political influences on his works in this exploration of the painter's career at the Spanish court.

13. **Fire in the Belly: The Life and Times of David Wojnarowicz by Cynthia Carr, 2012 – The author met** Wojnarowicz, perhaps most famous for having one of his artworks censored after Catholic outcry, shortly before he became a seminal figure of the eighties-era East Village art scene. In vital, measured prose, Carr recounts Wojnarowicz's cruel childhood, his years of success and his eventual role as a trailblazing AIDS activist. This book is notable, not only for its treatment of the artist, but also for its ability to evoke the dilapidation of New York City in the eighties; for its elegizing of a generation of artists lost to HIV; and for its insights into the so-called culture wars.

ARTIST GUIDES
Essential Titles for Budding Artists

Many people would love to draw but believe, based on a few frustrating attempts, that they lack the talent for it. Actually, drawing is very much a learnable skill, and now is a great time to learn it — traditional drawing is undergoing a renaissance after decades of relative dormancy. Here are a few recent and not-so-recent books on this foundational art, balanced with general books on creativity. There's something for everyone on the list — from beginners who think they can't draw anything more complex than a stick figure to those who have already devoted years to the practice and want to move to another level.

1. **The Artist's Complete Guide to Figure Drawing: A Contemporary Perspective on the Classical Tradition** by Anthony Ryder, 2000 – A fabulous resource for drawing students, this accessible but sophisticated book explains the principles of classical drawing from the nude model with clarity and passion. Each step of the way is illustrated with Ryder's magnificent drawings.

2. **The Artist's Way: A Spiritual Path to Higher Creativity** by Julia Cameron, 1992 – A program for freeing your natural creativity from fear, guilt, and other common problems that might be standing in your way.

EXCERPT: THE ARTIST'S WAY:

Many of us wish we were more creative. Many of us sense we are more creative, but unable to effectively tap that creativity. Our dreams elude us. Our lives feel somehow flat. Often, we have great ideas, wonderful dreams, but are unable to actualize them for ourselves. Sometimes we have specific creative longings we would love to be able to fulfill — learning to play the piano, painting, taking an acting class, or writing. Sometimes our goal is more diffuse. We hunger for what might be called creative living — an expanded sense of creativity in our business lives, in sharing with our children, our spouse, our friends.

3. **Artistic Anatomy** by Dr. Paul Richer, translated and edited by Robert Beverly Hale, 1971 – A sound understanding of anatomy can change the way you look at the human form — what used to be a confusing mass of shapes and details turns into an understandable, familiar (yet ever surprising) system. This is a work from the late nineteenth century, still renowned for its accuracy and clarity. It includes a series of illustrations of how muscles' shapes change in different positions and movements.

4. **Charles Bargue and Jean-Léon Gérôme: Drawing Course** by Gerald Ackerman, 2003 – From the Renaissance through the early modern era, young artists began their training by copying drawings or engravings of classical sculpture, and learning to recognize shapes and depict light and shadow in two dimensions, before moving on to drawing from sculptures and from life. This book contains the full course of nineteenth-century lithographs for an intensive study of academic drawing — it was used by traditional artists and early modernists such as Van Gogh and Picasso alike. Its extremely rigorous and meticulous approach is not for everyone, but if you burn to draw like the nineteenth-century masters, check it out!

5. **Drawing Lessons from the Old Masters** by Robert Beverly Hale, 1964 – This book focuses on learning to draw realistically from imagination, like Michelangelo and Rubens. Filled with reproductions of Old Master drawings that illustrate its principles, it will change the way you look at art as well as how you create it.

6. **Drawing On the Right Side of the Brain** by Betty Edwards, 1989 – Be prepared to be amazed! The exercises in this book are designed to switch your consciousness from the verbal, logical left brain to the spatial, intuitive right brain. Perfect for beginners, it will build your confidence and flexibility in drawing (try making a "before" and "after" comparison of your own work!). This landmark book may change the way you "look at things!"

7. **How to Be an Explorer of the World: Portable Life Museum** by Keri Smith, 2008 – This visually appealing, playful book directs budding artists to slow down and absorb the stuff of everyday life, pulling ideas from what would seem — at first — the unlikeliest places. With sections for pasting in samples that inspire you, coupled with thought-provoking exercises, this personalized museum gets the artistic juices flowing in children and adults alike.

8. **The Practice and Science of Drawing** by Harold Speed, 1989 (reprint) – Learn about materials and a few different ways of drawing and seeing that work together to help you approach any subject with assurance.

9. **The War of Art: Winning the Inner Creative Battle** by Steven Pressfield, 2012 – A guide for creators of all stripes, *The War of Art*: *Winning the Inner Creative Battle* helps you identify and eliminate the naysayer within, freeing you to realize your creative potential. Taking a tactical approach while avoiding clichés about hard work, this book promises a strategy for dealing with those skirmishes with self-doubt.

ASIAN-AMERICAN NOVELS
Caught Between Two Worlds

Shunted to the margins of American popular culture, literature and media for decades, Asian-Americans have now become a significant force in all areas of the arts. The days when actors like Alec Guinness, Katharine Hepburn and Mickey Rooney donned heavy make-up and spoke pidgin English to play egregious, stereotyped Asian characters in such films as *A Passage to India, Dragon Seed* and *Breakfast at Tiffany's* are long gone. In 1988, Chinese-American playwright David Henry Hwang won the Tony Award for his play, *M. Butterfly*; twelve years later, Indian-American author Jhumpa Lahiri's short story collection **Interpreter of Maladies** won the 2000 Pulitzer Prize. And Korean-American comedian Margaret Cho regularly blows the image of the dutiful, meek Asian woman to smithereens with her raunchy, politically-charged stand-up.

It is the literary realm where Asian-Americans have perhaps made the greatest inroads, due largely to Chinese-American writer Amy Tan, whose debut novel, **The Joy Luck Club,** spent eight months on the *New York Times* bestseller list, was translated into seventeen languages, and spawned a hit film. The daughter of Chinese immigrants, Tan writes perceptively about being torn between the world of her parents and American culture. It's a theme that resonates in all of the following novels, listed alphabetically, that evoke what it means to be of Asian descent in America.

1. **American Dervish** by Ayad Ahktar, 2012 – Growing up a secular Muslim in the Midwest, a young Pakistani-American boy becomes obsessed with memorizing the Quran, due to his infatuation with his mother's beautiful and devout friend, who's fled an abusive marriage in Pakistan. A poignant and timely coming-of-age story, written with great empathy and insight, about a Muslim-American struggling with questions of identity and religion.

2. **American Woman** by Susan Choi, 2003 – Inspired by real-life seventies-era radical Wendy Yoshimura, a member of the underground group that kidnapped

Patty Hearst, Choi's second novel focuses on a Japanese-American militant who forms a bond with a kidnapped heiress. An ambitious and bracing finalist for the 2004 Pulitzer Prize.

3. **The Bonesetter's Daughter** by Amy Tan, 2001 – Another gem from Tan. A San Francisco career woman investigates the early life of her Alzheimer's afflicted mother, a Chinese immigrant, who grew up in an isolated, mountain community ruled by superstition.

EXCERPT: THE BONESETTER'S DAUGHTER:

Throughout the years, LuLing lamented in Chinese, "Ai-ya, if only your father had lived, he would be even more successful than your uncle. And still we wouldn't spend so carelessly like them!" She also noted what should have been Ruth's rightful property: Grandmother Young's jade ring, money for a college fund. It shouldn't have mattered that Ruth was a girl or that Edwin had died. That was old fantasizing what her life might have been like had her father lived.

4. **The Buddha in the Attic** by Julie Otsuka, 2011 – Otsuka (***When the Emperor Was Divine***) won the PEN/Faulkner Award for Fiction for *The Buddha in the Attic*, which depicts the lives of a group of Japanese "picture brides" brought to San Francisco nearly one hundred years ago. Beautifully written and perceptively told from multiple points of view, Otsuka's second novel conveys the women's sense of cultural dislocation and isolation in elegant and economical prose.

5. **Donald Duk** by Frank Chin, 1991 – A breezy, good-naturedly funny coming-of-age novel set in San Francisco's Chinatown. The title character is a twelve-year-old boy in full rebellion mode against everything Chinese — particularly his name. However, he gradually comes to embrace his heritage through nightly dreams of building the transcontinental railroad in 1869.

6. **The Fruit 'N Food** by Leonard Chang, 1996 – Racism rears its ugly head for a Korean-American college student, who returns home to his economically depressed, crime-riddled Queens neighborhood in Chang's hard-hitting novel.

7. **The Gangster We All Are Looking For** by Thi Diem Thuy Le, 2003 – Haunting and sorrowful debut novel about Vietnamese refugees trying to let go of their traumatic past while making a new life in America.

8. **I Hotel** by Karen Tei Yamashita, 2010 – Beginning in 1968, Yamashita's National Book Award nominee chronicles ten years of political and social upheaval in San Francisco's Chinatown through the experiences of a finely drawn cast of characters, including students, political radicals, former World War II-era Japanese-American internees, avant-garde artists and more. Mixing prose, graphic art, playwriting and other literary forms, *I Hotel* was hailed as the "literary equivalent of an intricate and vibrant street mural depicting a clamorous and righteous era of protest and creativity" by *Booklist*.

9. **The Konkans** by Tony D'Souza, 2008 – Descended from a long line of Konkans — Hindus who converted to Catholicism in the sixteenth century — on his father's side, Francisco D'Sai is the biracial narrator of D'Souza's engaging novel, set in Chicago. While his father pursues the American dream of fortune and membership in an exclusive country club, Francisco's American mother pines for the culture and traditions of India, where she served in the Peace Corps. Caught between them, Francisco tries to find his own niche in what the *Boston Globe* called "an astute glimpse of the challenges, dangers, and rewards of assimilation."

10. **The Namesake** by Jhumpa Lahiri, 2003 – Lahiri hit the literary jackpot with her first book, the Pulitzer Prize-winning short story collection ***Interpreter of Maladies***. Her follow-up, *The Namesake*, makes very good on that promise. Trading Calcutta for Cambridge, Massachusetts, an Indian couple experiences culture shock; later, their first-born son, named Gogol after his father's favorite writer, tries to forge his own identity, but is unsure whether he's Indian or American.

11. **Native Speaker** by Chang-Rae Lee, 1995 – Lee's brilliant first novel has been called the Asian-American counterpart to Ralph Ellison's ***Invisible Man***. Feeling like a perpetual outsider in fifties-era America, a Korean-American who feels neither Korean nor American goes to work as a spy, only to suffer an identity crisis while spying on a rising Korean-American politician.

12. **When the De La Cruz Family Danced** by Donna Miscolta, 2011 – When his mother Bunny Piña dies, nineteen-year-old Winston finds a letter she wrote but never mailed to his father, Johnny De La Cruz. Leaving the Philippines for San Diego, Winston deals with issues of assimilation and belonging when he meets his father's Filipino-American family for the first time. An acclaimed short story writer, Miscolta scores a literary triumph with her debut novel.

AUSTRALIAN NOVELS
Classics from Down Under

Founded as an English penal colony in 1788, Australia has long since transcended its criminal past to become a major player on the world stage — particularly in the arts. The country's primal, harshly beautiful landscape and turbulent history have sparked the imagination of such internationally acclaimed Australian writers as Peter Carey, Thomas Keneally and Patrick White, who became the first (and so far only) Australian novelist to win the Nobel Prize for Literature in 1973. In his presentation speech to White, Artur Lundkvist of the Swedish Academy cited White "for an epic and psychological narrative art which has introduced a new continent into literature."

Picking up the literary mantle from White, who died in 1990, Carey, Richard Flanagan and Kate Grenville, among others, continue to explore the land down under in novels running the gamut from rollicking, colorful yarns to harrowing, fact-based historical fiction. Here are ten novels, listed alphabetically, from some of Australia's great writers, past and present.

1. **The Chant of Jimmie Blacksmith** by Thomas Keneally, 1972 – A protean talent who's tackled everything from Joan of Arc to World War II in his novels, Keneally won acclaim for this explosive, fact-based novel about the title character, a nineteenth century servant born to a white man and Aboriginal mother, whose efforts to get ahead are continually thwarted by racist "Christians" in New South Wales. Driven to the brink by their cruel bullying, Blacksmith snaps and vents his long-festering rage in a horrific killing spree. Short-listed for the Booker Prize.

2. **For the Term of His Natural Life** by Marcus Clarke, 1874 – While melodramatic and blatantly contrived by today's standards, Clarke's novel about an innocent man wrongfully convicted of murder and sentenced to the Australian penal colony is still a landmark in Australian fiction. Brutal and unsparing in its depiction of the suffering and cruelty hero Rufus Dawes endures, *For the Term of His Natural Life* effectively put Australia on the world's literary map.

3. **Gould's Book of Fish** by Richard Flanagan, 2001 – Dazzling and enthralling, *Gould's Book of Fish* shifts back and forth in time in Tasmania, where a contemporary art forger finds an invaluable manuscript penned and illustrated by a nineteenth century inmate on Sarah Island, a penal colony overseen by a sadistic commandant in a gold mask. Reminiscent of the novels of Joseph Conrad and Daniel Defoe, *Gould's Book of Fish* is a stunning achievement.

4. **The Great World** by David Malouf, 1993 – While not nearly as well-known as either Peter Carey or Thomas Keneally, Malouf has established himself as one of Australia's most exciting novelists, thanks to such books as **Remembering Babylon** and this spellbinding novel about two men, who form an enduring bond as World War II prisoners-of-war in a Japanese camp in Thailand. Spanning close to seventy years, *The Great World* is a great book that won the Commonwealth Prize.

5. **The Idea of Perfection** by Kate Grenville, 2002 – In a small, remote outback town, two divorced misfits stumble and fall their way into love. Winner of the Orange Prize for Fiction, *The Idea of Perfection* is a seriocomic romance of great tenderness and humor.

6. **My Brilliant Career** by Miles Franklin, 1901 – A pioneering feminist novel, *My Brilliant Career* introduces the reader to the irrepressible and spirited Sybilla Melvyn, a teenager in rural New South Wales determined to preserve her hard-

won independence at all costs — even it if means turning down a marriage proposal from a man she loves.

EXCERPT: MY BRILLIANT CAREER:

This was life — my life — my career, my brilliant career! I was fifteen — fifteen! A few fleeting hours and I would be old as those around me. I looked at them as they stood there, weary, and turning down the other side of the hill of life. When young, no doubt they had hoped for, and dreamed of, better things—had even known them. But here they were. This had been their life; this was their career. It was, and in all probability would be, mine too. My life — my career — my brilliant career!

7. **On the Beach** by Nevil Shute, 1957 – Written at the height of the cold war, *On the Beach* is a sobering account of the survivors of a nuclear war, bravely living out their final days in Australia in grim anticipation of the end. A subdued but chilling portrait of nuclear Armageddon from the author of *A Town Like Alice*.

8. **Things We Didn't See Coming** by Steven K. Amsterdam, 2010 – This award-winning first novel sends its narrator on a journey through a dystopian, post-apocalyptic future over the course of nine linked stories. But this vision of the future is anything but depressing. Through it all, both author and protagonist retain their humor and humanity.

9. **True History of the Kelly Gang** by Peter Carey, 2000 – The heir apparent to Patrick White, Carey brings Australia's outlaw folk hero, Ned Kelly, to bold life in this hugely entertaining historical novel, written in the form of a letter from Kelly to his infant daughter.

10. **Voss** by Patrick White, 1957 – Inspired by the mysterious, nineteenth century disappearance of Prussian naturalist Ludwig Leichhardt, *Voss* is a bona-fide masterpiece that brought White long overdue recognition in Australia. A German explorer leaves his bride in Sydney to embark on an ill-fated trek across the Outback, where he falls prey to his own hubris.

BIG STUFF
Books about ENORMOUS Things

As mind-blowing as tiny things can be, there's plenty out there to blow the mind at the other end of the scale. Here are some entertaining and informative books, listed alphabetically, about products of nature and culture that inspire awe by their sheer enormousness. For a well-balanced mind, read them in tandem with the books listed in the entry "Tiny Things."

1. **The Big Book of Sumo: History, Practice, Ritual, Fight** by Mina Hall, 1997 – Being enormous is all part of a day's work for Japan's sumo wrestlers. Hall, a dedicated fan of the sport, explains the rules of sumo along with its history and rituals, the wrestlers' highly regimented daily lives, and more. Photos and, in true Japanese fashion, cute cartoons enliven the text.

2. **Blue Whales** by John Calambokidis and Gretchen Steiger, 1997 – Learn all about the biggest animals on earth. How did these air-breathing mammals end up living underwater? What do they eat to grow so much? How do they communicate? The book gives answers to all these questions and provides magnificent photographs as well.

3. **Dinosaurus: The Complete Guide to Dinosaurs** by Steve Parker, 2003 – It may seem hard to believe that such formidable creatures ever existed, but the illustrations in this book will help you imagine them and their world with full-color vividness. The great predators, the duckbills, the giants, and many other categories of dinosaurs come to life in these pictures, and the author captures the grand adventure of paleontology.

4. **An Elephant's Life: An Intimate Portrait from Africa** by Caitlin O'Connell, 2011 – For nearly twenty years, O'Connell has studied elephants in their natural habitat in Namibia's Etosha National Park. Her close observations of the magnificent creatures inform every page of this entrancing tome that is lavishly illustrated with photos by O'Connell and Timothy Rodwell. The lives of these wonderful and endangered animals unfold in unforgettable pages that encompass every aspect of elephant life from reproduction to family life to competition among the males.

5. **Michelangelo and the Pope's Ceiling** by Ross King, 2003 – Michelangelo Buonarroti loved to sculpt, not to paint. But, genius that he was, when he was conscripted to decorate the Sistine Chapel, he rose to the challenge. His soaring frescoes are now among the immortal masterpieces of art. This book recounts the political wrangling behind the accomplishment.

EXCERPT: MICHELANGELO AND THE POPE'S CEILING:

A few months after the David was finished, early in 1505, Michelangelo received from Pope Julius II an abrupt that interrupted his work in Florence. So impressed was the pope with the Pietà, which he had seen in a chapel of St. Peter's, that he wanted the young sculptor to carve his tomb as well. At the end of February the papal treasurer, Cardinal Francesco Alidosi, paid Michelangelo an advance of one hundred gold florins, the equivalent of a full year's salary for a craftsman. The sculptor then returned to Rome and entered the service of the pope. So began what he would later call "the tragedy of the tomb."

Papal tombs were usually grand affairs. That of Sixtus IV, who died in 1484, was a beautiful bronze sarcophagus that had been nine years in the making. But

Julius, a stranger to all modesty, had envisioned for himself something on an entirely new scale. He had begun making plans for his sepulchre soon after his election to the papacy in 1503, ultimately conceiving of a memorial that was to be the largest since the mausoleums built for Roman emperors such as Hadrian and Augustus.

6. **Remarkable Trees of the World** by Thomas Pakenham, 2002 – Not all the trees described and pictured in this book are large — you'll find bonsai as well as massive baobabs. But there is a whole chapter devoted to "Giants," and another to "Methuselahs." The photographs of arboreal wonders all over the world are extraordinary.

7. **Skyscrapers: A History of the World's Most Extraordinary Buildings** by Judith Dupré, 1996 – Ogle some of mankind's most astonishing feats of architecture and engineering, from the Eiffel Tower to the Empire State Building to the Petronas Towers in Malaysia. To do justice to the amazing black-and-white photographs of its subject matter, this volume is an unusual rectangular shape, a foot and a half high. (Produced before the destruction of the World Trade Center, it includes the twin towers among its marvels.) You won't want to neglect the text, which is also eye-opening.

8. **The Stars of Heaven** by Clifford Pickover, 2001 – All the life on our planet depends on the most familiar star — the sun — for the light and heat it generates. This book uses some amusing science fiction to help us make sense of the real-world — er, real-universe — phenomena which are even more amazing than science fiction, from our old dependable sun to black holes and supergiants.

9. **The Statues that Walked: Unraveling the Mystery of Easter Island** by Terry Hunt and Carl Lipo, 2011 – The great stone heads of Easter Island in the South Pacific have intrigued the world for centuries. The European expedition that first spotted the place in the eighteenth century found a barren, sparsely populated island. The theory has long held that in building the monoliths, the islanders wrought war and environmental devastation on themselves. Archaeologists Hunt and Lipo expected to validate that theory during a 2001 expedition. Instead, as they report in this captivating book, they uncovered evidence that the islanders were staunch environmentalists and that the creation of the giant statues was part of their effort to achieve sustainability.

BIRD LOVERS' BOOKS
All about Our Feathered Friends

From the young woman who becomes a nightingale in the Greek legend of Philomela to Hans Christian Andersen's "The Ugly Duckling" to the albatross in Coleridge's

"Rime of the Ancient Mariner," birds have always been a theme for writers and storytellers. Yes, the dog may always be man's best friend. But various kinds of birds possess charming and even awe-inspiring attributes — singing, exquisite plumage, the ability to fly, intelligence, and devotion to family. Here is an alphabetical list of ten books about our feathered friends.

1. <u>**The Alex Studies: Cognitive and Communicative Abilities of Grey Parrots**</u> by Irene Maxine Pepperberg, 1999 – Just how intelligent are parrots? We all know they can mimic human speech, but do they know what they are saying? This book details a university professor's research with Alex, the reasoning parrot.

2. <u>**The Art of Bird Identification: A Straightforward Approach to Putting a Name to the Bird**</u> by Pete Dunne, 2012 – Pete Dunne, one of America's most renowned avian observers and the director of the New Jersey Audubon Society's Cape May Bird Observatory, adds a bright feather to his cap with this guide to becoming a better birder. Spotting birds is easier than identifying them, so the author provides logical methods for properly naming the birds you see, as well as what mistakes to avoid.

3. <u>**The Beak of the Finch: A Story of Evolution in Our Time**</u> by Jonathan Weiner, 1995 – The finches of the Galápagos Islands were the catalysts for Charles Darwin's theory of evolution by natural selection. This book recounts how two present-day scientists spent more than twenty years studying these birds and documenting the evolution still taking place from generation to generation.

4. <u>**The Bedside Book of Birds: An Avian Miscellany**</u> by Graeme Gibson, 2005 – This beautiful book is brimming with artwork, poems, and legends about birds of all kinds. It explores both the magic and the dark side of humans' relationship with birds.

5. <u>**The Big Year: A Tale of Man, Nature, and Fowl Obsession**</u> by Mark Obmascik, 2004 – Made into a 2011 movie starring Steve Martin and Jack Black, *The Big Year* chronicles three men in 1998 who fight tooth and nail (or is it beak and claw?) for the most coveted birdwatching record in North America. From January 1 to December 31, they traverse the continent, covering hundreds of thousands of miles on a compulsive quest to set a record for the number of bird species sighted in a single year.

EXCERPT: THE BIG YEAR:

Slowly, from some of his friends, a picture emerged: Thompson Marsh was a birdwatcher possessed. To chase rare birds, he would rise before dawn on weekends. He would take expensive vacations on desolate Alaskan isles and pray for foul weather. He would wait for phone calls in the middle of the night, then rush to the airport for the next red-eye flight. Only five others in history had seen more species of birds in North America.

6. **The Grail Bird: Hot on the Trail of the Ivory-billed Woodpecker** by Tim Gallagher, 2005 – The adventure of searching for — and finding — a magnificent bird long thought to be extinct. An exciting and heartening true story.

7. **The Sibley Guide to Bird Life & Behavior** by David Allen Sibley, 2001 – This book is not a field guide, but it offers a wealth of information about the behavior, anatomy, and evolution of the eighty families of North American birds. Illustrated with hundreds of full-color paintings as well as many diagrams and maps, it's great for reference or for browsing.

8. **The Sibley Guide to Birds** by David Allen Sibley, 2000 – For casual and serious birders alike, this is an excellent, in-depth field guide, with full-color illustrations and detailed text to help you identify hundreds of species of North American birds. It describes markings, songs, migration routes, and much more.

9. **The Singing Life of Birds** by Donald Kroodsma, 2005 – We all know and love the sound of birdsong, but why do they sing? Are their songs purely instinctive, or does each generation of birds learn them anew? The author explains the mysteries of one of nature's loveliest phenomena and helps readers hear the songs of many different birds with sensitivity and understanding. For an aural as well as a literary experience, listen to the compact disc that comes with the book.

10. **The Wild Parrots of Telegraph Hill: A Love Story...with Wings** by Mark Bittner, 2004 – The subject of a documentary, this is the real-life story of friendship between a man and a flock of birds. The author was a lost soul living in San Francisco when he met the parrots that had escaped from captivity and bred in the wild. He writes movingly about their individual personalities and how they transformed his life.

BROADWAY BOOKS
Biographies/Memoirs of Theatrical Legends

They are the giants of twentieth century American theater — the playwrights, composers, and choreographers of Broadway's "Golden Age," when theatergoers regularly clamored to see both musicals *and* serious dramas by such luminaries as Arthur Miller, Eugene O'Neill and Tennessee Williams. And legendary songwriters Irving Berlin, George Gershwin and Cole Porter wrote the standards that all of America was humming. Although the luster of Broadway has faded somewhat in recent years, the glory days of The Great White Way come vibrantly alive in the following biographies and memoirs, listed alphabetically, that offer a veritable feast of revealing anecdotes and insights about Broadway icons, both on and off stage.

1. **Cole Porter** by William McBrien, 1998 – "Swellegant" biography of the most urbane and sophisticated of tunesmiths, who ran in high society's most glittering circles.

2. **Dazzler: The Life and Times of Moss Hart** by Stephen Bach, 2001 – Although Hart's widow, Kitty Carlisle, refused to cooperate with him, Bach has nonetheless written an engrossing and scrupulously researched of the multi-talented Hart, the thirties-era Broadway "golden boy" playwright/director.

3. **Elia Kazan: A Life** by Elia Kazan, 1988 – Exceptionally frank autobiography from the Broadway/Hollywood icon, whose brilliant string of successes have been forever overshadowed by his decision to "name names" to the House Un-American Activities Committee during the "Red Scare."

4. **Eugene O'Neill: Beyond Mourning and Tragedy** by Stephen A. Black, 1999 – Taking a psychoanalytic approach to the Nobel Prize-winning playwright, Black persuasively argues that O'Neill exorcised his family demons in such plays as *Long Day's Journey Into Night* and *A Moon for the Misbegotten*.

5. **Finishing the Hat: Collected Lyrics (1954-1981) with Attendant Comments, Principles, Heresies, Grudges, Whines and Anecdotes** by Stephen Sondheim, 2010 – A must-read for musical theatre junkies, Sondheim's insightful, gossipy and thoroughly entertaining book succeeds as a lesson in the art and craft of songwriting, as well as a highly personal look at Sondheim's decades-spanning career. Read it in conjunction with Meryle Secrest's highly regarded biography of the Broadway icon, *Stephen Sondheim: A Life*.

6. **Jerome Robbins: His Life, His Theater, His Dance** by Deborah Jowitt, 2004 – In stark contrast to his exuberant, joyous choreography, Robbins was reputed to be a sour, even hateful man widely despised in the theater and dance world. In this thorough and skillfully written biography, Jowitt reveals the vulnerability and insecurity beneath Robbins' temperamental façade.

7. **The Kindness of Strangers: A Life of Tennessee Williams** by Donald Spoto, 1985 – Respectful and intelligent biography of Williams, who tragically fell from critical and popular grace in the sixties, when he plunged into alcohol and drug-fueled despair.

8. **Kurt Weill – On Stage: From Berlin to Broadway** by Foster Hirsch, 2004 - After penning the enduring "Mack the Knife" for *Threepenny Opera*, Weill fled Nazi Germany and settled in America to become one of its best-known composers. This well-researched biography, drawn largely from New York's Kurt Weill Foundation, takes up the argument of Weill's wife, Lotte Lenya: "…there is no American Weill, there is no German Weill…there is only Weill."

9. **Original Story By: A Memoir of Broadway and Hollywood** by Arthur Laurents, 2001 — With a career that spanned both coasts and saw such hits as *Gypsy* and *West Side Story*, it's no wonder that this memoir of director/screenwriter/playwright Arthur Laurents is as lively and entertaining as a night on Broadway. Liz Smith of *Newsday* calls this book a "must for show biz mavens."

10. **Rewrites: A Memoir** by Neil Simon, 1996 – Appealingly honest and down-to-earth memoir from one of America's most successful comic playwrights, who writes movingly about the tragic loss of his first wife to cancer.
11. **Somewhere for Me: A Biography of Richard Rodgers** by Meryle Secrest, 2001 – With partner Oscar Hammerstein, Richard Rodgers wrote the classic scores for *The Sound of Music* and *South Pacific*, among others. Despite his success, however, Rodgers was a deeply unhappy man, alcoholic and estranged from his family. A thoughtful and poignant biography.
12. **Timebends** by Arthur Miller, 1989 – An intelligent and nuanced memoir from the playwright of ***Death of A Salesman*** and ***The Crucible***.

EXCERPT: TIMEBENDS:

There was also an adenoidal young assistant stage manager popping in and out whom Grosbard, incredibly, told me I should keep in mind to play Willy Loman in a few years. My estimate of Grosbard all but collapsed as, observing Dustin Hoffman's awkwardness and his big nose that never seemed to get unstuffed, I wondered how the poor fellow imagined himself a candidate for any kind of acting career. Grosbard, however, was looking not at Hoffman but at an actor, at a spirit, and this kind of naked skin-on-skin contact with essentials was what his production had in every role.

BUSINESS BOOKS
Fortune Magazine Recommendations

In its March 21, 2005 issue, *Fortune* offered its readers a list of "75 books that teach you everything you need to know about business" drawn up by the magazine's staffers. Not all the selections are business books, they pointed out, but all of them can teach you something about it. *Fortune* divided its seventy-five recommendations into sixteen categories — here are two of these, "Economics" and "Investing," along with our brief description of each title.

ECONOMICS

1. **Capitalism, Socialism, and Democracy** by Joseph A. Schumpeter, 1942 – This book discusses the links between economics, politics, and social values, suggesting that they cannot be fully understood in isolation from one another. *Fortune* suggests skipping right to Chapter 7 ("The Process of Creative Destruction").
2. **Everything for Sale: The Virtues and Limits of Markets** by Robert Kuttner, 1996 – Kuttner outlines the dangers and pitfalls — both domestically and internationally — of blind faith in the benevolence of free markets.

3. **The General Theory of Employment, Interest, and Money** by John Maynard Keynes, 1936 – One of the most influential works on economics ever written, this book argues for measured government intervention to ward off violent booms and slumps. *Fortune* suggests that you focus on Chapter 12, "a timeless, witty, crystalline account of why financial markets confound and bewitch us."

4. **Pop Internationalism** by Paul Krugman, 1996 – "Pop internationalism" is the author's term for the conventional wisdom about international trade — which has little to do with reality. A controversial take on globalization that may make you more skeptical about things that most pundits seem to agree on.

5. **The Wealth of Nations** by Adam Smith, 1776 – In his pioneering work on the value of free markets, Smith lays out the fundamental assumptions of his vision of how economies function, offers clear, concrete examples to illustrate his arguments, and discusses what he sees as the proper role of government and taxation.

INVESTING

6. **The Essays of Warren Buffett: Lessons for Corporate America** compiled by Lawrence Cunningham, 1997 – Learn from one of the most successful investors of all time in this selection of Jimmy Buffet's annual letters to shareholders of Berkshire Hathaway. He shares principles learned from his teacher and mentor, Benjamin Graham, and from years of his own experience and decision-making.

7. **Fooled by Randomness: The Hidden Role of Chance in the Markets and in Life** by Nassim Nicholas Taleb, 2001 – Taleb is both a hedge fund manager and a professor of mathematics. His book is less an enumeration of strategies than a broad perspective on the nature of the stock market — and many other aspects of life in which dumb luck plays a bigger role than you might have thought.

EXCERPT: FOOLED BY RANDOMNESS:

Nero has seen many traders blow up, and does not want to get into that situation. Blow up in the lingo has a precise meaning; it does not just mean to lose money; it means to lose more money than one ever expected, to the point of being thrown out of the business (the equivalent of a doctor losing his license to practice or a lawyer being disbarred). Nero rapidly exits trades after a predetermined loss. He never sells "naked options" (a strategy that would leave him exposed to large possible losses). He never puts himself in a situation where he can lose more than, say, $1 million— regardless of the probability of such an event. That amount has always been variable; it depends on his accumulated profits for the year.

8. **The Intelligent Investor: A Book of Practical Counsel** by Benjamin Graham, 1949 – The author is the teacher and mentor of Warren Buffett mentioned above. The

fact that this book remains so well respected by successful investors over sixty years after Graham wrote it is a testament to the soundness of his concept of "value investment."

9. **Moneyball: The Art of Winning an Unfair Game** by Michael Lewis, 2003 — This is the story of Billy Beane, the general manager of the Oakland A's, and his success, based on creative thinking, hard study of statistics, and a willingness to stray from the beaten path.

CARTOON COLLECTIONS
The Far Side of Funny

Turning to your favorite comic strip in the Sunday paper is a pleasant ritual, but when you're a really committed fan, sometimes you want a little more — or a lot more. Luckily, there are some fabulous cartoon collections out there. Whether your tastes run to the warm and poignant or to trenchant satire, you'll find something to chuckle at in this list of ten cartoon collections, listed in alphabetical order.

1. **40: A Doonesbury Retrospective** by G. B. Trudeau, 2010 — This hefty collection contains 1,800 strips highlighting the evolving relationships among the more than forty major characters in this cartoon classic. At times sweet and sentimental, at others biting and satirical (especially when skewering politicians — for example, Trudeau drew President Bill Clinton as a giant waffle) this compendium demonstrates how the *Doonesbury* universe has remained fresh and funny despite four decades of profound change.

2. **Art Out of Time: Unknown Comics Visionaries 1900–1969** by Dan Nadel, 2006 — Twenty-nine little-known creators of comics get their due here. If you're interested in the history of comics and stylistic experimentation, these artists will pique your interest and even change some of your ideas about the genre's march of progress.

3. **The Complete Cartoons of The New Yorker** edited by Robert Mankoff, 2004 — Nearly as famous for its cartoons as for its prose, *The New Yorker* magazine has published thousands upon thousands of them since the twenties. This enormous book includes many of the best, from James Thurber to George Booth to Roz Chast, proving that a good laugh can defuse some of the anxieties of modern life.

4. **Cul de Sac Golden Treasury: A Keepsake Garland of Classics** by Richard Thompson, 2010 — Known for its smarts and light touch, as well as its gorgeous watercolor artwork, the *Cul de Sac* strip revolves around the comings and goings of a precocious preschooler in suburbia. Thompson is noted for being uniquely able to couch wit in the words of children, and his amusing and informative annotations will delight newcomers and longtime followers alike.

5. **The Indispensable Calvin and Hobbes: A Calvin and Hobbes Treasury** by Bill Watterson, 1992 – The intelligent, beloved cartoon about a little boy and his toy tiger depicts the joys and frustrations of childhood and the need for companionship in full-color and black-and-white drawings.

6. **Mad Art: A Visual Celebration of the Art of Mad Magazine and the Idiots Who Create It** by Mark Evanier, 2002 – The house style of *Mad Magazine* illustration is vigorous, vulgar, and even creepy, yet it has a strange kitschy charm. This fiftieth-anniversary collection offers a huge dose of the magazine's peculiar brand of madness.

7. **Peanuts: The Art of Charles M. Schulz** by Charles M. Schulz, 2001 – This book offers a colorful and intimate look at Charlie Brown, Linus, Peppermint Pattie, Snoopy and all the other well-loved characters of *Peanuts*. It has an insightful introduction by Schulz's wife and sketches from early in his career — a treat for any fan.

8. **The Prehistory of the Far Side: A 10th Anniversary Exhibit** by Gary Larson, 1989 – This book lets us watch Larson's drawings become simpler and his jokes more honed as he developed the hallmark style of *The Far Side*. More than just a collection of previously published cartoons, it also features Larson's commentary on everything from his obsession with cows (whether residing in barns, lifeboats, or suburban houses) to hilarious mix-ups in the funny pages (such as a pair of switched captions that made Dennis the Menace and a pal appear to be eating hamster sandwiches).

9. **A Right to Be Hostile: The Boondocks Treasury** by Aaron McGruder, 2003 – This edgy and sometimes controversial cartoon follows two young black boys from the city who find themselves living out in the boondocks of a mostly white suburb. There's hardly a rote or dull strip in this compound of humor and penetrating social commentary.

10. **The World of Charles Addams** by Charles Addams, 1991 – With his dreadful situations and spooky wash drawings, Chas Addams defines black humor. The Addams family in their creepy Victorian house are here, along with some delightfully horrible surprises.

CAT LOVERS' BOOKS
Purr-fect Fiction, Nonfiction and Verse

Cats are fascinating animals with many different sides to them — hilariously playful kittens, aloof loners, devoted companions, expert predators, lazy hedonists, skillful acrobats who get stuck in trees — they seem to have no end of contradictory qualities.

And they evoke all kinds of responses in humans — from worship (cats were considered sacred in ancient Egypt) to demonization (medieval Europeans believed Satan liked to take the form of a black cat). In modern times we're not *quite* so extreme in our reactions, but there are still those who adore cats and those who find them too peculiar or standoffish. If you fall into the former group, you're sure to love these ten books, listed alphabetically, that explore and celebrate the many aspects of this elegant creature. If you're decidedly not a cat person, be aware that conversions have happened before — and sometimes a good story is the "catalyst."

1. **250 Things You Can Do to Make Your Cat Adore You** by Ingrid Newkirk, 1998 – The author, one of the founders of People for the Ethical Treatment of Animals, offers practical advice on how to make your home more cat-friendly, natural remedies for your cat, and the finer points of feline communication.

2. **Asleep in the Sun** by Hans Silvester, 1997 – Napping is an important part of every cat's life. This book is filled with exquisite photographs of what appear to be some of the most idyllic catnaps on earth, in the Greek Cycladic Islands.

3. **Cat on the Edge: A Joe Grey Mystery** by Shirley Rousseau Murphy, 1996 – There are quite a few mysteries featuring detectives with feline sidekicks, but Murphy's popular Joe Grey mysteries feature a cat sleuth who's inexplicably learned to talk and understand people. As if that weren't vexing enough, Joe must crack a murder case or part with one of his nine lives. A charming blend of whimsical humor and murder mystery.

4. **The Cat Who Covered the World: The Adventures Of Henrietta And Her Foreign Correspondent** by Christopher S. Wren, 2000 – This is the true story of a cosmopolitan tabby named Henrietta who accompanied her owners — a foreign correspondent and his family —to Russia, China, South Africa, Egypt, and other distant lands. She brought the author a certain amount of trouble along the way but also humor and much-needed comfort.

5. **The Cat Who Went to Paris** by Peter Gethers, 1991 – Before he met Norton, a Scottish Fold cat, the author was a cat-hater. But this alert and refined creature ended up changing his life for the better. Gethers published two more books about Norton — *A Cat Abroad* and *The Cat Who'll Live Forever*.

6. **The Character of Cats: The Origins, Intelligence, Behavior, and Stratagems of Felis silvestris catus** by Stephen Budiansky, 2002 – A rigorous but entertaining survey of the domestic cat and our relationship with it. From feline evolution to our superstitions about cats, you'll learn the fascinating history and science of these animals. Cat owners are likely to punctuate their reading with exclamations of "So *that's* why they do that!"

7. **Dewey: The Small-Town Library Cat Who Touched the World** by Vicki Myron with Bret Witter, 2008 – This charming and light-hearted story about a stray tabby who becomes a library mascot is as sentimental as you'd expect, but it's hard not to

love Dewey, who provides friendship, inspiration and comfort to library patrons for nearly twenty years.

8. **Homer's Odyssey** by Gwen Cooper, 2009 – Another heart-tugger that's nearly as irresistible as Homer, an abandoned, eyeless kitten who becomes the fearless protector and best friend to Cooper, a novelist (***Diary of a South Beach Party Girl***).

EXCERPT: HOMER'S ODYSSEY:

A fuzzy shadow trails my steps through the apartment, leaping to the tops of any and all furniture along the way. Homer jumps effortlessly from floor to chair, from chair to dining room table, then back to the floor again, like Q*bert on speed. As I make my way from the living/dining area to the hallway, Homer's up on top of a side table, then hurls himself recklessly to the third shelf of the bookcase diagonally across the hall, perching for a precarious moment until I've passed. Then he's down on the ground once more, zipping along ahead of me and occasionally, in his enthusiasm, running smack into one of my other two cats until he reaches the doorway to the bedroom. Stopping at precisely the same point each time, he pauses for an infinitesimal moment, then cuts a hard left through the bedroom door, as if he were drawing a large capital L. He jumps to the top of the bed, where he knows I'll sit to remove my shoes, and crawls into my lap for another round of purring and face rubbing

9. **James Herriot's Cat Stories** by James Herriot, 1994 – Herriot was a dedicated veterinarian and a wonderful storyteller. Here is a collection of encounters with the cats in his rural Yorkshire community: Alfred, the cat who keeps watch over the counter of his owner's candy shop; Moses, a half-frozen kitten who takes up the life of a piglet; Oscar the socialite; and several other feline patients and friends.

10. **Old Possum's Book of Practical Cats** by T.S. Eliot, 1939 – The legendary Broadway musical *Cats* was based on this collection of verse, written by one of the central figures of modern poetry. Eliot's whimsical language brings to life a feline world whose inhabitants have characters as distinct as those of our own society.

CHICK LIT

Looking for Mr. Right — or Mr. Right Now

Need a break from the search for Prince Charming — or Mr. Right Now? Then kick off those stilettos, fix yourself a big, fat martini and curl up with one of these books before heading back into the dating trenches. It's time for a little vicarious ***Sex and*** *the Single Girl*, to quote the how-to book written by the late *Cosmopolitan* editor Helen Gurley Brown way back in the early sixties, before the sexual revolution made it okay for "nice girls" to take the occasional walk on the wild side.

Running the gamut from contemporary classics to juicy page-turners, the following books, listed alphabetically, open a window on the world of the single girl — or the soon-to-be-single girl — crossing paths with sexy cads, jet-setting zillionaires and the random decent guy.

1. **Bergdorf Blondes** by Plum Sykes, 2004 – Adhering to the writer's code of "write what you know," London-born socialite/fashionista Sykes trains her sights on the designer-clad, Botoxed and back-stabbing world of Park Avenue heiresses whose lives center around shopping, men and still more shopping.

2. **The Best of Everything** by Rona Jaffe, 1958 – Incredibly chaste by today's standards, Jaffe's well-crafted page-turner raised eyebrows in the fifties. Friends and co-workers in a swank New York publishing company, Jaffe's heroines navigate the tricky shoals of romance and career, not altogether successfully.

3. **Bombshell** by Lynda Curnyn, 2004 – The biological clock starts ticking for glamorous, cosmetics marketing executive Grace Noonan, who's had it up to her designer earrings with her commitment-phobic boyfriend. Bittersweet, good-natured fluff from the author of ***Engaging Men***.

4. **Breakfast at Tiffany's** by Truman Capote, 1958 – Has there ever been a more captivating heroine than Holly Golightly? Capote's beloved free spirit, immortalized on film by Audrey Hepburn, wafts her way through the pages of Capote's novella, looking for a rich husband and setting hearts aflutter — including the reader's.

5. **Bridget Jones' Diary** by Helen Fielding, 1996 – A lovable overweight bundle of neuroses, Fielding's zaftig heroine muddles her way through life and love in this pricelessly funny novel, written in diary form, which pays sexy homage to Jane Austen.

6. **Fear of Flying** by Erica Jong, 1973 – A seventies-era pop culture phenomenon, Jong's funny and unabashedly raunchy novel tracks the sexual misadventures of Isadora Wing, an erotic poet who prizes her freedom above all else, including her marriage. Praised by the *Wall Street Journal* as a "latter-day ***Ulysses***," *Fear of Flying* spawned two sequels, ***How to Save Your Own Life*** and ***Parachutes & Kisses***.

7. **The Girls' Guide to Hunting and Fishing** by Melissa Bank, 1999 – A critical and popular hit, Bank's short story collection is an intelligent and wryly funny alternative to the "chick lit" dreck littering bookstore shelves.

8. **I've Got Your Number** by Sophie Kinsella, 2012 – The author of the hugely popular ***Confessions of a Shopaholic*** series, Kinsella takes a break from her irrepressible

debt-ridden heroine to tell the story of Poppy Wyatt, whose seemingly perfect life gets upended when she loses both her engagement ring and her phone.

9. *Lipstick Jungle* by Candace Bushnell, 2005 – The *Sex and the City* novelist has become the sexy chick lit equivalent of a brand name. With *Lipstick Jungle*, Bushnell serves up "more of the same" in this nonetheless satisfying book about three high-flying Manhattan socialites running amok in their Manolo Blahniks.

EXCERPT: LIPSTICK JUNGLE:

"How ya doin, pretty lady?" Kirby asked casually, as if it were perfectly normal for an older woman to come to his apartment in the middle of the afternoon for sex. Nico suddenly felt shy. How was she supposed to behave? How did Kirby expect her to behave? How did he see her—and them? Having no other reference points by which to categorize the situation, she hoped he envisioned them as Richard Gere and Lauren Hutton in American Gigolo. Maybe if she pretended to be Lauren Hutton, she'd be able to get through this scene.

And what was up with that phrase, "pretty lady"?

10. **Valley of the Dolls** by Jacqueline Susann, 1966 – *The* bestselling novel of the sixties, Susann's randy roman à clef is a glossy page-turner about three beautiful young women caught up in the nasty, cutthroat world of showbiz, where "dolls," i.e., sleeping pills, provide irresistible escape from feckless men and predatory divas.

11. **Waiting to Exhale** by Terry McMillan, 1989 – Repeatedly unlucky in love, four African-American professional women find solace in their deep and abiding friendship in McMillan's intelligent and fiery bestseller.

12. **Wife 22** by Melanie Gideon, 2012 – Alice Buckle, a middle-aged woman whose life and marriage are on autopilot, decides to participate in an online study, "Marriage in the 21st Century." Free to express all her pent-up desires, frustrations and hopes anonymously (hence the title), Alice starts flirting online with the study researcher. As the flirtation develops into something deeper, she begins to question every aspect of her life in Gideon's smartly observed and addictively readable novel.

CHILDREN'S BOOKS
Alphabet Books for Toddlers (Up to 2-Years-Old)

Learning the alphabet takes time. Most toddlers begin to recognize some letters by the age of two, which makes it a good time to introduce the alphabet. Just keep in mind that they will not master the idea that letters form words, nor the ability to write their ABCs for some time. That is why choosing an ABC book is so important in the development of your child's literacy. Select one that has a particular appeal for you and your child, or pick a classic with staying power. Toddlers learn differently than preschoolers, so resist the urge to start with flashcards too early. Focus on reading and listening skills by calling out those first letters. Make a smart start, an art start or an animal start — learn to recognize shapes, animals and familiar objects. Or check out the hipster titles where A is for attitude. Select one, two or three titles from the ten colorful, original, amusing and all-around fun alphabet books below, listed in ABC order.

1. **ABC Kids** by Simon Basher, 2011 – Veer away from the traditional or classic in alphabet books to find the contemporary vision of Simon Basher. His distinctive graphic style suits the oddly wonderful characters your child will meet in alphabetical fashion. Fun and inventive, *ABC Kids* uses very creative alliteration and stylized imagery to bring an innovative take on learning the alphabet and having fun with language. Kids will love Maude, who has a mean monkey who makes marvelous milkshakes, and Vera, who vacuums vegetables. *ABC Kids* is a visual and lingual delight.

2. **Alternative ABCs (Chunky Edition)** by Dave Parmley, Eric Ruffing, 13th Floor Design (designer), 2011 – Learning the ABCs has never been so full of attitude! For all urban and hipster parents, this chunky board book spells out the alphabet in über cool fashion, borrowing its aesthetics and typography from street, skate and music subcultures. When B is for boombox and T is for tattoo, it's clear that this is indeed an alternative alphabet book. Do what the title suggests: Bask in its originality and wit.

3. **Charley Harper ABCs** by Charley Harper, 2008 – This ABC board book featuring the whimsical wildlife artwork of the modernist illustrator Charley Harper will engage you and your little one. Toddlers will learn their alphabet by paging through Harper's highly stylized animal imagery. Beautifully designed, this alphabet board book brings Harper's sensitive and nurturing outlook on our natural world to life, using it as an appreciated learning device.

4. **Chicka Chicka Boom Boom** by Bill Martin, John Archambault, Lois Ehlert (illustrator), 1989 – Bill Martin and John Archambault created *Chicka Chicka Boom Boom* as an infectious story of what happens when all twenty-six letters try to climb up a coconut tree that can't quite carry the weight. Parents adore reading the simple yet extraordinarily catchy narrative. Children love its nonsensical nature. It's an alphabet adventure, exuberant, full of lively, bold illustrations, and clearly worth being cited as one of the all-time best ABC books.

EXCERPT: CHICKA CHICKA BOOM BOOM:

A told b,
and b told c,
I'll meet you at the top of the coconut tree

5. **Curious George's ABCs** by H. A. Rey, 1998 – You and your toddler will enjoy reading along with George in a clever, easy-to-read version of *Curious George Learns the Alphabet*. The illustrations are smart and sassy with animals taking on the shape of the letter being introduced — all of which helps little ones focus on the alphabet.

6. **Dr. Seuss's ABC: An Amazing Alphabet Book!** by Dr. Seuss, 1963 – Learning the ABCs of reading is always fun with Dr. Seuss! In Seuss style, parents and children are stimulated and engaged by the amazing alliteration and rhyming fun. Try the sturdy board book version that's easy for your toddler to hold. You may recognize some of the entertaining animal and unusual characters from other Seuss books, but even if it's new to you and your child, this is a perennial favorite and has been for more than forty years. With Dr. Seuss leading the ABC charge, learning letters is nothing but fun and games.

7. **Eric Carle's ABC (The World of Eric Carle)** by Eric Carle, 2007 – Eric Carle's alphabet book features flaps that unfold and animals to discover. A is for ant, B is for bear, C is for camel and D is for duck. Beautifully illustrated with animal adventures, including some unusual choices that make learning your letters as easy as 1, 2, 3!

8. **LMNO Peas** by Keith Baker, 2010 – LMNO Peas is an inventive and entertaining take on learning the alphabet. Busy little peas, including an acrobat pea and a zoologist pea, engage you and your child in an original, career-centric journey through the ABCs. Along the way, letters are recognized and occupations, hobbies and interests named. It's a quirky alphabet book, yet hip and decidedly fun.

9. **Miss Spider's ABC Book** by David Kirk, 1998 – Celebrate along with your favorite arachnid, the guest of honor at a surprise party in a lush garden. Her friends, shown in alphabetical order, get the party started — butterflies blow balloons while caterpillars circle round and dragonflies decorate. The illustrations are signature Kirk; they're electric, expressive and evocative. Readers can hardly wait until it's party time! This is by far one of the prettiest, most elegantly illustrated ABC books and a good introduction to alliteration and practicing letters.

10. **The Sleepy Little Alphabet: A Bedtime Story from Alphabet Town** by Judy Sierra and Melissa Sweet (illustrator), 2009 – This is a drowsy little tale about nighttime in Alphabet Town. All twenty-six letters need or want something before they can be tucked in. With its rhyming cast of odd little letters, this story may remind you of *Chicka Chicka Boom Boom* but it will stand on its own both as an appealing alphabet tale and goodnight story. Melissa Sweet's illustrations are a lovely match to this entertaining story of little letters who need to rest.

CHILDREN'S BOOKS

Bedtime Stories for Preschoolers (Ages 3-5-Years-Old)

Bedtime stories are the ubiquitous family ritual. It's an act repeated every night and part of a healthy habit that can ease many childhood worries, from being scared of the dark to going to preschool. Bedtime storytelling begins before birth these days, but the optimum age is from three to five-years-old, when the process of reading begins to move from the caregiver to the child. Reading encourages language development, but perhaps more importantly, it creates an incredible bonding experience between parent and child. Choosing to read at bedtime sets a pattern for the importance of literacy and it makes nighttime a welcome adventure for little ones.

Here are ten of the best bedtime titles that focus on what to do at nighttime before going to sleep. Some are essential classics like *Goodnight Moon* and *Where the Wild Things Are*; some are new and hard to resist like *The Insomniacs*; and some are for all ages. We're sure there are many on this alphabetical list that will become family favorites — read again and again. After your tot slumbers off into dreamland, pick up your copy of ***Go the F**k to Sleep*** and laugh yourself to sleep!

1. **Dr. Seuss's Sleep Book** by Dr. Seuss, 1962 – *Dr. Seuss's Sleep Book* turned 50 in 2012. Written to be "read in bed" like most Dr. Seuss books, the story is clever, captivating, yet deceptively simple, beginning with a yawn that spreads and spreads until everyone in Seussville and your household is asleep. Yawning is quite catchy and the artwork, as always, contributes to family fun and drowsiness.

2. **Good Night, Gorilla** by Peggy Rathmann, 2000 – This is an amusing tale of a zookeeper whose normal evening routine is upset when a playful little ape mischievously frees the animals. The sleepy zookeeper doesn't notice they've followed him home. What happens next? Who leads the animals back to the zoo? This is a delightful story full of discoveries that heighten the storytelling experience. You and your child will soon be saying affectionate good nights to every animal in the zoo in the story's comforting ending.

3. **Goodnight Moon** by Margaret Wise Brown, Clement Hurd (illustrator), 1947 – The quintessential bedtime story of this little rabbit has been read and reread by parents for many decades. The little rabbit ceremonially says goodnight to everything in his room, eventually saying "Goodnight room, goodnight moon." The story's thoughtful and gentle simplicity makes it an endearing way to conclude the day.

4. **Guess How Much I Love You** by Sam McBratney, Anita Jeram (illustrator), 1994 – On many lists of all-time favorite children's books, this highly acclaimed story of Little Nutbrown Hare is one of the sweetest, with illustrations that match. Little Nutbrown expresses his love via a series of demonstrations that his father Big

Nutbrown tops. This is a tale of just how big and expressive love can be that happily ends in slumber, making it a perfect bedtime story.

5. **How Do Dinosaurs Say Good Night?** by Jane Yolen, Mark Teague (illustrator), 2000 – In simple verse and playful prose, father and mother dinosaurs ready their youngsters for bed. Each dinosaur child expresses itself differently as he or she says good night, but in the satisfying conclusion, they're very much like you and your family, kissing good night, turning out lights, tucking in and whispering good night.

6. **I Love You, Stinky Face** by Lisa McCourt, Cyd Moore (illustrator), 2004 – This lovely story is itself a bedtime tale of unconditional love and reassurance. As a delaying nighttime tactic, an inquisitive son relentlessly questions his mom's affection. Turning himself into a meat-eating dinosaur, a swamp creature and more, he tests that notion, only to discover that nothing will change a mother's love, no matter how slimy or stinky he might be.

EXCERPT: I LOVE YOU, STINKY FACE:
Mama, what if I were a big, scary ape? Would you still love me then?

7. **The Insomniacs** by Karina Wolf, The Brothers Hilts (illustrators), 2012 – Mr. Insomniac's big job move to a new time zone is keeping the entire family up at night. They try everything they can think of to help them fall asleep, including counting to one thousand, hot baths and sipping warm milk, but their internal clocks just don't adjust. Instead, the Insomniacs decide to "give night a try," finding nighttime's beauty just before they trundle off to bed as the sun is rising.

8. **Just Go To Bed** by Mercer Mayer, 2001 – In one of the most endearing of the Little Critter stories, a loveable preschool hero resists all efforts by his father to get him to go to sleep. Author Mayer really understands the necessity of rituals of bedtime, especially for energetic tots. Little Critter's dad is very nurturing, creating a routine for his son of bath time, pajama time and then sleep time.

9. **Pajama Time** by Sandra Boynton, 2008 – Sandra Boynton has presented many irresistible characters in stories that make you giggle with delight. *Pajama Time* is a goodnight book that doesn't take itself seriously. It's a silly singsong tale of a jump-roping chicken, a Scottie in plaid pajamas and an elephant in footed, one-piece jimjams. Everybody's wearing pajamas and your child will be too!

10. **Where the Wild Things Are** by Maurice Sendak, 1963 – Is there anyone who doesn't want to let the wild rumpus begin? Sendak's beloved classic is an essential must-have bedtime tale, rare in its ability to suit any age. Max's wild adventure into darkness is surprisingly calming, as we all learn to tame the beasts and monsters in our room, even before we imagine them.

CHILDREN'S BOOKS
Beloved Fictional Nannies (Ages 6-8-Years-Old)

In the world of childhood, parents are often busy with various responsibilities and concerns that can seem distant and unimportant to kids. But a good nanny or sensible governess, in fiction at least, watches over the children all the time — whether they initially like it or not — and is always there for them. Depending on her skills and personality, she can be a source of comfort, order, education and even enchantment for the entire family. Here are some of fiction's most notable caretakers, listed alphabetically by the characters' first names.

1. **Mary Poppins: Mary Poppins** by P. L. Travers, 1934 – Mary Poppins is the quintessential nanny (or perhaps sorceress) of all nannies. Blown by the "East Wind" to the house where Jane and Michael Banks live with their parents, she is strict, confident and totally in charge, but occasionally shows glimpses of gentleness as she introduces the children to all kinds of magical people, creatures and stories hiding just under the surface of ordinary life in London.

EXCERPT: MARY POPPINS:

Then the shape, tossed and bent under the wind, lifted the latch of the gate, and they could see that it belonged to a woman, who was holding her hat on with one hand and carrying a bag in the other. As they watched, Jane and Michael saw a curious thing happen. As soon as the shape was inside the gate the wind seemed to catch her up into the air and fling her at the house. It was thought it had flung her first at the gate, waited for her to open it, and then had lifted and thrown her, bag and all, at the front door. The watching children heard a terrific bang, and as she landed the whole house shook.

2. **Miss Penelope Lumley: The Incorrigible Children of Ashton Place: Book 1: The Mysterious Howling** by Maryrose Wood, Jon Klassen (illustrator), 2010 – There's nothing ordinary about the Incorrigible children or their governess, yet they are a perfect match. Find out if Miss Penelope Lumley can teach Alexander, Cassiopeia and Beowulf the civilities of everyday life. Full of mysterious adventure, the story helps you discover how these wild children, found running through the forests, came to live at Ashton Place. Can the young governess help them become socially adept in time for Lady Constance's ball? *The Incorrigible Children of Ashton Place: Book 1: The Mysterious Howling* is smart and funny and makes you want more.

3. **Nanny: Eloise** by Kay Thompson, Hilary Knight (illustrator), 1955 – Eloise is an enterprising child who lives in New York's Plaza Hotel with her pet pug and turtle and Nanny, who takes care of her; Eloise's glamorous mother always seems to be traveling, and her father is never mentioned (perhaps he fled when he saw what he had created). Here's how Eloise describes her caretaker: "Nanny is my nurse / She wears tissue paper in her dress and you can hear it / She is English and has 8 hairpins made out of bones / She says that's all she needs in this life for Lord's sake." The hair-raising yet delightful picture book will convince the entire family that this nanny is in fact a tolerant saint. *Eloise* is quite timeless and perfect for all ages.

4. **Nanny: The Willoughbys** by Lois Lowry, 2010 – Perfect for slightly older children with wicked senses of humor, Lowry's story depicts the misadventures of the Willoughby children, whose Nanny seems quite hateful at first, but turns out to be just what Timothy, Jane, Barnaby A and Barnaby B really need. *The Willoughbys* is an entertaining story that pays homage to *Mary Poppins* and many other classic children's tales.

5. **Nanny Cook and Nanny Butler: The 101 Dalmatians** by Dodie Smith, 1957 – This book is really about those dotted dogs (Pongo, Perdita and their scores of puppies), yet two nannies are a critical part of the household. Nanny Cook is Mrs. Dearly's old nanny and Nanny Butler is Mr. Dearly's old nanny; with their charges now parents and all grown up, the nannies stay on as cook and butler.

6. **Nanny Piggins: The Adventures of Nanny Piggins** by R. A. Spratt, Dan Santat (illustrator), 2010 – Nanny Piggins, who just happens to be a very common pink pig, shows up answering Mr. Green's ad. Perfect in many other ways, Nanny Piggins is a sassy, well-adorned chocolate lover of a pig who lovingly takes the children on one adventure after another.

7. **Nurse Matilda, a.k.a. Nanny McPhee: Nurse Matilda** by Christianna Brand, 1964 – The story of Nurse Matilda and her charges begins as follows: "Once upon a time there was a huge family of children; and they were terribly, terribly naughty." There are so many kids that the author doesn't bother trying to list them all at once. Luckily, Nurse Matilda is a match for them and for all the chaos they create — remarkable things happen when she thumps her big black stick on the floor.

8. **Ole Golly: Harriet the Spy** by Louise Fitzhugh, 1964 – In this novel for older children (ages eight and up), Harriet is a precociously intelligent girl whose parents don't understand her very well. But Ole Golly does. She is Harriet's nurse, a serious-minded woman who quotes Wordsworth and Emerson and "never wore anything as recognizable as a skirt, a jacket, or a sweater. She just had yards and yards of tweed which enveloped her like a lot of discarded blankets, which ballooned out when she walked, and which she referred to as her Things."

CHILDREN'S BOOKS
Junior Sleuths (Readers Ages 9-12-Years-Old)

Not many literary genres are as fun, intriguing and help improve reading skills as mystery and detective books. Children will become investigators before you know it, paying attention to small details that help solve a case, or remembering everything that might add up to a clue. Twists, turns, puzzling clues and surprise endings appeal to young readers and present satisfying challenges. The best mysteries and detective books can't be put down — kids want to read them under the covers with a flashlight because they simply cannot wait to find out what happens next.

A good mystery yarn is an ideal way to introduce critical thinking and problem-solving skills. Young readers hunt down the clues, track comings and goings, and search analytically for patterns and sequences. Some of the most addictive stories or series go back in time, feature codes that utilize math skills, focus on forensics or technology or involve art forgeries. Whatever the storyline, here are some of the best mysteries and detective books, listed alphabetically, that will keep a junior sleuth guessing, turning page after page as quickly as possible!

1. **The Angel Experiment: A Maximum Ride Novel (Book 1)** by James Patterson, 2005 – In this book for older readers, fourteen-year-old Maximum Ride, known as Max, soars above the world as a member of the "flock," a group of six winged kids who find themselves in a lot of danger. Fighting to survive, the six struggles to find out exactly what their purpose is while warding off the evil Erasers. The "flock" soars all across New York City, deciphering their purpose in the world. Are they good or evil? And will they save the world?

2. **Artemis Fowl: Book One** by Eoin Colfer, 2001 – Older readers will adore this series as it's magically chock full of deceptions, plots, computers and kidnapping of fairies who don't play by the rules. Artemis Fowl is a brilliant protagonist. At twelve-years-old, he's got the notoriety of being a genius criminal mastermind with millionaire status. When Artemis schemes to deprive the fairies of their gold, a thrilling adventure with twists, turns and tech wizardry unfolds. *Artemis Fowl* is seriously cool crime fodder, perfect for any age!

3. **The Case of the Cat with the Missing Ear: From the notebooks of Edward R. Smithfield D.V. M. (Adventures of Samuel Blackthorn)** by Scott Emerson, Vivo Mullet (illustrator), 2003 – Like Sherlock Holmes and Dr. Watson, Detective Samuel Blackthorn, a Yorkshire terrier, and Edward R. Smithfield, a retired veterinarian, come together to solve crimes. In their first case, they unravel the mysteries surrounding an elegant greyhound needing their fine deductive reasoning skills.

4. **Death Cloud (Sherlock Holmes: the Legend Begins)** by Andrew Lane, 2011 – For older readers who ache for the true master of detection, here's a series about the teenaged Sherlock Holmes. The legend and lore is set in 1868, with fourteen-year-old Sherlock visiting his aunt and uncle in Hampshire, England while on school holiday. There's a plethora of oddly eccentric and evil characters to study, from his own relatives to a particularly vile villain. When two people die from what looks like the plague, the often-troubled yet brilliant Sherlock, with the help of Amyus Crowe his tutor, begins to deduce the real truth and sets out to solve the case.

5. **Extreme Danger: Hardy Boys: Undercover Brothers #1** by Donald J. Cobol, 2005 – The Hardy Boys, like girl detective Nancy Drew, originally appeared in the thirties. Written by many writers under the pseudonym Franklin W. Dixon, the Hardy Boys mysteries have evolved over the years. In this first volume of the newest *Undercover Brothers* series, Frank and Joe Hardy are agents of A.T.A.C. (American Teens Against Crime), investigating the sabotage of an extreme sports event in Philadelphia. As with all the earlier books, there's murder, suspicious violence, adventure and the reappearance of many beloved characters, all within a Hardy Boys investigation that young sleuths will find an "extreme" read.

6. **Liar & Spy** by Rebecca Stead, 2012 – *Liar & Spy* is a story about a seventh grader named Georges (with a silent "s"), whose new life in Brooklyn sometimes leads him into spy games with his best friend Safer, a twelve-year-old detective by design. It's a fun read with memorably endearing characters, especially Georges, who is intelligent but has a naiveté that makes readers laugh. *Liar & Spy* will keep readers guessing to the very end.

7. **The London Eye Mystery** by Siobhan Dowd, 2007 – When a boy mysteriously disappears from a sealed London Eye capsule, the police are perplexed. It's up to Ted and his older sister Kat to solve this thriller, tracing clues across the city of London in search of their cousin. Ted's brain is hard-wired differently than most kids— his condition often strains the brother-sister relationship. Yet it is Ted's insistence and preoccupation with detail, paired with Kat's intuitive action, which helps them unravel the mystery.

EXCERPT: THE LONDON EYE MYSTERY:

My favourite thing to do in London is to fly the Eye.

On a clear day you can see for twenty-five miles in all directions because you are in the largest observation wheel ever built. You are sealed into one of the thirty-two capsules with the strangers who were next to you in the queue, and when they close the doors, the sound of the city is cut off. You begin to rise. The capsules are made of glass and steel and are hung from the rim of the wheel. As the wheel turns, the capsules use the force of gravity to stay upright. It takes thirty minutes to go a full circle.

From the top of the ride, Kat says London looks like toy-town and the cars on the roads below look like abacus beads going left and right and stopping and starting. I think London looks like London and the cars like cars, only smaller.

8. **The Secret of the Mansion: Trixie Belden #1** by Julie Campbell, 1948 – In the first of many Trixie Belden mysteries, our heroine Trixie is forecasting a dreary summer until she befriends a new girl in town, a millionaire's daughter. The girls search for a runaway boy hiding out in Sleepy side-on-Hudson and help him solve a mystery revolving around his uncle. In this entertaining series, the two girls solve mystery after mystery, most of which stump local authorities.

9. **The Secret of the Old Clock** by Carolyn Keene, 1930 – Nancy Drew is one of the most popular characters of all time and with good reason. The amateur detective is intelligent, well-traveled, and continually tests her sharp aptitude for solving mysteries. In the first of the *Nancy Drew Mystery Stories*, Nancy searches for a missing will. Young readers will get easily hooked on all of Nancy's thrilling adventures. Thankfully there are many to read.

10. **Wonderstruck** by Brian Selznick, 2011 – From the author-illustrator of ***The Invention of Hugo Cabret*** comes another enticing tale told in pictures and words. Set fifty years apart, two children, Rose and Ben, venture forth on individual adventures that unfold in surprisingly similar ways. Will Ben and Rose's stories ever intersect?

CHRISTIAN BIOGRAPHIES/MEMOIRS
Personal Journeys of Faith

Journeys of faith take these writers in different directions, but all share a common goal: To better understand their lives and their purpose, and the ways their spiritual belief has guided or redeemed them. Each story is inspiring in its own way, whether the author is expressing self-doubt or self-acceptance, and each has a unique message for readers, who may use these books to better understand themselves. These engaging memoirs are listed in alphabetical order.

1. **The Confessions of Saint Augustine** by St. Augustine, 397-398 AD – For over 1,500 years, *The Confessions of St. Augustine* has inspired readers with stories of struggle and redemption, collected in a volume that many believe to be the first spiritual memoir ever recorded. With candor, he relates the struggles of his youth, and his gradual movement toward a life of Christian faith.

2. **The Cross and the Switchblade** by David Wilkerson, 1962 – In this classic story of faith and redemption David Wilkerson describes how his work with troubled

youth on the streets of New York City lead to the creation of his faith-based organization Team Challenge International.

3. **Girl Meets God: On the Path to a Spiritual Life** by Lauren Winner, 2002 – While practicing Judaism, Lauren Winner was drawn to Christianity, and in *Girl Meets God: On the Path to a Spiritual Life,* she explains her conversion and the ways she was eventually able to bring together different facets of her religious identity.

4. **Memories of God: Theological Reflections on a Life** by Dr. Roberta Bondi, 1995 – A professor of church history, the author presents personal stories of adversity, and explains the ways she used those experiences to find new meaning in the teachings of Christ.

5. **My Life with the Saints** by James Martin SJ, 2006 – A Jesuit priest, James Martin frequently calls upon the saints for help and inspiration, and in this volume he writes about his favorite saints and the ways they have served as role models in his everyday life.

6. **Reading Jesus: A Writer's Encounter with the Gospels** by Mary Gordon, 2009 – Mary Gordon wonders whether she has "invented Jesus to fulfill my own wishes," and decides to revisit the fundamental stories of the Gospel and understand them in the context of today's modern world.

7. **Through My Eyes** by Tim Tebow, 2011 – NFL quarterback Tim Tebow shares the many ways his values and beliefs have guided his life, both on and off the playing field.

8. **Together and Apart: A Memoir of the Religious Life** by Ellen Stephen, OSH, 2008 – A window into the world of monastic life from an author who has been a nun for over forty years, including a detailed account of the lifestyle day to day, and the reasons they choose to live as they do.

9. **Traveling Mercies** by Anne Lamott, 1999 – With her typical insight and humor, Anne Lamott explains her indirect path to religion and the ways her faith has guided her through difficult times and away from her troubles with alcohol, drugs, and relationships.

EXCERPT: TRAVELING MERCIES:

My coming to faith did not start with the leap but rather a series of staggers from what seemed like one safe place to another. Like lily pads, round and green, these places summoned and then held me up while I grew. Each prepared me for the next leaf on which I would land, and in this way I moved across the swamp of doubt and fear. When I look back at some of these early resting places – the boisterous home of the Catholics, the soft armchair of the Christian Science mom, adoption by ardent Jews – I can see how flimsy and indirect a path they made. Yet each step brought me closer to the verdant pad of faith on which I somehow stay afloat today.

CHRISTIAN BOOKS
Christianity Today's Twentieth Century Classics

As the twentieth century drew to a close, heralding the start of a new millennium, the editors of *Christianity Today* polled more than 100 prominent religious leaders and writers as to the ten religious books with the most "enduring significance for the Christian faith and church." While it's doubtful many lay readers will attempt to wade through Karl Barth's thirteen-volume *Church Dogmatics*, several of the titles became bona-fide bestsellers, like Thomas Merton's *The Seven Storey Mountain*. Here are the top ten vote-getters, ranked in descending order, according to *Christianity Today*.

1. **Mere Christianity** by C.S. Lewis, 1952 – A Christian apologist, the Oxford Don delivered a series of BBC radio lectures in 1943; *Mere Christianity* is adapted from those lectures, in which Lewis strives to establish the commonality linking the Anglican, Methodist, Presbyterian and Roman Catholic denominations.

2. **The Cost of Discipleship** by Dietrich Bonhoeffer, 1937 – Executed by the Nazis in 1945 for his work with the German resistance, Bonhoeffer was a Lutheran minister who practiced what he preached — personal sacrifice is an integral part of religious faith. In *The Cost of Discipleship*, Bonhoeffer examines what it means for lay people to incorporate the teachings of Jesus Christ into everyday life.

3. **Church Dogmatics** by Karl Barth, 1932-1968 – Encompassing thirteen volumes (that's six million words!), *Church Dogmatics* is an exhaustive investigation into *all* aspects of Christianity from Barth, a Swiss Reformed Christian theologian.

4. **The Lord of the Rings** trilogy by J.R.R. Tolkien, 1954-1955 – While religious leaders embrace C. S. Lewis' ***The Chronicles of Narnia*** as Christian allegory, there is no such consensus regarding Tolkien's Middle Earth trilogy. A devout Roman Catholic, Tolkien insisted that there were no religious overtones to *Lord of the Rings*, but many see it as a celebration of innately Christian virtues over evil.

5. **The Politics of Jesus** by John Howard Yoder, 1972 – A Christian ethicist/Biblical scholar, Yoder ruffled more than a few theological feathers with this provocative book, which argues that Jesus was politically radical in his pacifism.

6. **Orthodoxy** by G. K. Chesterton, 1908 – A literary polymath, Chesterton wrote mysteries, short stories, poetry, newspaper columns and Christian apologetics. In *Orthodoxy*, he uses his considerable reservoirs of wit and insight to argue that Christianity provides man with his greatest source of happiness and stability.

7. **The Seven Storey Mountain** by Thomas Merton, 1948 – Merton's classic spiritual autobiography details his religious awakening in 1941, when Merton joined a Trappist monastery in rural Kentucky. A surprise hit with the general public, *The Seven Storey Mountain* eventually sold more than a million copies in paperback and has been translated into fifteen languages.

EXCERPT: THE SEVEN STOREY MOUNTAIN:

The whole landscape, unified by the church and its heavenward spire, seemed to say: this is the meaning of all created things: we have been made for no other purpose than that men may use us in raising themselves to God, and in proclaiming the glory of God. We have been fashioned, in all our perfection, each according to his own nature, and all our natures ordered and harmonized together, that man's reason and his love might fit in this one last element, this God-given key to the meaning of the whole.

8. **Celebration of Discipline** by Richard J. Foster, 1978 – A Quaker theologian, Foster provides readers with simple methods for cultivating spirituality through meditation and prayer in this accessible text.

9. **My Utmost for his Highest** by Oswald Chambers, 1935 – Published eighteen years after Chambers' death from a ruptured appendix, *My Utmost for his Highest* offers 365 daily readings that distill Christian doctrine into accessible, often witty language.

10. **Moral Man and Immoral Society: A Study of Ethics and Politics** by Reinhold Niebuhr, 1932 – A major influence on both Dietrich Bonhoeffer and Martin Luther King Jr., Niebuhr examines the intersection of religious faith and politics with penetrating insight in this book.

CHRISTIAN BOOKS
Seminal Works

As St. Augustine of Hippo so eloquently wrote, "Grant me chastity and continence, but not yet." Throughout the ages, the works of European scholars, theologians, monks and writers have explored and defined Western spirituality. But perhaps no other thinker so neatly captured the tension between earthly pleasure and divine restraint as St. Augustine.

Inspired by the work of Greek statesman Cicero and trained in rhetoric, St. Augustine wrote the first true (spiritual) autobiography, tracing his journey from reckless hedonism to spiritual conversion. He combined his love of philosophy with a scrupulous honesty about his life — his now oft-quoted prayer spoke simultaneously to his more rambunctious youth and to the kind of man he wanted to be — and came to be regarded as one of the world's greatest Christian theologians. His *Confessions* survives as the most complete record of any individual living in the fourth and fifth centuries, and has inspired some of the most profound literature from the Middle Ages and beyond. Presented chronologically, the following works trace the development of Christian thought from the early Middle Ages into the nineteenth and twentieth centuries.

1. **The City of God** by St. Augustine of Hippo, completed 426 AD - A seminal theological work written after the sack of Rome, *The City of God* contrasts the Roman Empire's spiritual decay with the "City of God" to which Christianity might deliver humanity. An incisive apologia for the whole of Christianity, this monumental and provocative work set the course and tone of Christian thought for hundreds of years after.

2. **Summa Theologica** by St. Thomas Aquinas, fourteenth century AD - As its name suggests, this five-volume masterwork synthesizes all that can be known about God and man's relationship to God. A Dominican priest and one of the 33 Doctors of the Church, Aquinas took inspiration from St. Augustine and is regarded as the Church's greatest philosopher.

3. **The Imitation of Christ** by Thomas à Kempis, fifteenth century AD – Thomas à Kempis was a German copyist and writer who eventually became sub-prior of the Monastery of Mount St. Agnes. Considered one of the greatest devotionals in Christendom, this manuscript comprises a series of "admonitions" on how best to "imitate [Christ's] life and character." The 1441 autograph manuscript survives in the Bibliothèque Royale in Brussels.

4. **The Freedom of a Christian** by Martin Luther, 1522 – Leader of the Protestant Reformation, German monk and theologian Martin Luther argued that freedom from God's punishment for sin is not earned but granted freely by God through faith in Jesus Christ. *The Freedom of a Christian*, which includes his letter to Pope Leo X, comprises Luther's third major treatise on Christian life and salvation. His writings and translations of the Bible helped make Christian thought accessible to thousands more converts and reshaped centuries of accepted belief.

5. **The Institutes of Christian Religion** by John Calvin, 1536 - A key figure of the Protestant Reformation, French theologian John Calvin was forced to flee the religious uprisings of the time, and subsequently wrote this *apologia* in defense of his faith. *Institutes* marks the first printed expression of his beliefs, which he also intended to serve as instruction for those interested in Christianity. This version represents an abridgment of a previous translation, yet maintains the coherence of Calvin's arguments while updating the language for a contemporary audience.

6. **Interior Castle (or The Mansions)** by St. Teresa of Avila, 1577 - A Carmelite nun, mystic and writer of the Catholic Church's Counter Reformation, St. Teresa experienced a vision of a castle that would become her metaphor for the soul and the basis of this beautifully rendered guide to spiritual awakening. St. Teresa was canonized in 1622 by Pope Gregory XV, and in 1970, named the first female Doctor of the Church.

EXCERPT: INTERIOR CASTLE (OR THE MANSIONS):

I thought of the soul as resembling a castle, formed of a single diamond or a very transparent crystal and containing many rooms, just as in heaven there are many mansions. If we reflect, sisters, we shall see that the soul of the just man is but a paradise, in which, God tells us, He takes His delight. What, do you imagine, must that dwelling be in which a King so mighty, so wise, and so pure, containing in Himself all good, can delight to rest? Nothing can be compared to the great beauty and capabilities of a soul; however keen our intellects may be, they are as unable to comprehend them as to comprehend God, for, as He has told us, He created us in His own image and likeness.

7. **Paradise Lost** by John Milton, 1664 (first edition) - The English poet and scholar composed his magnum opus about the Fall of Man in the wake of the Restoration (of the English monarchy under Charles II), embittered, broke and completely blind. The epic poem remains the subject of scholarly debate, but its place in the literary canon is secure.

8. **The Pilgrim's Progress** by John Bunyan (Originally published in two parts: 1678 and 1684) - English writer and preacher John Bunyan composed this Puritan allegory while persecuted, and occasionally imprisoned, for his teachings. One of the most widely read books in English literature, it contributed to the development of the contemporary novel. It follows the hero, Christian, on his pilgrimage to the Celestial City, along with his friends Faithful and Hopeful.

9. **Orthodoxy** by G. K. Chesterton, 1908 – This English writer became respected for the reasoned faith espoused in his prolific writings, including *Orthodoxy*, in which he explains how he arrived at his Christian beliefs — and how Christian religion is an answer to human need, not an "arbitrary truth." Even Chesterton's critics acknowledge his wide-ranging appeal and persuasiveness.

10. **Mere Christianity** by C.S. Lewis, 1942-1944 - Perhaps best known for his ***Chronicles of Narnia***, Irish writer C.S. Lewis was invited to give a series of BBC radio addresses that were subsequently adapted into the book *Mere Christianity*. This apologia makes an argument for reasoned faith and sets out the very basic tenets of Christianity that undergird all denominations. Offering hope and sanity during the turmoil of World War II, *Mere Christianity* is anything but mere speechifying and remains relevant today.

CHRISTIAN FICTION

Christy Award Winners: Contemporary Standalone Novels, 2006-2012

Described by the *New York Times* as "the world's most inspirational author," Catherine Marshall penned more than two dozen works, twenty-five million copies of which are currently in print. It's estimated that thirty million people have read Marshall's novel ***Christy***, a work of historical fiction inspired her mother's work with impoverished children in Appalachia.

Established in 1999 to honor Marshall's work, the Christy Awards recognize excellence in Christian fiction, nurturing and encouraging creativity within the genre while honoring both bestselling and unsung writers.

Though a variety of subgenres are recognized each year, reflecting the depth and breadth of Christian literature, the following list highlights the winners of the Contemporary Standalone category from 2006 (the first year the category was recognized) through 2012. The winning titles are listed in reverse chronological order.

1. **Promises to Keep** by Ann Tatlock, 2011 (2012 winner) - Fleeing an abusive home life, eleven-year-old Roz Anthony and her family move to Mills River, Illinois. They soon discover, however, that their house's previous owner, the aging Tillie, is determined to stay and die in the place she's always called home. They agree to take her in and Tillie likewise adopts them as her own. But an old threat returns to stalk the family. This sweet coming-of-age tale engages readers with a finely drawn portrait of its pre-teen narrator.

2. **Almost Heaven** by Chris Fabry, 2010 (2011 winner) - "Hillbilly genius" Billy Allman has a special gift for playing the mandolin and a desire to make his life an "ode to God." When he builds a radio station in his home, he gets the attention of more than just his neighbors — the angel Malachi is sent to watch over him. This sweet, gentle tale surprises with unexpected turns.

EXCERPT: ALMOST HEAVEN:

I believe every life has hidden songs that hang by twin threads of music and memory. I believe in the songs that have never been played for another soul. I believe they run between the rocks and along the creekbeds of our lives. These are songs that cannot be heard by anything but the soul. They sometimes run dry or spill over the banks until we find ourselves wading through them.

3. **The Passion of Mary-Margaret** by Lisa Samson, 2009 (2010 winner) - This quirky blend of mysticism and social realism tells the story of Mary-Margaret Fischer,

who's studying in a convent school when she meets the troubled but magnetic Jude. He soon exits her life into a seamy underworld, only to reappear years later after Mary-Margaret has already committed herself to God. With Jude now a broken man in need of salvation, Mary-Margaret faces the prospect of making the ultimate sacrifice for her friend.

4. *Dogwood* by Chris Fabry, 2008 (2009 winner) - In the eponymous town of Dogwood, West Virginia, Karin and Will, a couple torn apart by tragedy and forced to bury their past, are united again through the young boy who survived the trauma. But it's a withered old woman who will expose the past and lead Karin down a dangerous path. *Dogwood* shines with a twisting plot and evocative imagery.

5. *Chasing Fireflies* by Charles Martin, 2007 (2008 winner) - This sentimental Southern charmer tells the story of "John Doe 117," a young boy abandoned by his suicidal mother, and Chase Walker, the reporter assigned to the boy's story and confronting a similarly painful past. As Chase discovers, finding the truth can be "as elusive as chasing fireflies on a summer night."

6. *Winter Birds* by Jamie Langston Turner, 2006 (2007 winner) - Octogenarian widow Sophia Hess' marriage of convenience was shattered by a startling secret. Taken in by her nephew and his wife, she becomes witness to the possibilities of true love, even when that love is tested by tragedy. In true Southern style, the story takes its time unfolding but ultimately draws the reader in with its poignancy.

7. *Levi's Will* by W. Dale Cramer, 2005 (2006 winner) - Amid a tainted past, Will Mullet flees his Amish community to enlist in the Army during World War II, eventually settling down with a new wife and family. As he attempts to reconcile with his unyielding father, Levi, Will realizes "that every man's failure dips its roots into the previous generation and drops its seeds into the next." Jumping between locales and points in time, the story of forgiveness was called "an accomplished work" by the American Library Association.

CHRISTIAN SELF-HELP
Finding Self-Awareness through Faith

The struggle to find fulfillment and meaning in our lives requires a variety of ideas and inspiration, and in the Christian self-help genre, the paths to self-awareness and to understanding one's faith are one and the same. By sharing their experiences and techniques, these authors provide guidance through the obstacles of life by asking readers to examine their lives in the context of their beliefs. These inspirational books are listed in alphabetical order.

1. **Boundaries: When to Say Yes, When to Say No to Take Control of Your Life** by Drs. Henry Cloud and John Townsend, 2004 – Being a faithful Christian doesn't require that you always go along with other's ideas, even when it's difficult to draw the line. The authors explain how to take a stance guilt-free, and how readers can look to their faith when setting boundaries.

2. **Grace for the Good Girl: Letting Go of the Try-Hard Life** by Emily P. Freeman, 2011 – For women who believe that the Christian life requires a sunny disposition against all obstacles, Emily Friedman offers advice on how to quit striving for perfection and goodness, and open oneself to Christ.

3. **Messy Spirituality: God's Annoying Love for Imperfect People** by Michael Yaconelli, 2002 – For those who silently wonder if they're doing Christianity the right way, Yaconelli helps readers redirect their focus away from their self-perceived flaws to recognize the essential role that imperfection plays in Christianity.

EXCERPT: MESSY SPIRITUALITY:

Spirituality is not a formula; it is not a test. It is a relationship. Spirituality is not about competency; it is about intimacy. Spirituality is not about perfection; it is about connection. The way of the spiritual life begins where we are now in the mess of our lives. Accepting the reality of our broken, flawed lives is the beginning of spirituality not because the spiritual life will remove our flaws but because we let go of seeking perfection and, instead, seek God, the one who is present in the tangledness of our lives. Spirituality is not about being fixed; it is about God's being present in the mess of our unfixedness.

4. **The Purpose Driven® Life: What on Earth am I Here For?** by Rick Warren, 2002 – Renowned religious leader Rick Warren presents this guide through a personal forty-day spiritual journey, a road map to finding contentment and reducing stress by understanding God's purpose for creating you.

5. **Radical: Taking Back Your Faith from the American Dream** by David Platt, 2010 – Author David Platt makes the case that many American Christians have forgotten how Jesus asked us to live, and he offers a solution with his plan for a personal one-year journey in discipleship.

6. **Treasures of Healthy Living** by Annette Reeder and Dr. Richard Couey, 2010 – The answers to many of our health problems lie in the pages of the Scripture, the authors explain, and they offer a practical study course to set you on your way towards a better life physically, emotionally, and spiritually.

7. **True Woman 101: Divine Design: An Eight-Week Study on Biblical Womanhood** by Mary A. Kassian and Nancy Leigh DeMoss, 2012 – The co-authors present the

reader with a week-by-week study program to help women rediscover and delight in the marvel of God's design.

8. **Wild at Heart: Discovering the Secret of a Man's Soul** by John Eldredge, 2001 – To help women better understand the men in their lives, the authors created this guide to understanding the true nature of man as God designed him to be: imbued with a spirit of adventure and risk.

9. **Your Scars Are Beautiful to God: Finding Peace and Purpose in the Hurts of Your Past** by Sharon Jaynes, 2006 –Jaynes reflects on the meaning of one's scars both physical and emotional, and the ways those wounds serve as an invitation for Christ to restore and mend our damaged bodies or our broken hearts.

CIVIL WAR NONFICTION
Essential Books about Abraham Lincoln

With approximately 16,000 books (and counting) about Abraham Lincoln, what is there left to say about America's sixteenth president? Apparently quite a bit, according to an October 12, 2012 article in *The Wall Street Journal* by Stefanie Cohen, who reports that "at least twenty more books about the president will be published before next summer [June 2013]."

Of course, many of these books about "Honest Abe" take considerable liberties with the facts of his life. Case in point: ***Abraham Lincoln: Vampire Hunter*** (!). Others have been slammed for glaring factual inaccuracies or dwelling on minutiae, i.e., what Lincoln ate and drank. Here are eight essential reads about Abraham Lincoln, listed alphabetically, that reveal the man behind the myth.

1. **The Fate of Liberty: Abraham Lincoln and Civil Liberties** by Mark E. Neely, Jr., 1991 – One of the aspects of Lincoln's presidency that remains controversial is his record on civil liberties. Here, Neely puts his decisions in historical context.

2. **The Fiery Trial: Abraham Lincoln and American Slavery** by Eric Foner, 2010 – The winner of the 2011 Pulitzer Prize for History, Foner's nuanced and insightful book examines Lincoln's often paradoxical attitude towards slavery and African-Americans. Although he once told a group of African-American leaders that they were "far removed from being placed on an equality with the white race," Lincoln eventually came to regard slavery as inherently wrong.

3. **Lincoln** by David Herbert Donald, 1995 – A wonderfully readable book that takes you back to Lincoln's time, the struggles he faced, and his growing abilities and wisdom just when the country needed a resolute, humane, and unifying leader.

4. **Lincoln Day by Day: A Chronology** edited by Earl Schenck Miers, 1960 – A great resource for anyone who needs to know the details of where Lincoln was and what he was doing at any given point in his life.

5. **Prelude to Greatness: Lincoln in the 1850s** by Don E. Fehrenbacher, 1962 – This book examines Lincoln's political career in the decade before he became president of the deeply divided nation.

6. **Rise to Greatness: Abraham Lincoln and America's Most Perilous Year** by David Von Drehle, 2012 – Focusing on 1862, Von Drehle (***Triangle: The Fire That Changed America***) paints a fascinating portrait of a president grappling with an ego-driven cabinet, an ineffectual Union commander and an aggressive Confederate army. Over the course of this pivotal year, however, Lincoln eventually finds his footing to put the Union on the road to ultimate victory.

7. **Team of Rivals: The Political Genius of Abraham Lincoln** by Doris Kearns Goodwin, 2005 – One of the most popular and critically acclaimed books about the sixteenth president, Goodwin's account of Lincoln's often-strained relationship with his cabinet, which included three former rivals for the presidency, was hailed as "elegant, incisive study" by Civil War historian James McPherson in the *New York Times*.

EXCERPT: TEAM OF RIVALS:

The Republicans had chosen to meet in Chicago. A new convention hall called the "Wigwam" had been constructed for the occasion. The first ballot was not due to be called until 10 a.m. and Lincoln, although patient by nature, was visibly "nervous, fidgety, and intensely excited." With an outside chance to secure the Republican nomination for the highest office of the land, he was unable to focus on his work. Even under ordinary circumstances many would have found concentration difficult in the untidy office Lincoln shared with his younger partner, William Herndon. Two worktables, piled high with papers and correspondence, formed a T in the center of the room. Additional documents and letters spilled out from the drawers and pigeonholes of an outmoded secretary in the corner. When he needed a particular piece of correspondence, Lincoln had to rifle through disorderly stacks of paper, rummaging, as a last resort, in the lining of his old plug hat, where he often put stray letters or notes.

8. **Tried by War: Abraham Lincoln as Commander in Chief** by James McPherson, 2008 – The author of the Pulitzer Prize-winning ***Battle Cry of Freedom*** examines Lincoln's skills as a military strategist in McPherson's acclaimed book, which the *Washington Post* called "the definitive portrait of Lincoln as war leader."

CIVIL WAR NONFICTION
True Stories of the Blue and the Gray

Approached by Random House editor Bennett Cerf to write a short, one-volume history of the Civil War, Shelby Foote initially agreed to produce a 200,000-word manuscript. Twenty years later, when the Mississippi-born novelist finally completed his landmark, three-volume history in 1974, *The Civil War: A Narrative* numbered 1,650,000 words and ran to 3,000 pages. Yet despite glowing reviews, Foote's masterpiece didn't catch on with the general public until 1990, when the courtly Southerner became a surprise television star, thanks to his appearance in Ken Burns' eleven-hour, PBS documentary about the Civil War.

Named the fifteenth best nonfiction book of the twentieth century by Modern Library, Foote's *The Civil War: A Narrative* joins Ulysses S. Grant's memoirs and a Southern belle's war diary on the list of twelve nonfiction books about the war between the states.

1. **Abraham Lincoln and Civil War America: A Biography** by William E. Gienapp, 2002 – This unusually concise history of the most complex and enigmatic of U.S. presidents synthesizes years of scholarship, but still manages to capture Lincoln's nuances, as well as his maturation from untested leader to savvy commander-in-chief.

2. **April 1865: The Month That Saved America** by Jay Winik, 2001 – Winik's panoramic and briskly paced look at the last month of the war from a variety of perspectives was praised by *Publishers Weekly* as "popular history at its best."

3. **Battle Cry of Freedom: The Civil War Era** by James T. McPherson, 1988 – McPherson's Pulitzer Prize winner is, hands-down, the best one-volume history of the Civil War.

4. **Chancellorsville** by Stephen W. Sears, 1996 – Was Lee's victory at Chancellorsville due to his military strategy or just plain luck? That's the provocative question Sears considers in his skillfully written and researched account of this pivotal battle.

5. **The Civil War: A Narrative** by Shelby Foote, 1958-1974 – If you read only one book about the Civil War, go with Foote's masterpiece, written with novelistic flair.

6. **A Diary from Dixie** by Mary Boykin Chesnut, 1905 – Published twenty-six years after Chesnut's death, her diary is an invaluable, meticulously detailed account of Confederate life spanning from February 15, 1861, to August 2, 1865.

7. **Fateful Lightning: A New History of the Civil War and Reconstruction** by Allen C. Guelzo, 2012 – Guelzo does more than just chronicle the battles and politics of the war; he widens his scope to provide a fascinating overview of Reconstruction and the long-term impact of the Civil War on American society, literature and pop

culture. *Booklist* called *Fateful Lightning* "an outstanding effort to recount and explain our greatest national trauma to general readers."

8. **The Long Road to Antietam: How the Civil War Became a Revolution** by Richard Slotkin, 2012 – The first major battle of the Civil War on Union soil, the Battle of Antietam claimed nearly 46,000 casualties in one day. In Slotkin's justly praised account of this horrific battle, he explores the politics and personalities involved in Antietam, which transformed the struggle into a "holy war" on slavery.

EXCERPT: THE LONG ROAD TO ANTIETAM:

Whatever his ideas about the likelihood of McClellan taking Richmond, Lincoln was becoming convinced that it was no longer possible for the Union to defeat the Confederacy in a short war. He did not share the troubled drift of his ideas with anyone. For all his affability he was an extremely secretive man who kept his deepest thoughts to himself until he was ready to act upon them. But the effects were visible in his dark mood and loss of appetite, his frequent outbursts of dissatisfaction with his generals, and his new willingness to contemplate a major restructuring of the army command.

9. **The Negro's Civil War: How American Blacks Felt and Acted During the War for the Union** by James T. McPherson, 1965 – A necessary and eye-opening book, vigorously written, that smashes racist preconceptions about African-Americans during the Civil War.

10. **Personal Memoirs of Ulysses S. Grant,** 1885 – Completed one week prior to his death from throat cancer, Grant's two-volume memoir was hailed by no less than Mark Twain as "the most remarkable work of its kind since the ***Commentaries of Julius Caesar***."

11. **Race and Reunion: The Civil War in American Memory** by David W. Blight, 2001 – This authoritative masterwork examines the lingering scars left on the American psyche by the Civil War. Did the U.S. buy national unity at the expense of those African-Americans for whom we had fought? How did we allow it to happen? *Race and Reunion* delves deep into cultural memory and the myths we tell ourselves about our past.

12. **Robert E. Lee: A Biography** by Emory M. Thomas, 1995 – Both lionized and demonized in other biographies, Lee emerges as an admirable, life-sized figure with his share of foibles in this terrific biography.

CLASSICAL MUSIC COMPOSERS
Biographies of the Great Masters

The great Hungarian composer/concert pianist Franz Liszt lived, wrote and performed music with a passionate intensity that left the ladies swooning — and produced three illegitimate children, one of whom, Cosima, later married Richard Wagner. In his day, the tall, long-haired virtuoso was the classical music world's equivalent of a rock star: a charismatic, innovative performer whose mastery of the keyboards reportedly prompted his female fans to fight for scraps of his handkerchiefs and gloves. Liszt's extraordinary life and illustrious musical career — he's credited with inventing the symphonic poem — has the sweep and romance of great fiction. Fortunately, English music historian Alan Walker is more than up to the task of chronicling the life and loves of Franz Liszt, as his three-part biography so marvelously demonstrates. The first volume, *Franz Liszt: The Virtuoso Years, 1811-1847,* is one of twelve nonfiction books about classical music composers, listed below alphabetically, that appeal to classical music scholars and general readers alike.

1. **An Autobiography** by Igor Stravinsky, 1966 - The Russian composer of *The Rite of Spring* and other classics offers readers a concise overview, and a wealth of blunt opinions, of his frequently turbulent life and musical career.

2. **Beethoven** by Maynard Solomon, 2001 – A revised edition of Solomon's gracefully written and involving biography distinguished by the sheer breadth of information about the German composer, who helped usher in the Romantic period in classical music.

3. **Chopin in Paris: The Life and Times of the Romantic Composer** by Tad Szulc, 1998 – A lively account of Chopin's eighteen years in the French capital, where his glamorous circle included Victor Hugo, Franz Liszt and the great love of Chopin's life, the novelist George Sand.

4. **Evening in the Palace of Reason: Bach meets Frederick the Great in the Age of Enlightenment** by James R. Gaines, 2005 – Intriguing and uncommonly elegant cultural history about the events that led to a memorable meeting between Bach and Frederick the Great one night in Potsdam in 1747.

5. **Franz Liszt: The Virtuoso Years, 1811-1847** by Alan Walker, 1983 – Walker's prodigiously researched and entertaining first volume in his three-part biography of the Hungarian composer.

6. **Gustav Mahler: Letters to His Wife** by Gustav Mahler, 2004 – An annotated compilation of 350 letters and postcards Mahler wrote to his much younger wife Alma over the course of a decade. An emotionally intimate look at a complex and tempestuous union.

7. **Johannes Brahms: A Biography** by Jan Swafford, 1997 – Emotionally potent biography of the mercurial genius unfolds like a gripping historical novel.

8. **The Memoirs of Hector Berlioz** by Hector Berlioz, 2002 – Captivating, anecdote-laden memoir distinguished by Berlioz's razor-sharp wit. Edited by David Cairns, the author of a two-volume biography of Berlioz.

9. **Mozart: A Cultural Biography** by Robert W. Gutman, 1999 – Gutman's exhaustively researched and lucidly written biography presents a multi-faceted portrait of the musical genius.

10. **Sergei Prokofiev: A Biography** by Harlow Robinson, 1987 – Highly accessible and dramatic biography of the Russian composer victimized by the Stalinist regime.

11. **Sibelius: A Composer's Life and the Awakening of Finland** by Glenda Dawn Goss, 2012 – Jean Sibelius (1865-1957), a romantic composer whose main oeuvre consists of seven symphonies, lived a long life that coincided with the rise of his mother country, Finland. In this page-turner of a biography, author Goss deftly explores the relationship between the artist and the nation he helped forge, which, for the first fifty years of Sibelius's life, was basically a colony of Russia.

EXCERPT: SIBELIUS:

Incited by the push-pull of the giants on either side of Finland, Sibelius and a handful of his predecessors and contemporaries set out to compose, conduct, draw, paint, poetize, sculpt, and versify what it meant to be Finnish, to inculcate a sense of pride in being Finnish, and through these activities to awaken their fellow Finns to their uniqueness, their separateness, and ultimately the possibilities of nationhood. They succeeded spectacularly, creating a world that so impressed its lustrous accomplishments upon those who encountered it that the epithet "golden age" was bestowed on their era and its artistic expressions. It was fitting that such a gilded epoch should have been born in regal surroundings — Imperial Russia, a realm of nearly unimaginable wealth and splendor. Of its surface glitter, Sibelius was supremely aware. He recognized it — and adored it. As he once wrote, "It's the surface sparkle people fall for. But I love this sparkle, because when you march over worries and so on with a tiara on the back of your head, then life becomes so dramatic. Not this drab gray."

12. **Tchaikovsky: The Man and His Music** by David Brown, 2007 – The *Sunday Times of London* called this book "a magnificent achievement," and so it is — a distillation of Brown's exhaustive, four-volume exploration of Tchaikovsky's life and work into a book designed for the everyday reader. Covering the beloved

Russian composer's creations as well as his tormented personal life, Brown, who teaches musicology in England, creates a vivid portrait of the man who gave us such immortal works as *The Nutcracker, Swan Lake* and the *1812 Overture*.

COMING-OF-AGE NOVELS
Innocence Lost

What we know as the coming-of-age novel is technically a bildungsroman, or "novel of formation," in literal translation from German. Typically, the hero or heroine undergoes an emotional, intellectual, and/or spiritual awakening over the course of a narrative that's often bittersweet in tone, even when their stories end on a happy note. Their hard-won epiphanies can strike a deeply personal chord for readers, who often read their favorite coming-of-age novels over and over again.

Most reading lists of essential "coming-of-age" novels invariably include J.D. Salinger's ***The Catcher in the Rye***, Harper Lee's ***To Kill A Mockingbird***, and Mark Twain's ***The Adventures of Huckleberry Finn***. Rather than go the usual route, this alphabetical list of twelve coming-of-age novels departs from the standard recommendations to focus on worthwhile, contemporary entries in the genre.

1. **Annie John** by Jamaica Kincaid, 1985 – Kincaid's slender but emotionally rich novel is set in her native Antigua, where a young girl's idyllic childhood ends with the onset of an unusually painful adolescence.

2. **Bastard Out of Carolina** by Dorothy Allison, 1992 – Allison's searing debut novel, a National Book Award finalist, is the loosely autobiographical story of Ruth Anne "Bone" Boatwright, the dirt-poor, illegitimate daughter of a waitress in rural South Carolina. When her mother marries a local man, Bone's initial joy turns to despair after her alcoholic stepfather begins sexually abusing her.

3. **The Buddha of Suburbia** by Hanif Kureishi, 1990 – Languishing in the suburbs of seventies-era London, a bisexual Anglo-Indian teenager escapes to the city, where he throws himself headlong into sex, drugs and rock and roll. An acerbic, lively satirical novel from the screenwriter of *My Beautiful Laundrette*.

4. **The Fortress of Solitude** by Jonathan Lethem, 2003 – The author of ***Motherless Brooklyn*** returns to the New York borough with this wonderfully evocative, decades-spanning portrait of two men, black and white, who meet as teenagers and bond over their shared love of music and comic books.

5. *Graceland* by Chris Abani, 2004 – Intense, stunningly rendered first novel about a Nigerian boy desperate to escape the nightmarish squalor of a Lagos ghetto, where he lives with his stern taskmaster of a father.

6. **Jim the Boy: A Novel** by Tony Earley, 2000 – A simple, unaffected and deeply moving story of a ten year-old boy growing up in fatherless in Depression-era North Carolina.

7. **The Miracle Life of Edgar Mint** by Brady Udall, 2001 - "If I could tell you only one thing about my life it would be this: when I was seven-years-old the mailman ran over my head." Thus begins Udall's Dickensian story of Mint, the half-white, half-Apache hero, who later embarks on a mission to find and forgive the mailman who inadvertently changed Mint's life forever.

8. **Once Upon a River** by Bonnie Jo Campbell, 2011 – With just a few supplies and her favorite biography of Annie Oakley, sixteen-year-old Margo Crane embarks on a solo boat trip up Michigan's Stark River in search of her long-lost mother. Critics compared Crane's resourceful and observant heroine to Twain's Huck Finn. Another winner from Campbell, a National Book Award finalist for her short story collection ***American Salvage***.

EXCERPT: ONCE UPON A RIVER:

She waded through serpentine tree roots to grab hold of water snakes and let the river clean the wounds from the nonvenomous bites. She sometimes tricked a snapping turtle into clamping its jaws down hard on a branch so she could carry it home to Grandpa Murray. He boiled the meat to make soup and told the children that eating snapping turtle was like eating dinosaur. Margo was the only one the old man would take along when he fished or checked his animal traps because she could sit without speaking for hours in the prow of The River Rose, his small teak boat. Margo learned that when she was tempted to speak or cry out, she should, instead, be still and watch and listen. The old man called her Sprite or River Nymph. Her cousins called her Nympho, though not usually within the old man's hearing.

9. **The Perks of Being a Wallflower** by Stephen Chbosky, 1999 – Frequently banned, due to its frank portrayal of teenaged homosexuality and drug use, Chbosky's novel about an introverted teenager finding his voice has become a favorite of many teens, who feel a deep affinity for the misfit hero.

10. **A Prayer for Owen Meany** by John Irving, 1989 – Irving serves up another winning mixture of farce and tragedy in this story of a dwarfish, misfit boy who announces that he's an instrument of God — after he accidentally kills his friend's mother with a stray foul ball during a little league game.

11. **She's Come Undone** by Wally Lamb, 1992 – Extraordinarily moving, tragicomic novel spans nearly forty years in the hard-knock life of Dolores Price, whose intelligence and wit make her one of the most likable heroines in recent fiction.

12. **We the Animals** by Justin Torres, 2011 – First-time novelist Torres knocks it out of the park with his emotionally raw and vividly written story of three brothers,

born to a Puerto Rican father and white mother, growing up in a poverty-stricken, dysfunctional family in upstate New York.

COMMUNITY LIFE IN FICTION
It Takes a Village

They say it takes a village to raise a child — and, let's not forget, it takes all kinds to make a village. Here are ten books, listed alphabetically, that weave tapestries of characters, showing how our individual lives are shaped by the collective life of the places where we live.

1. **Cannery Row** by John Steinbeck, 1945 – Steinbeck's novel describes the lives of various men and women living in a poor neighborhood in Monterey, California. Their attempts to live and find joy in their unconventional lifestyles, canning sardines, shopping at Lee Chong's grocery, and throwing parties, are touching and sad.

2. **Drop City** by T. C. Boyle, 2003 – A National Book Award finalist, Boyle's ninth novel depicts the ill-fated attempt by a group of California hippies, circa 1970, to establish a commune in the Alaskan interior, where they receive a chilly welcome from locals. The *New York Times Book Review* hailed *Drop City* as "one of the funniest, and at the same time, most subtle, novels we've had about the hippie era's slow fade to black."

EXCERPT: DROP CITY:

It was a bus. A school bus. And Norm, sleepless Norm, fueled on amphetamine and black coffee, was at the wheel, the suede cowboy hat pulled down to the level of the black broken frames of his glasses and Premstar perched in his lap like a ventriloquist's dummy. The gears ground with a shriek, the massive face of the thing swung into the yard and beat the mud into submission and the rain sculpted the two long streaming banks of windows in a smooth wrap. There was the wheeze of the air brakes, a heavy dependable sloshing, and then the bus was idling there before them, as if all they had to do was pick up their schoolbags and lunchboxes and climb aboard.

3. **Dubliners** by James Joyce, 1914 – The residents of Dublin are the subjects of this classic collection of short stories. Joyce uses to the fullest his uncanny ability to get into the heads of all kinds of people and describe the incidents, whether tiny or stunning, that define and reveal their lives. ONLINE DETAILS

4. **Lake Wobegon Days** by Garrison Keillor, 1985 – Drawn from episodes of the radio show *A Prairie Home Companion*, this is the history of Lake Wobegon, an

imaginary small town in the American Midwest. With humor and nostalgia, Keillor describes the down-to-earth characters who manage to live through hard winter after hard winter.

5. **Main Street** by Sinclair Lewis, 1920 – A lovely, idealistic young woman marries a doctor who lives in provincial Minnesota town. She harbors fantasies of creating a renaissance of high culture in the town, but the staid and stuffy locals refuse to cooperate in this wryly satirical novel by the Nobel Prize-winning author of ***It Can't Happen Here***.

6. **Midaq Alley** by Naguib Mahfouz, 1947 – The alley is a street in a poor section of Cairo; its inhabitants struggle to find contentment despite difficult circumstances and their own weaknesses and passions. You will meet Radwan Hussainy, a respected wise man who is gentle and philosophical in his dealings with his neighbors but tyrannizes his wife; Zaita, a sadist who helps beggars improve their prospects by crippling them; and Hamida, an ambitious and beautiful girl who is seduced into prostitution.

7. **Spoon River Anthology** by Edgar Lee Masters, 1915 – This is an unusual collection of stories — poems, really — about the inhabitants of the imaginary town Spoon River, told from their own perspectives after death. The residents of the village cemetery, from criminals to pillars of the community, share their secrets, dreams, and philosophies.

8. **Telegraph Avenue** by Michael Chabon, 2012 – Dubbed "the Michael Jordan of American novelists" by the *Denver Post*'s John Broening, Chabon (***The Yiddish Policemen's Union***) sets his exuberantly entertaining and heartfelt eighth novel in San Francisco's Brokeland neighborhood, on the border between Berkeley and Oakland, circa 2004. Here old friends and longtime business partners Archy and Nat run Brokeland Records, selling vinyl and holding court in the tight-knit community. All that is threatened, however, when a former NFL player announces plans to build a megastore on Telegraph Avenue.

9. **The Wettest County in the World** by Matt Bondurant, 2008 – Bondurant takes inspiration from his own family history in this riveting novel of dark deeds in Franklin County, Virginia, at the height of Prohibition. In the wake of the Great Depression, the citizens of Franklin County turn to bootlegging, operating openly until the Feds move in with demands for graft, something the three Bondurant brothers reject outright. Also, on the scene is *Winesburg, Ohio* author Sherwood Anderson, an outsider eager to get a firsthand look at the illicit alcohol trade. Bondurant has created a finely etched portrait of a family, a community and an era.

10. **Winesburg, Ohio** by Sherwood Anderson, 1919 – A classic of American literature, Anderson's novel in short stories was inspired by his own Midwestern childhood. As a young man named George Willard comes of age in a small town, Anderson

captures the loneliness and disillusionment of Winesburg's residents with insight and compassion.

CREATIVE NONFICTION
Blurring the Lines between Fact and Fiction

Creative nonfiction makes strange literary bedfellows: both the dapper, old school Southern gentleman Tom Wolfe and "gonzo journalist" Hunter S. Thompson excel at this hybrid of literary fiction techniques and reportage that encompasses such disparate genres as travel writing, personal essay, and nonfiction novels like Truman Capote's *In Cold Blood*. Although they use dialogue and write scenes to give their work the emotional depth and narrative momentum of fiction, practitioners of this form must be scrupulous in their attention to facts — or suffer the consequences. Case in point: James Frey, whose bruising, allegedly true account of his stint in rehab for alcohol and drug abuse, *A Million Little Pieces,* was revealed to be largely fabricated.

Ranging far and wide over such subjects as Hollywood, the AIDS crisis and Central American politics, the following twelve books, listed alphabetically, are some of the most compelling works of creative nonfiction published since the fifties.

1. **And the Band Played On** by Randy Shilts, 1987 – Chilling, infuriating and heartbreaking, Shilts' exhaustive account of the early days of the AIDS crisis weaves disparate storylines into a masterly narrative. Tragically, Shilts would later die of AIDS in 1994.

2. **The Armies of the Night: History as a Novel, the Novel as History** by Norman Mailer, 1968 – Mailer scored a one-two punch, winning both the National Book Award and the Pulitzer Prize for his nonfiction novel about the anti-Vietnam War movement. Such real-life figures as Abbie Hoffman, Dr. Benjamin Spock and Mailer himself play prominent roles in *Armies of the Night.*

3. **Black Hawk Down: A Story of Modern War** by Mark Bowden, 1999 – Grueling and unforgettable, Bowden's pulse-pounding chronicle of the U.S. Army's ill-fated, 1993 mission into the streets of Mogadishu, Somalia thrusts you headlong into the eighteen-hour firefight between U.S. soldiers and Somalis.

4. **The Children** by David Halberstam, 1998 – A giant of post-war American journalism, Halberstam wrote classic books on the Vietnam war, media tycoons, and baseball. With *The Children*, Halberstam immerses readers in the early days of the civil rights movement in the Jim Crow-era South. An exceptional achievement from the Pulitzer Prize-winning journalist.

5. **Fear and Loathing in Las Vegas** by Hunter S. Thompson, 1971 – Fueled by alcohol and prodigious amounts of drugs, Thompson and his lawyer zoomed off to Las Vegas to attend a narcotic officers' convention. The father of "gonzo

journalism" later transformed their experiences into the freewheeling acid trip of book that's a surreal meditation on the "American Dream."

6. __The Electric Kool-Aid Acid Test__ by Tom Wolfe, 1968 – Wolfe's indelible record of his psychedelic bus ride with Ken Kesey and his LSD-swilling Merry Pranksters into hippiedom is a superlative example of "new journalism."

7. __Here Is a Human Being: At the Dawn of Personal Genomics__ by Misha Angrist, 2010 — As the fourth participant in the Personal Genome Project, Angrist gained an unusual window into modern science and the cataloguing of the entire human genome. Both informative and entertaining, this surprising account asks all the right — thought-provoking — questions.

8. __Me Talk Pretty One Day__ by David Sedaris, 2000 — This side-splitting collection of stories wittily depicts the humans to communicate with one another. (The title is transliterated from the author's mangling of the French language.) The *New York Times Book Review* referred to Sedaris' humor as something that would result if Dorothy Parker and James Thurber had had a love child. At turns silly and sophisticated, *Me Talk Pretty One Day* will leave you breathless with laughter.

EXCERPT: ME TALK PRETTY ONE DAY:

The agent came for me during a geography lesson. She entered the room and nodded at my fifth-grade teacher, who stood frowning at a map of Europe. What would needle me later was the realization that this had all been prearranged. My capture had been scheduled to go down at exactly 2:30 on a Thursday afternoon. The agent would be wearing a dung-colored blazer over a red knit turtleneck, her heels sensibly low in case the suspect should attempt a quick getaway.

"David," the teacher said, "this is Miss Samson, and she'd like you to go with her now."

No one else had been called, so why me? I ran down a list of recent crimes, looking for a conviction that might stick. Setting fire to a reportedly flameproof Halloween costume, stealing a set of barbecue tongs from an unguarded patio, altering the word 'hit' on a list of rules posted on the gymnasium door; never did it occur to me that I might be innocent.

9. __Picture__ by Lillian Ross, 1952 – A regular contributor to *The New Yorker*, Ross got permission from director John Huston to watch him direct *The Red Badge of Courage* in 1950. First published in serial form in *The New Yorker*, *Picture* is widely considered the best book ever written about Hollywood — a revealing, warts-and-all portrait of movie studio politics, hubris and Machiavellian intrigue.

10. __Random Family: Love, Drugs, Trouble and Coming of Age in the Bronx__ by Adrien Nicole LeBlanc, 2003 — For ten years, LeBlanc followed the lives of two, working-class Latina women and their extended families in the Bronx. The result is a stunning and sympathetic chronicle of resilience in the midst of squalor,

rampant crime, and lives gone to drugs. A finalist for the National Book Critics Circle Award.

11. **Salvador** by Joan Didion, 1983 – Didion brings her clinical eye to this mesmerizing account of her two-week visit to El Salvador in 1982, when the country was torn apart by nightmarish civil war.

12. **Thy Neighbor's Wife** by Gay Talese, 1981 – How the sixties-era sexual revolution trickled down to suburbia is the subject of Talese's eye-opening book, which details the author's sexual research in prose that's frank yet never prurient.

CREATURES OF THE NIGHT
They're Heeeere — to Scare the Bejesus Out of You

Forget Lestat or any of the vampire dandies who walk the night in Anne Rice's phenomenally popular novels about the undead, *__Interview with the Vampire__* and *__The Vampire Lestat__*. Ignore the mopey vampires of Stephanie Meyer's *__Twilight__* young adult series. None of these angst-ridden bloodsuckers have the bite of Bram Stoker's immortal creation, Count Dracula.

Since its publication in 1897, Stoker's *Dracula* has been imitated, parodied and filmed countless times, but few, if any of its subsequent incarnations, conjure the nightmarish dread of Stoker's epistolary novel, which draws heavily upon Central European folklore. Initially regarded as just a Gothic potboiler — albeit a supremely chilling example of the genre — *Dracula* is now considered a bona-fide literary classic. It's also one of ten books, listed alphabetically, that feature supernatural, mythological and man-made characters who will haunt your dreams.

1. **American Gods** by Neil Gaiman, 2001 – The winner of the Bram Stoker, Hugo and Nebula Awards, this ambitious and boldly realized novel by Gaiman (*__Anansi Boys__*) envisions a United States where the ancient gods and mythological creatures of European lore clash with homegrown deities representing everything from the Internet to credit cards.

2. **The Books of Blood,** Books 1-3 by Clive Barker, 1984-1985 – Here's where Clive Barker began his remarkable career in fantasy, horror and terror. His later works are larger in scope, and deal with deeper philosophical issues, but read these stories and understand why Stephen King once said, "I have seen the future of horror, and his name is Clive Barker." *__Books 4-6__* are in a second volume.

3. **A Dark Matter** by Peter Straub, 2010 – Although he's best known for his supernatural and fantasy-themed novels, including two collaborations with Stephen King, *__The Talisman__* and *__Black House__*, Straub has also written mysteries, poetry and nonfiction. In *A Dark Matter*, Straub returns to the supernatural with this marvelous novel, told *Rashomon*-style, about the evil

unleashed by four friends, who participated in an occult ceremony forty years earlier. Proclaimed a "masterpiece" by novelist Michael Chabon, *A Dark Matter* won the Bram Stoker Award.

4. **A Discovery of Witches** by Deborah Harkness, 2011 – An instant bestseller, the critically praised debut novel by Harkness plunges the reader into a richly imagined world where witches, vampires and demons are fighting for possession of an ancient alchemical manuscript. The first in a trilogy — ***Shadow of Night*** followed in 2012 — *A Discovery of Witches* is a compulsively readable mixture of romance, fantasy and supernatural thriller.

5. **Dracula** *by Bram Stoker*, 1897 – Best read with the lights on, Stoker's most acclaimed novel (he wrote thirteen in all, including ***The Lair of the White Worm***), remains an atmospheric and genuinely frightening page-turner that set the bar for all novels of the supernatural that followed. Leaving a trail of corpses stretching from Transylvania to London, Dracula meets his match in the Dutch vampire hunter, Van Helsing.

6. **The Exorcist** by William Peter Blatty, 1971 – Faithfully adapted for the screen by Blatty and director William Friedkin in 1973, *The Exorcist* has a visceral intensity, even on the page, that's not for the easily spooked. Based on an actual exorcism performed in 1949, Blatty's disturbing novel pits two priests against an ancient demon who's taken possession of a movie star's adolescent daughter.

7. **Frankenstein** by Mary Shelley, 1818 – Along with *Dracula*, Shelley's *Frankenstein* set a literary standard for Gothic horror that has rarely been equaled. Inspired by a dream, Shelley's first and most famous novel about the obsessive quest of Dr. Victor Frankenstein to create life has lost none of its power to get under your skin, nearly 200 years after it was published.

8. **The Last Werewolf** by Glen Duncan, 2011 – Written as a memoir, Duncan's scary, smartly conceived and sexually explicit novel recounts the experiences of Jake Marlowe, a 201-year-old chain-smoking, philosophy-reading werewolf whose wit is as sharp as his fangs. Although he's as spry as ever, Jake has fallen into a depression that has him contemplating suicide — even as he tries to evade a mysterious organization that's targeted him for execution.

EXCERPT: THE LAST WEREWOLF:

All wolf and no gang. Humour darkens. I looked out of the window. The snow was coming down with the implacability of an Old Testament plague. In Earl's Court Road pedestrians tottered and slid and in the cold swirling angelic freshness felt their childhoods still there and the shock like a snapped stem of not being children anymore. Two nights ago I'd eaten a forty-three-year-old hedge fund specialist. I've been in a phase of taking the ones no one wants. My last phase, apparently.

9. **Let Me In** by John Ajvide Lindqvist, 2007 – A bullied twelve-year-old living in a Stockholm suburb, Oskar finds an unlikely friend and protector in Eli, who only emerges at night to feed on transients and unsavory characters. Originally titled *Let the Right One In*, *Let Me In* marked a spectacular debut for Lindqvist, who's been called "Sweden's Stephen King."

10. **The Strange Case of Dr. Jekyll and Mr. Hyde** by Robert Louis Stevenson, 1886 – One afternoon Mrs. Stevenson heard her sleeping husband utter cries of horror. Terrified, she woke him, and he replied, "Why did you wake me? I was dreaming a fine bogey tale." That "bogey tale" became this nightmarish classic, a meditation on horror, good and evil and what lurks inside all of us. Hyde's horrific acts in the book had to be toned down for the stage and screen.

CRIME FICTION
Hard-Boiled Classics

Duplicitous femme fatales, corrupt cops on the take, sadistic criminals who delight in torturing their victims to death — these are the denizens of the shadowy underworld of hard-boiled crime fiction, that peculiarly American literary genre. Born in the pages of the twenties-era magazine pulp magazine *Black Mask* (founded by H.L. Mencken and George Jean Nathan), the genre was honed and refined by the legendary Dashiell Hammett, the author of **The Maltese Falcon** and **Red Harvest**. His stories about cynical, world-weary detectives unraveling mysteries of Byzantine complexity basically set the template for the genre, which continued to flourish in the novels of Raymond Chandler, Mickey Spillane and more recently, James Ellroy.

Although most readers associate hard-boiled crime fiction with detective yarns, the genre is not the sole province of Sam Spade, Philip Marlowe and other private eyes. The novels of James M. Cain (**The Postman Always Rings Twice**) and Jim Thompson (**The Grifters**) aren't mysteries, but lurid, sex-soaked narratives of amoral characters whose crimes eventually catch up with them. Dubbed "literary noir," these novels are still classified as hard-boiled fiction. Here are twelve classics of the genre, listed alphabetically, from masters of hard-boiled crime fiction past and present.

1. **The Big Nowhere** by James Ellroy, 1988 – Exceptionally dark and grimly compelling novel about two Los Angeles police detectives searching for a serial killer targeting gay men while simultaneously rooting out suspected "Commies" in Hollywood, circa 1950. The second novel in Ellroy's "L.A. Quartet," which also includes **The Black Dahlia**, **L.A. Confidential** and **White Jazz**.

2. **The Dain Curse** by Dashiell Hammett, 1929 – Looking for clues in a diamond heist, a detective uncovers a wealthy family's disturbing involvement with the occult in this vintage Hammett novel.

3. **The Deep Blue Good-by** by John D. MacDonald, 1964 – MacDonald introduces his Florida-based "salvage consultant" Travis McGee, an ex-football player with a knack for finding missing persons and property, in *The Deep Blue Good-by*.

4. **Double Indemnity** by James M. Cain, 1936 - The source for Billy Wilder's classic film noir is a marvel of narrative economy about a two-bit insurance salesman seduced into committing murder by a calculating femme fatale.

5. **Farewell, My Lovely** by Raymond Chandler, 1940 – According to Ross MacDonald, "Chandler wrote like a slumming angel and invested the sun-blinded streets of Los Angeles with a romantic presence." In *Farewell, My Lovely*, Chandler's legendary detective, Philip Marlowe, goes in search of an ex-convict's missing girlfriend and gets ensnarled in a murder linked to a jewel thief ring.

6. **The Hunter** by Richard Stark, 1962 – "Richard Stark" was one of several pseudonyms used by the late Donald E. Westlake, who wrote more than one hundred books during his prolific career. *The Hunter* is a tough, in-your-face crime drama about a criminal, shot and left for dead by his former partner, out for vengeance. The first of Stark's Parker novels.

7. **I, The Jury** by Mickey Spillane, 1947 – When a friend is murdered, New York private eye Mike Hammer vows to find the killer. A brawler with a foul mouth and an eye for beautiful broads, Hammer dispenses his own brand of justice without remorse in Spillane's pulp favorite.

8. **The Killer Inside Me** by Jim Thompson, 1952 – Overlooked during his lifetime, Thompson has been posthumously embraced as one of the all-time great pulp writers. *The Killer Inside Me* is arguably his best and most disturbing work. Outwardly placid, a small town Texas deputy is fighting a losing battle to suppress his urge to commit acts of savage violence.

EXCERPT: THE KILLER INSIDE ME:

I'd been trying to place him, and finally it had come to me. It's been several years since I'd seen that big ugly mug in one of the out-of-town papers, and the picture hadn't been so good a resemblance. But I remembered it, now, and some of the story I'd read about him. He'd taken his degree at the University of Edinburgh at a time when we were admitting their graduates to practice. He'd killed half a dozen people before he picked up a jerkwater Ph.D., and edged into psychiatry.

9. **The Killer Is Dying** by James Sallis, 2011 – The lives of three men become linked when a murder takes place in Phoenix and each must come to grips with their connection to the crime. One is pursuing the killer; another may be set up for the crime; and a third is pulled in by the information he's receiving against his wishes: He's dreaming the real killer's dreams.

10. **Live By Night** by Dennis Lehane, 2012 – The author of ***Mystic River*** and ***Gone, Baby Gone*** ventures into *Boardwalk Empire* territory with this masterful Prohibition-era crime novel. The youngest son of a Boston police captain, Joe Coughlin strays off the straight and narrow to work for a local mobster. Burning the proverbial candle at both ends, Joe revels in his outlaw status, but it comes at a steep price in *Live by Night*, which *Booklist* called "an utterly magnetic novel on every level."

11. **Solomon's Vineyard** by Jonathan Latimer, 1941 – A textbook example of hard-boiled crime fiction at its best. A tough St. Louis private detective's got his work cut out for him when he must save a beautiful heiress from a lunatic religious cult. Oozing sleaze and kinky sex, *Solomon's Vineyard* was initially banned in the United States.

12. **Swag** by Elmore Leonard, 1976 – By adhering to ten, strictly delineated rules of conduct, two small-time crooks pull off a string of heists in Detroit without a hitch. The fun begins when they start bending the rules. A fast-paced, funny and tautly drawn crime drama from a modern master of the genre, known as "the Dickens of Detroit."

DOGS IN LITERATURE
Unforgettable Canine Characters

Contrary to many opinions of late, modern literature has not gone to the dogs — it happened centuries ago. One of the earliest literary tributes to dogs appears in Homer's **The *Odyssey*.** When the hero Ulysses finally returns home after twenty years abroad, only his faithful dog Argus recognizes him. Lying near-death on a dung heap, Argus weakly raises his head and wags his tail one last time at his master's approach. Now *that's* devotion.

Although most dogs in literature come across as steadfast, brave and lovably exasperating as their real-life counterparts, a few canine villains lurk in the shadows, waiting to pounce on unwary readers (***The Hound of the Baskervilles***). Here are some of the most memorable dog characters in fiction, listed alphabetically by character name.

1. **Buck**: **The Call of the Wild** by Jack London, 1903 – Jack London's most popular book introduces Buck, the St. Bernard/Scotch Sheepdog mix who survives kidnapping and cruel masters to find freedom in the frozen Yukon during the Gold Rush.

2. **Chet**: **A Fistful of Collars: A Chet and Bernie Mystery** by Spencer Quinn, 2012 – Kicked out of the police academy's K-9 school for an incident he can't remember (though he does admit that blood *may* have been involved), Chet is the canine

narrator of Quinn's clever and witty mystery series that pairs the crime-solving mutt with private investigator Bernie Little. In the fifth book of the series that began with **_Dog On It_,** Chet and Bernie play bodyguard to a sleazy Hollywood actor with a criminal past.

3. **Cujo: Cujo** by Stephen King, 1980 – Every dog lover's worst fear comes to disturbing life in King's novel about a rabid St. Bernard who terrorizes his owners.

4. *Dog of Tears:* **Blindness** by José Saramago, 1998 - In this chilling dystopian novel by the Nobel Prize-winning novelist, the unnamed Dog of Tears is the companion/protector of a doctor's wife and her companions in a city plagued by mass blindness. In a 2002 poll conducted by *Book Magazine*, the Dog of Tears was ranked seventy-eighth in the list of the top one hundred fictional characters of the twentieth century.

5. **Enzo**: **The Art of Racing in the Rain** by Garth Stein, 2008 – Only the most hard-hearted cynic will be able to resist Enzo, the narrator of Stein's bestselling novel The wise and faithful companion of race car driver Denny Swift, Enzo ponders reincarnation and questions of morality as he watches the ups and downs of Denny's life, both on and off the race track.

6. **Lassie**: **Lassie, Come Home** by Eric Knight, 1938 – Arguably the most famous bitch in the world (among dogs, anyway), Lassie made her first appearance in this *Saturday Evening Post* short story. When her impoverished masters are forced to sell her to a rich duke, Lassie escapes to make the arduous trek home to her beloved family.

7. *Maf:* **The Life and Opinions of Maf the Dog, and of His Friend Marilyn Monroe** by Andrew O'Hagan, 2010 – A Maltese who claims to be descended from pets owned by Mary, Queen of Scots and Marie Antoinette, Maf (short for Mafia) becomes the confidante of the legendary film star in O'Hagan's delightful novel. Chronicling his run-ins with Hollywood and literary heavyweights (he bites Lillian Hellman at a cocktail party), Maf offers a compassionate "dog's eye view" of the emotionally fragile Monroe.

EXCERPT: THE LIFE AND OPINIONS OF MAF THE DOG, AND OF HIS FRIEND MARILYN MONROE:

There are several things every civilised person ought to know about your average dog. The first is that we love liver and think it's a zizz and a yarm and a rumph and a treat, especially when it comes with sausage. The second is that we usually hate cats, not for the typical reasons, but because they show an exclusive preference for poetry over prose. No cat ever spoke for long in the warmth of good prose. A dog's biggest talent, though, is for absorbing everything of interest — we absorb the best of what is known to our owners and we retain the thoughts of those we meet. We are retentive enough and we have none of that fatal human weakness for making large distinctions between what is real and what is imagined. It is all the same, more or less.

8. **Nana**: **Peter and Wendy** by James M. Barrie, 1911 – The adored protector of the Darling children, this Newfoundland stays behind when Wendy, Michael and John fly off to Never-Never Land with Peter Pan and Tinkerbell.

9. **Old Yeller**: **Old Yeller** by Frederick Gipson, 1956 – Has there ever been more of a tearjerker than *Old Yeller*? Set in rural Texas just after the Civil War, Gipson's novel depicts the close bond between a young boy and his courageous dog that comes to a tragic end.

10. **Pongo and Perdita**: **101 Dalmatians**, by Dodie Smith, 1957 – The intrepid, surprisingly docile (considering the breed) couple who rescue their brood from the clutches of Cruella De Vil, public enemy no. 1 to Dalmatians and PETA activists everywhere.

11. **Skip**: **My Dog Skip** by Willie Morris, 1995 – Growing up in Depression-era Mississippi, a lonely young boy slowly emerges from his shell, thanks to the companionship of the title character, an irrepressible Jack Russell terrier who drives a car and drinks from the toilet with equal aplomb.

12. **White Fang:** **White Fang** by Jack London, 1906 – Half-wolf, half-Indian dog, the title character of London's novel is a wild, savage fighter who gradually warms to human contact through the patient efforts of a kind master.

DYNAMIC DUOS OF LITERATURE
Couples Who Write

Romantic passion, as we all know, is one of the great driving forces of literature. When both partners are gifted writers, their intensity and eloquence only seem to grow, even if love isn't their subject matter. Brief affairs between writers are innumerable, of course, but here are some couples of longer standing who have made great contributions to literary culture. Their relationships ranged from idyllic to tortured and everything in between, but all were highly productive. Note that the tradition of writers marrying continues among today's young writers, such as Nicole Krauss (***The History of Love***) and Jonathan Safran Foer (***Everything Is Illuminated***), and Dave Eggers (***What is the What***) and Vendela Vida (***The Lovers***).

1. **Percy Bysshe Shelley (1792–1822) & Mary Wollstonecraft Shelley (1797–1851)** - Mary Wollstonecraft Shelley was herself the product of a literary couple: her parents were William Godwin, a novelist and political radical, and the early feminist Mary Wollstonecraft, who died a year after her daughter was born. Percy Bysshe Shelley was an English nobleman whose rebellious streak went against

his conservative background. As a teenager he eloped with his first wife, after whose suicide he and Mary were wed. He is the author of such poems as "To a Skylark" and "Adonais," which are included in ***Percy Bysshe Shelley: The Complete Works***. She wrote ***Frankenstein*** as part of a friendly contest with Percy, Lord Byron, and another friend. Their union was cut off when Percy was drowned in 1822.

2. **Robert Browning (1812–1889) & Elizabeth Barrett Browning (1806–1861)** - The two poets met after Elizabeth Barrett, who lived as a cloistered invalid, referred to Browning's work in one of her poems. Against her father's wishes, they fell in love and eloped to Italy. Their romance produced a number of beautiful letters and verses, including the famous line "How do I love thee? Let me count the ways" from one of Elizabeth's sonnets to her husband. ***Sonnets from the Portuguese*** includes forty-four interlocking poems she wrote for Browning. Some of his most important work is featured in the compendium ***Robert Browning: Selected Poems***.

3. **Jean-Paul Sartre (1905–1980) & Simone de Beauvoir (1908–1986)** - This French pair first met as students in 1929. Pioneers of the Existentialist movement in philosophy, they became famous for books such as Sartre's ***Being and Nothingness*** and de Beauvoir's ***The Second Sex*** . They spent most of their lives together as friends and lovers, although their relationship was not exclusive and they never married. They are now buried in the same grave.

4. **Sylvia Plath (1932–1963) & Ted Hughes (1930–1998)** - Plath met the handsome British poet at a party in 1956, and they were soon married. They had two children and both of them began to gain recognition for their work, but they were separated by the time Plath committed suicide in 1963. Hughes edited her Pulitzer-prize winning ***Collected Poems*** after her death, and decades later, shortly before his own death, a book of poems addressed to her called ***Birthday Letters*** was published.

5. **Raymond Carver (1938–1988) & Tess Gallagher (born 1943)** - These American authors had both been married before when they began to live together in the late seventies after meeting at a writers' conference in Texas. They collaborated on projects, figured in each other's poetry (Carver was also a noted fiction writer — ***What We Talk About When We Talk About Love: Stories***), and finally married in the spring of 1988, when Carver was dying of cancer. Gallagher's ***Midnight Lantern: New and Selected Poems*** was deemed "worthy of the Pulitzer Prize" by the *Seattle Times*.

6. **Louise Erdrich (born 1954) & Michael Dorris (1945–1997)** - Erdrich, the author of ***The Beet Queen*** and Dorris, the author of ***A Yellow Raft in Blue Water***, shared a love of literature as well as their mixed Native American and European heritage. The married couple raised three adopted children and three children of

their own, and collaborated extremely closely on much of their work. They separated in 1995, and, plagued by family troubles, Dorris committed suicide in 1997.

ENVIRONMENTAL STUDIES
Readings about Global Warming

As the evidence adds up from around the world, there is little debate that the carbon dioxide our industries and automobiles send into the atmosphere is trapping more of the sun's heat and contributing to the earth warming up. However, there is an intense (and economically high-stakes) debate about the likely effects of this warming on our lives, and the relative costs of trying to limit it versus letting it take its course. Some argue that switching from fossil fuels to cleaner sources of energy such as wind power would be too disruptive to the economy. Others argue that such changes are manageable and that failing to make them will create problems much more expensive and difficult to control — not just hotter summers and more powerful hurricanes, but coastal cities being flooded and droughts disrupting agricultural production. Here are eight books, listed alphabetically, by a range of experts weighing in with their opinions.

1. **Climate of Uncertainty: A Balanced Look at Global Warming and Renewable Energy** by William Stewart, 2010 – In a book that gives the appearance of effortlessness as it condenses complicated issues into easily digestible prose, Stewart meticulously avoids overblown rhetoric of any kind. Readers of all political persuasions have hailed it for taking a step back from the emotionally charged debate and giving a holistic view of where our planet is today. Though well-researched, Stewart doesn't have all the answers — nor does he claim to. Somewhat paradoxically, *Climate of Uncertainty* is therefore the rare offering on global warming that actually has something for everyone.

2. **Field Notes from a Catastrophe: Man, Nature, and Climate Change** by Elizabeth Kolbert, 2006 – Kolbert travels around the world documenting signs of the warming earth, from permafrost — no longer permanent — melting in Fairbanks, Alaska, to butterflies in England choosing habitats farther north. She also uses history to explore how droughts can affect a civilization and looks into the ways communities and governments are dealing with the changes that have already occurred and those that are likely to happen. Responses include energy conservation; inaction; the construction of floating roads (in the low-lying Netherlands); and packing up and leaving home (a native village in Alaska).

3. **Global Warming: The Complete Briefing** by John Houghton, 1994, updated 2004 – This is an accessible overview of the science of global warming and what it

means for our society. You'll come away from it with a clear understanding of the basic climatological, political, and economic aspects of the issue.

4. **Meltdown: The Predictable Distortion of Global Warming by Scientists, Politicians, and the Media** by Patrick J. Michaels, 2004 – The author does think that the earth is warming as a result of our emissions of carbon dioxide, but also thinks that the threat has been exaggerated and that warming is unlikely to lead to any serious problems. He argues that we should adjust to any changes as they occur rather than interfere in the process with regulation.

5. **The Skeptical Environmentalist: Measuring the Real State of the World** by Bjørn Lomborg, 1998 – As the title implies, this is another skeptic. His book deals with a number of environmental questions, but he devotes a sixty-page chapter to global warming. He writes, "There is no doubt that mankind has influenced and is still increasing atmospheric concentrations of CO_2 and that this will influence temperature." But he also thinks we should be careful to choose cost-effective responses.

6. **Thin Ice: Unlocking the Secrets of Climate in the World's Highest Mountains** by Mark Bowen, 2005 – Ice melting at the poles gets a lot of press, but there's also much to learn about the history and current state of the earth's climate from the icy mountains in the tropical and semitropical latitudes. This book follows an Ohio State University geologist on his high-altitude expeditions studying this ice. It argues that global warming could have drastic effects, leading to saltwater flooding coastal settlements and not enough freshwater available for farming.

EXCERPT: THIN ICE:

Since it [El Nino] generally appears at around Christmastime, the phenomenon was named for the Christ child by anchovy fishermen living less than a thousand miles northwest of here, in the coastal villages of Peru and Ecuador. They noticed that the cold waters that they fished, normally one of the most productive fisheries on earth, rose in temperature with El Niño, and the anchovy disappeared. This disrupts the entire aquatic food chain and the economy based upon it. Seabirds, which feed off the anchovy and produce the mountains of guano that the local farmers use as fertilizer and export all over the world, disappear as well. And while the sea withholds its bounty, it drives huge thunderheads into the skies above the equatorial coastal plain, normally one of the driest places on earth, producing storms, flash floods, and the occasional deadly landslide.

7. **Tropic of Chaos: Climate Change and the New Geogrolenceaphy of Vi** by Christian Parenti, 2011– Parenti, a journalist with *The Nation* magazine, makes the case that climate change is breeding conflict and strife in the postcolonial societies centered around the equator. As a result, he asserts, Western military forces are creating a new "climate fascism" in which

wealthier countries become armed fortresses willfully ignorant to the hardships of people in these equatorial regions, despite there being ample evidence that such hardships tend to metastasize in unexpected ways. Closing with prescriptions to avoid catastrophe, Parenti paints a deeply personal and unexpectedly optimistic climate-change picture.

8. **The Weather Makers: How Man Is Changing the Climate and What It Means for Life on Earth** by Tim Flannery, 2005 – This lively book explains the evidence for global warming and the importance of a stable climate for our economic system as well as our ecological system. The author also delves into the various options that are now available for cleaner energy and what individuals can do to reduce carbon emissions.

EPICS
Grand Old Stories

One of the oldest traditions in literature is the epic, a long heroic tale often composed in verse. Many epics were originally passed down orally from generation to generation, with different bards combining memory and invention to entertain and instruct their listeners. Others have been the work of single authors with grand visions. While the days of belief in dragons, sea monsters, and rulers descended from gods may be past, the best epics still do more than tickle our fancies; they provide us with metaphors for the struggles of our own lives (which ring no less true for the tales' exaggerations). Here is an alphabetical list of some of the greatest epics ever written. Their heroes vary considerably, from brawny fighting men to militant angels. But almost all of them exalt courage, rectitude, and wisdom — qualities that hold universal appeal.

1. **The Aeneid** by Virgil, 19 BC – After the famous war with the Greeks, the Trojan warrior Aeneas and his followers leave their destroyed city. A storm blows their ships to Carthage, the goddess Juno's favorite city. In Carthage Queen Dido receives them and falls in love with Aeneas (who recounts how the Greeks used the "gift" of a monumental wooden horse to enter Troy). Tragedy and adventure ensue, leading toward the founding of Rome—although Virgil died before completing the poem.

2. **Beowulf** by Anonymous, circa eighth century – The hero Beowulf battles a voracious monster named Grendel in order to save his allies, the Danes, upon whom Grendel has been banqueting. Soon he discovers that he must also take Grendel's vengeful mother into the reckoning. Later, the hero becomes a king and undergoes a final fight with an enraged dragon. *Beowulf* brings the world of the Dark Ages to life, drawing the reader into the concerns of the chieftains and their followers — loyalty, courage and cowardice, wealth, and strength.

EXCERPT: BEOWULF:

Shield had fathered a famous son:
Beow's name was known through the north.
And a young prince must be prudent like that,
giving freely while his father lives
so that afterwards in age when fighting starts
steadfast companions will stand by him
and hold the line. Behaviour that's admired
is the path to power among people everywhere.

3. **The Divine Comedy** by Dante Alighieri, 1321 – The narrator finds himself lost in a dark forest and menaced by beasts when none other than Virgil (***The Aeneid***) appears to guide him to safety. The way will not be easy: it takes him through Hell (*Inferno*), Purgatory (*Purgatorio*), and Heaven (*Paradiso*), where the saintly Beatrice replaces the pagan bard as guide. In these forbidding settings the reader may be surprised to find politics, love, and even humor, all expressed in lively and beautiful verse.

4. **Don Juan** by Lord Byron, 1819–1824 – This satirical epic poem follows the romantic (in both senses) career of Don Juan, ladies' man. After the young hero has an affair with an older woman, his overprotective mother sends him away from his home in Spain, thinking the trip will improve his morals. But shipwreck, slavery, and the attentions of powerful women make his travels much more eventful than Donna Inez would have hoped.

5. **Mahabharata,** Anonymous, circa fourth century – An extraordinarily long and complex poem, the *Mahabharata* describes (among many topics) a war of succession between the Kauravas and the Pandavas, two branches of the same family. It's rich with mythological episodes that illustrate the power of virtue and tackle thorny philosophical problems such as the morality of warfare.

6. **Le Morte d'Arthur** by Sir Thomas Malory, 1485 – Malory had the misfortune to spend about a third of his life in jail (where he died around the age of sixty), but he made the best of his time by writing down old folktales of King Arthur, the legendary king of medieval England. Chivalry, tournaments, fair ladies, the magician Merlin, the quest for the Holy Grail — it's all here.

7. **The Odyssey** by Homer, ninth century BC – Follow the adventures of the strong, resourceful, and long-suffering Odysseus as he makes his way back to his faithful wife Penelope after the Trojan War. He overcomes a man-eating Cyclops, ensnaring sirens, a possessive sea nymph, and many other dangers and delays, only to find impudent suitors for Penelope's hand overrunning his home. (Hint: don't mess with a hero like Odysseus or his loved ones, no matter how many years he's been away.)

8. **Orlando Furioso** by Ludovico Ariosto, 1532 – This witty tale in verse builds on an unfinished epic (***Orlando Innamorato***) by another Italian poet, Matteo Maria Boiardo. Orlando, or Roland, is a knight of Charlemagne in love with a Saracen princess. Duels, enchantments, and distant travels (even to the moon) make this an entertaining story.

ESPIONAGE NOVELS
Cloak and Dagger Classics

Stirred, but rarely shaken, Ian Fleming's Agent 007, James Bond, is one of the most enduring characters in popular culture, due largely to the long-running film series that began with 1962's *Doctor No*. For the most part, however, these splashy, spectacle-driven films bear only the slightest resemblance to Fleming's original novels, which are darker and comparatively more realistic in tone. The gimmickry and gadgets that drive the Bond films are MIA from the twelve novels and two short story collections Fleming wrote between 1953 and his death in 1964. Today, most critics name Fleming's fifth book, *From Russia with Love*, as the best of the series — it was also the only novel that made President John F. Kennedy's list of ten favorite books for the March 17, 1961 issue of *Life* magazine.

From *Russia with Love* is one of twelve, crackling good espionage yarns, listed alphabetically, that plunge readers into the shadowy and byzantine world of conspiracies, cover-ups and covert operations that's all in a day's work for master spies.

1. **A Coffin for Dimitrios** by Eric Ambler, 1939 - Looking for artistic inspiration, a British mystery writer in thirties-era Istanbul gets embroiled in a deadly web of intrigue while investigating the murder of the enigmatic Dimitrios — who may not be dead after all. A rattling good thriller from one of the acknowledged masters of the espionage genre.

2. **From Russia with Love** by Ian Fleming, 1957 - A gorgeous Soviet siren, Tatiana Romanova, lures the unflappable Bond into a trap set up by 007's chief cold war nemesis, the SMERSH organization, in Fleming's gripping page-turner.

3. **The Ipcress File** by Len Deighton, 1962 - The antithesis of 007, Deighton's middle-aged, cynical anti-hero is more of a paper-pusher whose dogged research into the mysterious disappearance of British scientists thrusts him into a bizarre plot involving mind control. Convoluted, sometimes to the point of confusion, *The Ipcress File* is nonetheless an ingenious and sardonically funny thriller — the first in what became known as Deighton's Harry Palmer series.

4. **The Kill Artist** by Daniel Silva, 2000 - Ranked the equal of John Le Carré and Graham Greene by *The Washingtonian*, CNN correspondent-turned novelist Silva

is at his relentless, pulse-pounding best in *The Kill Artist*, which depicts a former Israeli intelligence operative's hunt for a deadly Palestinian terrorist.

5. **The Moscow Club** by Joseph Finder, 1991 - Finder's ambitious debut novel is a densely plotted, post-cold war era thriller about a CIA analyst investigating a mysterious document reportedly dictated by Lenin on his deathbed. Thus begins a hair-raising, globe-trotting thriller that places Finder's hero in perpetual harm's way — from both the KGB and the CIA.

6. **The Tourist** by Olen Steinhauer, 2009 – The first in Steinhauer's Milo Weaver trilogy introduces the title character, a retired CIA operative forced to go back undercover following the arrest of a notorious assassin. A two-time Edgar Award nominee, Steinhauer has been favorably compared to John Le Carré by the *New York Times*.

7. **Night Soldiers** by Alan Furst, 1988 - Furst's literary career took off with this riveting, atmospheric thriller, set in 1934, about a young Bulgarian recruited by Soviet intelligence. Doubled-crossed while on assignment during the Spanish Civil War, Furst's traumatized hero takes refuge in Paris, where he eventually joins the French resistance in World War II.

8. **Our Man in Havana** by Graham Greene, 1958 - A giant of twentieth century English literature, Greene excelled at writing novels, plays, short stories, travel books, screenplays and criticism. One of his best and most diverting "entertainments" (as Greene called his mysteries/espionage thrillers) is this witty, razor-sharp novel about a vacuum cleaner salesman turned unlikely spy in pre-Castro era Cuba. Greene himself served in Great Britain's Secret Intelligence Service from 1941 to 1944.

EXCERPT: OUR MAN IN HAVANA:

Suddenly, without warning, one of the policemen slapped his face. He felt shock rather than anger. He belonged to the law-abiding class: the police were his natural protectors. He put his hand to his cheek and said, "What in God' name do you think . . . ?" The other policeman with a blow in the back sent him stumbling along the pavement. His hat fell off into the filth of the gutter. He said, "Give me my hat," and felt himself pushed again. He began to say something about the British Consul and they swung him sideways across the road and sent him reeling.

9. **The Riddle of the Sands** by Robert Erskine Childers, 1903 - Regarded as one of the first modern espionage novels, *The Riddle of the Sands* eerily anticipates World War I in its story about two Englishmen on a yachting holiday in the Baltic Sea who tangle with German spies.

10. **The Thirty-Nine Steps** by John Buchan, 1915 - The basis for Alfred Hitchcock's classic suspense thriller, Buchan's novel introduces Richard Hannay, a resourceful

Scotsman and free-lance spy, who runs afoul of German spies plotting to assassinate the Greek premier in London. Relying on his wits and several disguises, Hannay turns the tables on the spies, in Buchan's old-fashioned page-turner par excellence.

11. **Tinker, Tailor, Soldier, Spy** by John Le Carré, 1974 - Arguably the greatest living writer of espionage thrillers, Le Carré launched his brilliant Karla Trilogy with this bestseller, that finds middle-aged and embittered British agent George Smiley on the hunt for a Soviet "mole," who may have penetrated British Intelligence decades earlier. ***The Honourable Schoolboy*** and ***Smiley's People*** are the other novels in Le Carré's Karla Trilogy.

12. **Waiting for Sunrise** by William Boyd, 2012 – A young English actor gets swept up in the shadowy world of espionage in Boyd's fast-paced World War I-era novel that the *Financial Times* called "a historical thriller that genuinely thrills."

EXPATRIATE NONFICTION
Dispatches from Abroad

Living in a place for an extended period of time yields a different kind of knowledge than just visiting it as a tourist. Not all of us are lucky enough to be offered a position as a correspondent in Paris, or to be able to buy a villa in Tuscany. But we can still learn about far-off countries from expatriates living there — an intimate perspective, yet with the foreigner's sense of curiosity and appreciation (and, sometimes, crankiness). Listed alphabetically, these ten books will take you to some of the world's most beautiful, fabled, and dynamic locales.

1. **Bad Times in Buenos Aires** by Miranda France, 1999 – The author, a young British journalist, brings a keen sense of history to her descriptions of Buenos Aires. As the title suggests, she doesn't wear rose-tinted glasses: there are rats, bad phone lines, and other urban ills a-plenty. But there is also the glamour of the tango, and unexpected aspects of the culture to ponder — everyone seems to be in psychoanalysis, for example.

2. **City of Djinns: A Year in Delhi** by William Dalrymple, 1993 – Dalrymple shares his fascinating time living in the capital of India, a city of destruction, renewal, and remarkable people and traditions. Daily life, popular pastimes, festivals, and the multifarious past all come to life in his account.

3. **Foreign Babes in Beijing: Behind the Scenes of a New China** by Rachel DeWoskin, 2005 – In this perceptive and funny book, a young American public-relations specialist literally has a starring role in China's rapidly changing culture. DeWoskin plays what she really is — a foreign babe in Beijing — in the popular Chinese soap opera the book is named after. Her unusual tale makes for a great read and will teach you a lot about modern China, too.

4. **The Japan Journals: 1947–2004** by Donald Richie, edited by Leza Lowitz, 2005 – A writer and film director, Richie moved to Japan to work as a typist just after the end of World War II. His journals and diaries reflect his own active life there — social and sexual — and the changes in Japanese culture over the course of a half century.

5. **Paris to the Moon** by Adam Gopnik, 2000 – *The New Yorker* magazine sent Gopnik to Paris for five years with his wife and young son to write about his experiences there. The result is a lively, precisely observed series of adventures in the beautiful but complicated city. Gopnik enjoys the traditional charms of Paris even as he and the city deal with strikes, a formidable bureaucracy, and the pressures of globalization.

EXCERPT: PARIS TO THE MOON:

It is the weather reports on CNN that will scare you the most. They must come from a studio in Atlanta, like most things on the cable network, but they tell about the European weather, and only the European weather, and they treat Europe as if it were, for CNN's purposes, one solid block of air with dirt down beneath, one continuous area of high- and low-pressure systems bumping into one another over a happy common land, just like the tristate area, or "here in the Southland," or "up in the heart of the North country," or any of the other cheerful areas into which American television stations divide the country.

6. **A Street in Marrakech** by Elizabeth Warnock Fernea, 1976 – This book focuses on the relationships between the American author and the women of the street where she lives in the historic city of Marrakech. We may think of Morocco as exotic, but to them, of course, *she* was the strange one, at least at first.

7. **Trailing: A Memoir** by Kristin Louise Duncombe, 2012 – Duncombe, a psychotherapist by training, falls in love with a Médecins Sans Frontières doctor and drops her career plans in New Orleans to live with him in Kenya. At first suffering the usual culture shock, she eventually crafts a life for herself before a carjacking vaults her into a world of anxiety and doubt. Dealing with questions of personal and cultural identity, marital relations and career, as well as providing insight into humanitarian crises in the region, this compulsive page-turner is frank, poignant and, at times, heartrending.

8. **Under the Tuscan Sun** by Francis Mayes, 1996 – Vicariously savor the rich, relaxed lifestyle of Cortona, Italy as you read this memoir. The work of restoring an old villa in the hills proves as much a pleasure for the author as the beautiful landscape and culture of Tuscany.

9. **Voluntary Nomads: A Mother's Memories of Foreign Service Family Life** by Nancy Pogue LaTurner, 2011 – When her husband gets a job with the U.S. State Department, LaTurner, full of gung-ho spirit, moves with him and their two infant

children to Tehran during the tumultuous waning days of the Shah's regime. The family goes on to seven more countries, and, in the process, develops a knack for adaptability and an appreciation for cultural differences. Full of shocking, tender, joyful and traumatic moments, *Voluntary Nomads* is an earthy, honest book about an American family in exotic and ever-changing circumstances.

10. **A Year in Provence** by Peter Mayle, 1989 – Month by month, Mayle details he and his wife's first year in their new home in the south of France — replete with eccentric neighbors, gifted workmen, quaint customs, and enormous, vividly described meals. Prepare to be charmed—and hungry.

FAMILIES OF WRITERS
Chips Off the Old (Writer's) Block

What combination of genes and environment goes to make a great writer? We don't know for sure, but in spite of all the cases of lone geniuses who have to battle philistine relatives in order to get their work done, literary ability certainly does sometimes run in families. Here are some of the most notable examples.

1. **Kingsley Amis (1922–1995) and Martin Amis (born 1949)** - Kingsley Amis was a prolific English novelist and poet, best known for his novels ***Lucky Jim*** and ***The Old Devils***. He was politically volatile, once considered one of England's "Angry Young Men" who rebelled against snobbery and the establishment in general, but later became a conservative and was knighted near the end of his life. Kingsley's son Martin Amis inherited his gift for language, earning accolades for such novels as ***Dead Babies***, ***The Rachel Papers*** and ***Time's Arrow***, as well as his essays. Like his father, Martin is a highly opinionated, entertaining, and sometimes controversial figure — a force to reckon with in the second generation.

2. **The Brontë Sisters: Charlotte (1816–1855), Emily (1818–1848), and Anne (1820–1849)** - The Reverend Patrick Brontë, an Irishman who moved to England and became a minister, was a published poet and kept his home well stocked with books. Their family was unlucky: his wife died when Anne, the youngest, was less than two, and two of his daughters died from the conditions at an awful boarding school, later immortalized in ***Jane Eyre*** Like the passionate children in ***Wuthering Heights***, the Brontë sisters and their brother Branwell spent much of their youth playing on the Yorkshire moors. They also passed the time reading and making up stories. In 1847, the three surviving sisters all published novels — *Jane Eyre* by Charlotte, *Wuthering Heights* by Emily, and ***Agnes Grey*** by Anne. Female writers were severely frowned on in that day, so they used the pen names Currer, Ellis, and Acton Bell, respectively — although "Currer Bell" received correspondence from his publisher care of a Miss Brontë.

1. **A. S. Byatt (born 1936) and Margaret Drabble (born 1939)** - Byatt and Drabble are also sisters from Yorkshire who grew up in a family that loved to read. Their relationship has been more troubled and competitive than the Brontës', but this does not seem to have harmed their work terribly, as both became prolific and successful writers. Byatt published a novel called *The Game* which was about a rivalry between two sisters, and Drabble published one called *The Peppered Moth* that was largely based on their mother. Byatt is also the author of *Possession: A Romance* and *Angels and Insects* among many other books, and Drabble is the author of *A Summer Bird-cage The Needle's Eye*, and *The Witch of Exmoor,* among many others.

2. **Alexandre Dumas, père (1802–1870) and fils (1824–1895)** - The elder Dumas was an extraordinarily prolific novelist and playwright. His lively imagination produced *The Count of Monte Cristo* and *The Three Musketeers.* When he was a young man, a woman with whom he had an affair bore him a son (fils), whom he seldom saw for the next seven years. Once the father (père) became successful, however, he got custody of the boy and sent him to school. After a spendthrift youth the younger Dumas became a writer in order to pay off his debts, eventually producing such celebrated works as the play *La Dame aux Camélias*.

3. **The Brothers Grimm: Jacob (1785–1863) and Wilhelm (1786–1859)** – Jacob and Wilhelm Grimm were scholars who helped develop the study of German linguistics. But we know them for their marvelous collections of fairy tales, first published in the early nineteenth century. It may seem incongruous that the men who familiarized the world with "Hansel and Gretel," "Cinderella," and "Little Red Riding Hood" — magical tales, but containing plenty of hardship and some gruesome scenes — had wonderful childhoods, at least until their father died. Life became much harder, but, as resourceful as any of their fairy tale heroes, they worked hard in school and ended up achieving success and renown. Read all their classics in *The Complete Fairy Tales of the Brothers Grimm*.

4. **The Huxley family: Thomas Henry (1825–1895), Julian (1887–1975), and Aldous (1894–1963)** – This family possessed a dual genius for science and literature. T. H. Huxley, the author of *Man's Place in Nature* and *Ethics and Evolution*, was known as "Darwin's bulldog" for his role in defending, explaining, and popularizing the theory of evolution by natural selection. One of his sons married a niece of the Victorian poet and philosopher Matthew Arnold; Julian and Aldous Huxley were among their children. Julian became a biologist and popularizer of science in such books as *Evolution: The Modern Synthesis*; his brother Aldous became a novelist and essayist who also shared an interest in science — probably his best-remembered work today is *Brave New World*, a dystopian novel about the dark side of technology.

5. **William James (1842–1910) and Henry James (1843–1916)** – These American brothers, whose father was a journalist and theologian, traveled all over Europe

with their family as they grew up. William became a psychologist and philosopher, producing such groundbreaking works as ***The Principles of Psychology*** and ***The Varieties of Religious Experience***. Henry became a novelist, penning such masterpieces as ***The Portrait of a Lady*** and ***The Turn of the Screw***. An anonymous writer commented on the relationship between the brothers' styles and concerns: "Mr. James, I mean Mr. William James, the humorist who writes on psychology, not his brother, the psychologist who writes novels." Their sister Alice, an invalid, is also remembered for her diary.

FEMALE SLEUTHS IN FICTION
From Miss Marple to V. I. Warshawski

In her tweeds and sensible shoes, Miss Jane Marple of the quaint village of St. Mary Mead initially seems to be like any other elderly British spinster — the type of sweet old lady who lives for cucumber sandwiches at tea time and natters on about her rose garden.

But as the saying goes, first impressions can be deceiving — and none more so than in the case of Miss Marple, the shrewd and methodical amateur sleuth heroine of thirteen Agatha Christie mysteries. The most famous female sleuth in all literature, Miss Marple cracked her last case in ***Sleeping Murder***. Today, there are scores of female sleuths — private detectives, forensic anthropologists, bounty hunters — solving crimes in the pages of best-selling mysteries. Here are ten notable mysteries featuring female sleuths, written by women, listed alphabetically.

3. **B is for Burglar** by Sue Grafton, 1985 – The second entry in Grafton's Kinsey Milhone Alphabet Mystery Series and arguably the best. Santa Barbara private investigator Kinsey Milhone encounters a veritable rogue's gallery of suspects in this winner of the Shamus Award from the Private Eye Writers of America organization.

4. **A Bitter Feast** by S. J. Rozan, 1998 – What first appears to be a missing persons case gradually turns into something far more complex and deadly for Chinese-American private investigator Lydia Chin and her partner in Rozan's gripping mystery, the fifth in the series.

5. **Body of Evidence** by Patricia Cornwell, 1991 – The second of Cornwell's mysteries featuring Dr. Kay Scarpetta, the chief medical examiner of Virginia. In this solidly plotted novel, teeming with twists and turns, Scarpetta investigates the murder of a local romance novelist.

6. **Body Work: A V. I. Warshawski Novel** by Sara Paretsky, 2010 — This critically praised novel explores Chicago's avant-garde art scene as Warshawski solves the murder of a performance artist at Club Gouge. The initial suspect is a soldier suffering PTSD, but Warshawski believes more is going on behind the scenes at

the club. *Body Work* marks the fourteenth entry in the series, but neither Paretsky nor her cunning detective show signs of slowing.

EXCERPT: BODY WORK:

Nadia Guaman died in my arms. Seconds after I left Club Gouge, I heard gunshots, screams, squealing tires, from the alley behind the building. I ran across the parking lot, slipping on gravel and ruts, and found Nadia crumpled on the dirty ice. Blood was flowing from her chest in a thick tide.

7. **Both Ends of the Night** by Marcia Muller, 1997 – Tracking down the killer of her flight instructor, hard-boiled private investigator Sharon McCone must leave her native San Francisco for the frozen Minnesota wilderness. A *Publishers Weekly* "Best Book" of 1997.

8. **Devil Bones: A Novel (Temperance Brennan)** by Kathy Reichs, 2008 - Forensic anthropologist Temperance Brennan is called upon to investigate a grisly scene in a forgotten cellar. Is the odd collection of human and animal remains the work of devil-worshippers? Reichs fills her story with meticulous forensic, cultural and historic detail as Brennan struggles to find the answer.

9. **A Murder is Announced** by Agatha Christie, 1950 – Most critics and fans regard *A Murder is Announced* as the best of the Miss Marple mysteries. Responding to a newspaper advertisement, townspeople arrive to play what they think is a murder game – until a stranger is shot dead before them.

10. **Restless in the Grave** by Dana Stabenow, 2012 – Kate Shugak, the private investigator heroine of Stabenow's popular series, is an Aleut living in an Alaskan state park with only her half-husky, half-wolf Mutt for company. When an aviation entrepreneur dies under mysterious circumstances, however, Kate reluctantly leaves her isolated home to investigate his death in the series' nineteenth book, which *Kirkus Reviews* called "a combination of fast and furious adventure and the beauty and complexity of Alaska."

11. **The Sugar House** by Laura Lippmann, 2000 – Top-notch, atmospheric mystery that finds Baltimore reporter-turned-private investigator Tess Monaghan tracking down the identity of a teenaged Jane Doe, murdered by a teenaged boy, who later dies mysteriously in prison.

12. **An Unsuitable Job for a Woman** by P. D. James, 1972 – Chilling mystery introduces novice sleuth Cordelia Gray, who just inherited a detective agency and now must solve her first crime: the bizarre murder of a wealthy man's son, found hanging by the neck.

FUTURISTIC FICTION
Dystopian Visions

Most novels seek to interpret the world around us through the stories of fictional characters. But the novel also gives writers the chance to create new worlds. Depending on an author's temperament — and beliefs about the proper role of literature in society — these worlds can be visions of hope, despair or pure fantasy.

Sir Thomas More coined the term "utopia," based on the Greek words for "no" and "place," in the sixteenth century. He used it as the title of his narrative about an imaginary land where a humanistic government had succeeded in eliminating crime, poverty and other social ills. Since the publication of More's **_Utopia_**, many writers have dreamed up their own ideal systems, as well as the reverse — nightmarish societies, often made possible by misuses of science. The term "dystopia" was first used by economist John Stuart Mill in an 1868 speech to the British House of Commons.

The following alphabetical list of novels list offers some of literature's most indelible visions of dystopian societies.

1. **1984** by George Orwell, 1949 – In the totalitarian state run by Big Brother, individuality, love, privacy and truth itself are forbidden. Elements of Orwell's classic dystopian novel have become part of the everyday vernacular, as has the author's last name: "Orwellian" is used to describe a repressive society that evokes *1984*'s nightmarish world.

2. **Atlas Shrugged** by Ayn Rand, 1957 – In a socialized United States where the strong must sacrifice themselves to the weak, the intelligent and able go on strike in the hope of bringing back capitalism. Extolling the virtues of "rational self-interest," Rand's objectivist philosophy has been embraced and scorned by politicians and economists.

3. **Brave New World** by Aldous Huxley, 1932 – In London circa 2540 AD, embryos are raised in bottles, a wonder drug takes the place of genuine happiness, and individuality and moral choice are considered obsolete. Taking its title from a line in Shakespeare's **_The Tempest_**, Huxley's chilling vision of the future was named one of the hundred best English-language novels of the twentieth century by Modern Library.

4. **The Children of Men** by P. D. James, 1992 – Best known for her mystery novels featuring detective Adam Dalgliesh, James won raves for *The Children of Men*, set in England in the year 2021, when global infertility threatens mankind with extinction. Called a "trenchant analysis of politics and power that speaks

102

urgently" by the *New York Times*, *The Children of Men* was adapted for the screen in 2006.

5. **A Clockwork Orange** by Anthony Burgess, 1962 – Another bleak portrait of England's future, *A Clockwork Orange* envisions a world where teenaged hooligans, like the protagonist Alex and his gang — "droogs" — spend their nights committing "ultra-violence." Arrested after a botched robbery leaves an elderly woman dead, Alex undergoes a radical treatment to cure his violent impulses — with decidedly mixed results.

6. **Fahrenheit 451** by Ray Bradbury, 1953 – In the twenty-fourth century, books are outlawed and television is used to control the masses. A "fireman" whose job it is to burn books meets a young woman who has defied the law, inspiring him to steal one of the books he is commanded to burn.

EXCERPT: FAHRENHEIT 451:

The woman knelt among the books, touching the drenched leather and cardboard, reading the gilt titles with her fingers while her eyes accused Montag.

"You can't ever have my books," she said.

"You know the law," said Beatty. "Where's your common sense? None of those books agree with each other. You've been locked up here for years with a regular damned Tower of Babel. Snap out of it! The people in those books never lived. Come on now!"

She shook her head.

7. **Far North** by Marcel Theroux, 2009 – A National Book Award finalist, Theroux's novel depicts a world reduced to pre-industrial technologies by global warming. Makepeace, the scarred narrator of *Far North*, searches for remnants of civilized society, but only finds religious cults and heavy labor work camps in the frozen landscape.

8. **The Handmaid's Tale** by Margaret Atwood, 1984 – A theocracy has taken over the United States and deprived women of the right to hold property or jobs. Instead, they themselves become property whose sole value lies in child-bearing.

9. **The Hunger Games** by Suzanne Collins, 2008 – A bona-fide literary phenomenon, this young adult novel transports the reader to the post-apocalyptic nation of Panem, where twenty-four boys and girls ages twelve to eighteen-year-old fight to the death annually in a televised competition called the Hunger Games. Narrated

by the sixteen-year-old heroine Katniss Everdeen, *The Hunger Games* is the disturbing and gritty first book in an acclaimed ***trilogy***.

10. **Never Let Me Go** by Kazuo Ishiguro, 2005 – Shortlisted for the Booker Prize, Ishiguro's quietly unsettling novel unfolds at Hailsham, an English boarding school where "guardians" prepare the students for their express purpose of being "donors:" clones whose organs are harvested for "originals."

GAY & LESBIAN NOVELS
The Publishing Triangle's Top Twelve

In this era of *Glee, Modern Family* and the reality series *The Real L Word*, it seems the "love that dare not speak its name" is loudly present and relatively accepted in mainstream culture. Yet not so very long ago, such matter-of-fact, non-stereotypical depictions of gay and lesbian life were rare, if not downright impossible to see in films and television. Only in the pages of novels could people find honest and emotionally complex representations of gay and lesbian life, but many writers paid the price for tackling such a controversial subject. When twenty-three-year-old Gore Vidal published his groundbreaking gay novel ***The City and the Pillar*** in 1948, the staid *New York Times* excoriated Vidal and refused to review his next five novels. And closeted British novelist E.M. Forster scribbled the note "Publishable, but worth it?" on the manuscript for ***Maurice,*** which would only be published with his death in 1971 — nearly sixty years after Forster wrote it.

In 2004, the Publishing Triangle, an association of gays and lesbians in publishing, asked a panel of thirteen judges to rank the hundred best lesbian and gay-themed novels of all time. Here are the panel's top twelve choices, per their ranking.

1. **Death in Venice** by Thomas Mann, 1912 – The exquisite agonies of romantic obsession consume an older novelist, whose unrequited love for a beautiful Italian youth spells his downfall in Mann's classic novella, reportedly inspired by Austrian composer Gustav Mahler.

2. **Giovanni's Room** by James Baldwin, 1956 – The author of ***Go Tell It on the Mountain*** courted controversy with his second novel, a ruminative and deeply melancholy first-person account of a closeted American man's furtive love affair with an Italian bartender in post-World War II Paris.

3. **Our Lady of the Flowers** by Jean Genet, 1942 – Written during one of Genet's many prison stints, *Our Lady of the Flowers* is an explicit, unabashedly autobiographical novel that immerses the reader in the decadent Parisian underworld of male prostitutes, drag queens and career criminals. Despite its sordid topic, *Our Lady of the Flowers* is a remarkable mixture of harsh realism and poetic imagery.

4. **Remembrance of Things Past** by Marcel Proust, 1913-1927 – Along with James Joyce's *Ulysses*, Proust's seven volume magnum opus is regularly hailed as the crowning achievement in twentieth century literature. Over 2,000 characters, many of them gay and lesbian, inhabit the pages of Proust's epic roman à clef.

5. **The Immoralist** by Andre Gide, 1902 – While recovering from tuberculosis, a Parisian scholar experiences a profound sexual awakening and devotes himself to the pursuit of pleasure, albeit with grave consequences in this novel from the Nobel Prize-winning novelist.

6. **Orlando** by Virginia Woolf, 1928 – According to British politician Nigel Nicholson, Woolf's *Orlando* was the author's love letter to his mother, Vita Sackville-West. Blurring the lines between fiction and nonfiction, *Orlando* chronicles the gender-bending experiences of the title character, an ageless young man in Elizabethan England who becomes a woman centuries later.

7. **The Well of Loneliness** by Radclyffe Hall, 1928 – Initially banned in Great Britain, Hall's sorrowful tale of Stephen, a masculine "invert," i.e., lesbian, who endures heartbreak remains a classic of the genre, even though Hall's prose style is a bit clunky at times.

EXCERPT: THE WELL OF LONELINESS:

That evening she and Mary walked over the fields to a little town not very far from their billets. They paused for a moment to watch the sunset, and Mary stroked the new Croix de Guerre; then she looked straight up into Stephen' eyes, her mouth shook, and Stephen saw that she was crying. After this they must walk hand in hand for a while. Why not? There was no one just then to see them.

8. **Kiss of the Spider Woman** by Manuel Puig, 1976 – Later adapted for the stage and screen, Puig's novel primarily consists of an extended conversation between two prisoners in an Argentine jail cell: a movie-loving drag queen and a socialist revolutionary. Over time, these two radically different men develop a friendship that ripens into a sexual bond.

9. **The Memoirs of Hadrian** by Marguerite Yourcenar, 1951 –Named one of the hundred best novels published since 1923 by *Time* magazine, Yourcenar's tour de force takes the form of a letter, written by the Roman Emperor Hadrian to his successor, Marcus Aurelius. Some of the novel's most memorable passages address Hadrian's love for the Greek youth Antonius, whose death plunged his older lover into deep despair.

10. **Zami** by Audre Lorde, 1983 – Lorde called *Zami* her "biomythography," since it blends autobiography and fiction to spellbinding effect. The daughter of West Indian immigrants, Lorde was a self-described "black feminist lesbian poet

warrior" whose poetry celebrates the spiritual and erotic connection between women.

11. **The Picture of Dorian Gray** by Oscar Wilde, 1890 – Wilde's only published novel famously depicts the Faustian bargain the narcissistic title character makes to stay forever young and handsome.

12. **Nightwood** by Djuna Barnes, 1936 – Lauded by such writers as William Burroughs and T. S. Eliot as one of the greatest novels of the twentieth century, *Nightwood* follows Robin Vote, a woman who flits from lover to lover as she searches in vain for happiness. Novelist Jeanette Winterson (***Oranges Are Not the Only Fruit***) likened reading *Nightwood* to "drinking wine with a pearl dissolving in the glass."

GHOST STORIES
Classic Chillers

Ghost stories are most often tales of retribution where the past bumps into the present with chilling results. The variety comes from the many ways ghosts make themselves known to the living — mists, omens, symbols, groans, taps, disembodied voices or gross wanton destruction. Yet a good part of the pleasure we derive from reading or hearing these tales (because there's nothing so desirable as a well-told ghost story around a crackling fire) is because they are so personally familiar. Ghosts must surely be around us, and frequently. Who among us hasn't been tickled or jostled or startled by something we couldn't explain any other way? The following eight books are listed alphabetically by author.

1. **The Best Ghost Stories of Algernon Blackwood** by Algernon Blackwood, 1939 – Considered one of the greatest ghost story writers, Blackwood published nearly 200 ghost stories and twelve novels in his day, including such classics as ***The Wendigo*** and ***The Willows***.

2. **The Haunting of Hill House** by Shirley Jackson, 1959 – The concept is familiar: Try to find proof of the supernatural. In this classic chiller, the characters get hopelessly entangled and threatened by the evil forces haunting a legendary estate. In ***Danse Macabre***, Stephen King explains why he regards *The Haunting of Hill House* as one of the finest horror stories of the twentieth century.

EXCERPT: THE HAUNTING OF HILL HOUSE:

It started again, as though it had been listening, waiting to hear their voices and what they said, to identify them, to know how well prepared they were against it, waiting to hear if they were afraid. So suddenly that Eleanor leaped back against the bed and Theodora gasped and cried out, the iron crash came against their door, and both of them lifted their eyes in horror, because the hammering was against the upper edge of the door, higher than either of the them could reach, higher than Luke or the doctor could reach, and the sickening, degrading cold came in waves from whatever was outside the door.

3. **The Turn of the Screw** by Henry James, 1898 – Among writers of psychological acuity, few are in the class of Henry James. So when he turns that skill to a study of possessed children under the care of a neurotic governess, the result is subtle and satisfyingly eerie.

4. **The Collected Ghost Stories of M. R. James** by M. R. James, 1931 – As a medieval scholar and antiquarian, James wrote stories with familiar settings and premises, but the scares can be nerve-wracking as well as thought-provoking. Given credit for helping shift horror fiction away from the Gothic and into the realistic, James was admired by H.P. Lovecraft and others. Read "Oh, Whistle and I'll Come to You, My Lad" for a good scare.

5. **Best Ghost Stories of J. S. LeFanu** by J. Sheridan LeFanu, 1964 edition – One of a handful of horror fiction geniuses, LeFanu said he sought to explore "the equilibrium between the natural and the supernatural." "Carmilla," of course, is his most famous story, the seminal tale of a lesbian vampire who wreaks havoc through the ages, and an inspiration for Stoker's ***Dracula***.

6. **Hell House** by Richard Matheson, 1971 – The author of ***I Am Legend*** puts his own, terrifying spin on the haunted house narrative in *Hell House*, which follows a physicist and two mediums as they investigate a ghost-infested mansion that's been abandoned for years.

7. **Dracula's Guest and Other Weird Stories** by Bram Stoker, 1897 – Stellar collection of short stories from a master of Gothic horror.

8. **Ghost Story** by Peter Straub, 1979 – A modern classic from a writer who's been called one of America's foremost writers of supernatural-themed fiction. Four old friends discover they cannot bury the past; it literally comes back to haunt them in the form of an alluring and malevolent ghost.

HARLEM RENAISSANCE
The Classics of Afro-Americana

The twenties saw the dawn of what African-American philosopher and Rhodes scholar Alain Locke famously called the era of the "New Negro" — a period of unprecedented artistic growth in literature, art, and music by African-Americans, many of whom called New York's Harlem home. As WASP blue bloods and Greenwich Village bohemians trekked uptown to hear Duke Ellington and his orchestra perform at The Cotton Club, poets and writers like Countee Cullen, Langston Hughes, and Zora Neale Hurston explored the questions of racial identity and African-American culture in their self-published magazine, *Fire! Devoted to Younger Negro Artists*.

Although the "Harlem Renaissance" would more or less end with the onset of the Depression in the thirties, its legacy endures in the unusually high number of classic novels published by Hughes, Hurston, and other, lesser-known writers. Here are twelve of the most celebrated novels by "Harlem Renaissance" authors, listed alphabetically:

1. **The Blacker he Berry** by Wallace Thurman, 1929 – Controversial upon its release for being the first novel to explore racial prejudice and self-hatred among members of the African-American community, *The Blacker the Berry* was written by one of the Harlem Renaissance's most active members. In honest, beautifully descriptive prose, the protagonist, a dark-skinned woman named Emma Lou Morgan, travels from her hometown of Boise, Idaho, to attend college at UCLA, and from there moves to Harlem for work. In the process, she comes to terms with the discrimination of lighter-skinned peers and finds fulfillment.

2. **Cane** by Jean Toomer, 1923 – A commercial disappointment upon publication, Toomer's extraordinary novel is an amalgam of poetry, short fiction and character sketches that was truly ahead of its time. Adeptly mixing these literary forms, Toomer illuminates the plight of the African-American in the American South.

EXCERPT: CANE:

Karintha is a woman. She who carries beauty, perfect as dusk when the sun goes down. She has been married many times. Old men remind her that a few years back they rode her hobby-horse upon their knees. Karintha smiles, and indulges them when she is in the mood for it. She has contempt for them. Karintha is a woman.

3. **The Conjure-Man Dies: A Mystery Tale of Dark Harlem** by Rudolph Fisher, 1932 – This is the first African-American mystery novel and has been praised highly by Walter Mosley, the most successful African-American writer in the genre. Darkly atmospheric and chock-full of plot twists, it's a whodunit about the bizarre murder of an African prince and Harvard graduate, who makes his living in thirties-era Harlem as a tribal psychic. The language and imagery paint an indelible image of a particular time and place, both sensually and in terms of social norms.

4. **The Fire in the Flint** by Walter White, 1924 – Light-skinned, with blonde hair and blue eyes, White nonetheless identified himself as black and served as the executive director of the NAACP from 1931 to 1955. In this overlooked classic that's never received its due, White tackles racism head-on in his taut narrative about a Harvard-educated black doctor running afoul of the Klu Klux Klan in rural Georgia.

5. **Home to Harlem** by Claude McKay, 1927 – A black World War I U.S. Army deserter returns from Europe to live the high life in twenties-era Harlem, where he encounters a veritable rogue's gallery of dreamers, schemers and hustlers in McKay's boldly realized, atmospheric novel.

6. **Infants of the Spring** by Wallace Thurman, 1932 – Thurman fires off satirical barbs at Langston Hughes, Zora Neale Hurston and other leading figures of the Harlem Renaissance in this witty and daring (for its time) roman à clef, about the artists, writers, and entertainers living in a rooming house nicknamed "Niggeratti Manor."

7. **Jonah's Gourd Wine** by Zora Neale Hurston, 1934 – Praised as "one of the greatest writers of our time" by Nobelist Toni Morrison, the novelist, folklorist and anthropologist depicts the rise and fall of a womanizing preacher in her challenging but rewarding first novel, written in black Southern dialect.

8. **The Living is Easy** by Dorothy West, 1948 – While she hobnobbed with the leading lights of the Harlem Renaissance in the twenties, the short story writer/journalist didn't publish her first novel until 1948. Set in Boston during World War I, *The Living is Easy* is a wryly funny and sophisticated portrait of a manipulative Southern black woman clawing her way into the city's black elite.

9. **Not Without Laughter** by Langston Hughes, 1930 – Renowned as a poet, Hughes tried his hand at fiction with this sensitively written coming-of-age story about a poor young black boy, dreaming of a life beyond the suffocating confines of rural Kansas.

10. **Plum Bun** by Jessie Redmon Fauset, 1928 – Able to "pass," a beautiful, light-skinned black woman deludes herself into thinking that being taken for white will bring her everlasting happiness, only to grapple with other issues, in Fauset's insightful novel.

11. **Quicksand** by Nella Larsen, 1928 – Born to a black father and a Danish mother, Helga Crane feels inexorably caught between two worlds. She embarks on a journey to find her niche, but as time passes, becomes increasingly disillusioned, in Larsen's tragic, largely autobiographical novel.

12. **When Washington Was in Vogue** by Edward Christopher Williams, 1926 – The twenties-era "black bourgeoisie" of Washington, D.C., provides the enthralling backdrop for Williams' epistolary romance, originally serialized, that's a bittersweet charmer.

HISTORICAL FICTION
Dreaming Up the Past

Even during the age of antiquity, writers were looking back nostalgically at past times that seemed more heroic, more romantic and more picturesque than their own contemporary societies. Historical fiction is a genre whose possibilities are all the richer for its combination of verisimilitude and pure, unfettered imagination. If we could read an attempt by a twenty fifth-century author to write historical fiction about our times, would it seem like an authentic picture of our sense of reality? Impossible to know, but we *can* tell when we've got hold of a good historical novel — feeling swept away into a distant time and place is a good indicator.

Perhaps the greatest work of historical fiction in the modern sense is Tolstoy's ***War and Peace,*** which is set in Napoleonic times, about a half-century before it was written. Here are twelve other acclaimed novels, listed alphabetically, set as far back as the biblical era. Most of them do take liberties with the facts, but they succeed in making the characters, social milieus and events feel convincing in their own way.

1. **The Betrothed** by Alessandro Manzoni, 1827 – Set in the seventeenth century against a backdrop of warfare, plague, and riots, this is the story of two young lovers — peasants named Renzo and Lucia — separated by circumstances. Politics, religion, and vengeance all intensify the drama.

2. **Ivanhoe** by Sir Walter Scott, 1819 – The adventures of a dishonored knight redeeming himself in medieval England's struggle between Norman and Saxon. Robin Hood and Friar Tuck make appearances here, plus some unforgettable ladies.

3. **Les Misérables** by Victor Hugo, 1862 – The story of Valjean, a decent peasant who becomes a criminal and later a mayor, serves as the basis for a passionate exploration of the nature of morality, crime, innocence and even the sewers of Paris. The upheavals of early nineteenth century France come to life in this long and winding tale.

4. **The Other Boleyn Girl** by Philippa Gregory, 2001 – There's more drama in the true history of Henry VIII's court than most soap-opera writers could ever make up — conflicting loyalties, devious power plays, illicit sex and executions. Experience all this through the eyes of Mary Boleyn, Anne's less ambitious (and ultimately more fortunate) sister.

5. **Paradise Alley** by Kevin Baker, 2002 – Baker is a talented crafter of personal stories, set against the backdrop of actual events — in this case the bloody Civil War-era draft riots in New York City circa 1863, when working-class resentment over the unequal imposition of the Civil War draft erupted in horrific violence. Richly detailed, with an ever-changing cast of narrators, *Paradise Alley* follows three Irish women during the five-day uprising. The picture it paints is dark, but gripping.

6. **Ragtime** by E. L. Doctorow, 1975 – Playing much more loosely with real-life historical figures (Harry Houdini, Sigmund Freud, and the Archduke Franz Ferdinand all show up in this wonderfully entertaining book), Doctorow evokes

the vitality and tensions of early twentieth-century America with wit and narrative flair.

7. **The Red Tent** by Anita Diamant, 1997 – Dinah is the daughter of Jacob, briefly mentioned in the Old Testament. She becomes the central character here, a vehicle for the author to imagine the world of biblical women in rich, poetic detail.

8. **The Scarlet Letter** by Nathaniel Hawthorne, 1850 – In seventeenth century Salem, Massachusetts (the town of witchcraft-trial infamy), Hester Prynne refuses to identify the father of her illegitimate child; as punishment, she is forced to wear a scarlet "A" for the sin of adultery. But this is only the beginning of a story that questions the nature of sin and purity and religious hypocrisy.

9. **The Song of Achilles** by Madeline Miller, 2012 – Miller spent ten years writing her Orange Prize-winning debut novel about the sexually fluid relationship between Achilles and Patroclus. Although *The Song of Achilles* is appealingly written in a pared-down style that's a tip of the hat to oral tradition, its thematic core — the abiding love between two same-sex characters caught up in war — is contemporary.

10. **A Tale of Two Cities** by Charles Dickens, 1859 – In the years leading up to the French Revolution, tensions simmer between oppressive aristocrats and bitter common folk. A man wrongly imprisoned in Paris for nearly two decades is reunited with his long-lost daughter and escapes to London, but their family is still not immune from the violence of the times in this affecting tale of love and sacrifice.

11. **The Thousand Autumns of Jacob de Zoet** by David Mitchell, 2010 – Set in the year 1799 on the man-made island of Dejima, the most distant outpost of the Dutch East Indies Company, and the only place in isolationist Japan where natives and foreigners mix, this superb novel succeeds as an adventure, a romance and, of course, as a window onto a unique period in history. Exploring the give-and-take between East and West, between science and superstition, Mitchell (*Cloud Atlas*) has an eye for telling detail and period-specific linguistic quirks in *The Thousand Autumns of Jacob de Zoet*, which was a *New York Times* Notable Book of the Year.

EXCERPT: THE THOUSAND AUTUMNS OF JACOB DE ZOET:

Snitker upends the table and lunges at Vorstenbosch. Jacob glimpses Snitker's fist over his patron's head and attempts to intercept; flaming peacocks whirl across his vision; the cabin walls rotate through ninety degrees; the floor slams his ribs; and the taste of gunmetal in his mouth is surely blood. Grunts and gasps and groans are exchanged at a higher level. Jacob peers up in time to see the first mate land a pulverizing blow on Snitker's solar plexus, causing the floored clerk to wince with involuntary sympathy. Two more marines burst in, just as Snitker totters and hits the floor.

12. **The Three Musketeers** by Alexandre Dumas, 1844 – Set in France and England in the seventeenth century, the swashbuckling classic depicts the adventures of d'Artagnan, a young man who joins the famous three musketeers who fight to protect their king, Louis XIII. A zesty and entertaining read by the author of ***The Count of Monte Cristo***.

HISTORICAL MYSTERIES
Sleuths through the Centuries

Setting your mystery in a far-off land a long time ago time opens the door for writers to break free from the conventions of contemporary mystery writing. It gives them dramatic license to create new kinds of challenges for strange and unusual characters. Social and cultural differences and technological oddities enhance the background against which the characters interact. Series protagonists are the rule rather than the exception, as authors come to discover new chords and scales to play. Here are ten spellbinding historical mysteries, listed alphabetically by author.

1. **The Alienist** by Caleb Carr, 1994 – In New York City circa 1896, alienists (psychologists) were treated with distrust, if not actual disdain. So when the city's police commissioner Theodore Roosevelt forms a team headed by alienist Dr. Laszlo Kreizler to find a serial killer, people are suspicious. The result is a thrilling ride down the dark alleys and ugly souls of the time. Great history as well as great crime drama.

2. **Alexandria** by Lindsey Davis, 2009 – This entry is the nineteenth in the series of Lindsey Davis' tales concerning super first-century Roman sleuth Marcus Didius Falco. Like the best of this sub-genre, Davis ties together quality history with intelligent and exciting crime-solving. Davis is also known for slyly modern embellishments to her stories as well.

3. **The Name of the Rose** by Umberto Eco, 1980 – Eco's novel was hailed as groundbreaking for its adroit blend of philosophical inquiry and murder mystery narrative. The hero of the Italian philosopher/semiotician's bestselling historical mystery is a fourteenth-century Franciscan friar, William of Baskerville, who has a similar bearing and depth of knowledge reminiscent of Sherlock Holmes. But that's just one of Eco's many inside jokes in *The Name of the Rose*, which unfolds in a Benedictine monastery where the monks are dying under mysterious circumstances.

4. **The Gods of Gotham** by Lyndsay Faye, 2012 – Being a policeman in mid-nineteenth century New York City was especially dangerous in the crime-plagued

slums of the Sixth Ward. But the terror and the blood become a source of redemption for the severely wounded hero Timothy Wilde in this gripping serial killer murder mystery that features a rogue's gallery of colorful and fascinating characters.

5. **Mistress of the Art of Death** by Ariana Franklin, 2007 – Written by historical romance writer Diane Norman under a pseudonym, *Mistress of the Art of Death* features a protagonist who is the medieval equivalent of a forensic practitioner. But in twelfth century England, even examining a corpse was deemed desecration. And the crime-solving heroine hunting for a child killer has one of the best names ever: Vesuvia Adelia Rachel Ortese Aguilar.

EXCERPT: MISTRESS OF THE ART OF DEATH:

Here they come. From down the road we can hear harnesses jingling and see dust rising into the warm spring sky.

Pilgrims returning from Easter in Canterbury. Tokens of the mitered, martyred Saint Thomas are pinned to cloaks and hats – the Canterbury monks must be raking it in.

They're a pleasant interruption in the traffic of carts whose drivers and oxen are surly with fatigue from plowing and sowing.

These people are well fed, noisy exultant with the grace that their journey has gained them.

But one of them, as exuberant as the rest, is a murderer of children. God's grace will not extend to a child-killer.

6. **The Historian** by Elizabeth Kostova, 2006 – When a sixteen-year-old American girl finds a cache of ancient letters in Amsterdam, she begins what becomes an epic search through ancient letters, other documents, codes, secrets, and lies for truth about the legendary Vlad the Impaler, who may have actually become the undead "Dracula" of myth. It's exciting stuff in Kostova's nimble literary hands.

7. **A Morbid Taste for Bones** by Ellis Peters, 1977 – Peters' twelfth-century monk is truly a man of his times who fought in the Crusades and womanized before becoming a dutiful man of the cloth. The "Bones" in the title refer to a saint's personal relics which become the matter of contention between two towns.

8. **Slayer of Gods** by Lynda S. Robinson, 2001 – A favorite technique of historical mystery writers is to mix in real historical figures to add flavor, color and veracity. But Robinson does much more in *Slayer of Gods*; she makes the central conflict of her tale involve no less than King Tut and Pharaoh Akhenaten in this mystery about the death of Akhenaten's wife, Queen Nefertiti.

9. **The Fire Kimono** by Laura Joh Rowland, 2008 – One of the most successful series detectives is Rowland's eighteenth-century samurai Sano Ichiro. This is the thirteenth of sixteen Ichiro mysteries currently in print, and piles period color on daring sleuthery. It starts when the shogun gives Ichiro only three days to solve a mystery that dates back forty years.

10. **The Shadow of the Wind** by Carlos Ruiz Zafon, 2005 – The *New York Times* described Zafon's novel as "Gabriel Garcia Marquez meets Umberto Eco meets Jorge Luis Borges for a sprawling magic show." The plot coils around a rare book, *The Shadow of the Wind*, which a young boy finds in post-World War II Barcelona. What he discovers in its pages will plunge him into a terrifying world of murder and dark secrets.

HISTORICAL OVERVIEWS
The Family of Man

For all our flaws, we humans have got to hand it to ourselves for at least one thing: We're a fascinating species. The variety of languages, cultures, discoveries, and experiences that form our shared history is pretty amazing. There are lots of wonderful books that look at small slices of history — what it was like to live through a certain war, or why that war took place; how a new religion evolved after its founding; how great political experiments were tried; the struggles and joys of a single extraordinary person in a particular time and place. But in order to appreciate all that, sometimes we need to step back and get a broad view of ourselves and our history. Here are some selections that can help you put all the other stuff in context.

1. **The Discoverers: A History of Man's Search to Know His World and Himself** by Daniel J. Boorstin. 1983 – This is actually a history of science, but it provides insight into many of the most important developments in history, from the development of solar timekeeping to the modern world. As sweeping as the scope of the book is, it depicts individuals and societies with a wonderful vividness, explaining the hindrances to innovation and the ways people have overcome them.

2. **The Disappearing Spoon: And Other True Tales of Madness, Love, and the History of the World from the Periodic Table of the Elements** by Sam Kean, 2010 – Human history, scientific discovery, scandal, and adventure play out in this disarming volume. Kean takes an anthropological approach to the periodic table and in so doing offers both a science lesson that teaches what each element means and the story behind it. "Kean succeeds in giving us the cold hard facts, both human and chemical, behind the astounding phenomena without sacrificing any of the wonder," writes *Entertainment Weekly*.

3. <u>**Guns, Germs, and Steel: The Fates of Human Societies**</u> by Jared Diamond. 1997 – Why did Westerners, rather than New Guineans, Africans, or Native Americans, come to dominate much of the rest of the world? Diamond aims to answer this by examining the geographical and environmental circumstances that early on allowed people of the West to domesticate plants and animals and become immune to devastating diseases. The book offers an important angle on the development of civilizations, although it has been criticized for implying that explanations are either environmental or racist, ignoring cultural factors that change over time and have nothing to do with skin color (read ***The Discoverers,*** above, for a good perspective on this aspect of history).

EXCERPT: GUNS, GERMS, AND STEEL:

Cro-Magnon garbage heaps yield not only stone tools but also tools of bone, whose suitability for shaping (for instance, into fishhooks) had apparently gone unrecognized by previous humans. Tools were produced in diverse and distinctive shapes so modern that their functions as needles, awls, engraving tools, and so on are obvious to us. Instead of only single-piece tools such as hand-held scrapers, multipiece tools made their appearance. Recognizable multipiece weapons at Cro-Magnon sites include harpoons, spear-throwers, and eventually bows and arrows, the precursors of rifles and other multipiece modern weapons. Those efficient means of killing at a safe distance permitted the hunting of such dangerous prey as rhinos and elephants, while the invention of rope for nets, lines, and snares allowed the addition of fish and birds to our diet.

4. <u>**Heroes of History: A Brief History of Civilization from Ancient Times to the Dawn of the Modern Age**</u> by Will Durant, 2001 – Durant is most famous for the multi-volume ***The Story of Civilization***, which he wrote with his wife, Ariel Durant. This single volume, published after his death, is a more compact exploration of the course of (mostly Western) thinkers and leaders, from Buddha to Leonardo da Vinci. It's a fascinating tour of changing philosophies, religions, and world views.

5. <u>**The Journey of Man: A Genetic Odyssey**</u> by Spencer Wells, 2002 – Historians are not the only people who can tell us about our pasts, and we have more than written documents to teach us about our common history. The fossil record and, just as exciting, the genetic record that lives on in all of us has much to reveal about our common history. Wells explains what studying the relatively stable male Y chromosome has taught us about our origins and migrations, confirming that we all developed in Africa and that our racial differences are superficial.

6. <u>**The New History of the World**</u> by John M. Roberts, 2002 – This revision of an earlier work covers the history of mankind from its earliest civilizations to the fall

of the Berlin Wall and September 11. Remarkably thorough, it can be considered a one-book survey course.

7. **The Story of Mankind** by Hendrik Willem van Loon, originally published in 1921, since updated by John Merriman — Van Loon wrote this book for young people, but it's also delightfully informative and engaging for those of us with a few more decades under our belts. It makes history into a sort of real-life adventure story, helping us imagine ourselves right back into long-ago events as they were unfolding, fresh and new.

8. **Timelines of History** by DK Publishing, 2011 – The story of human life unfolds chronologically in this enthralling survey that begins with prehistoric man's origins in Africa and continues through to the present era. Entertaining summaries of key historical events are lavishly illustrated and cross-referenced, allowing the reader to skip back and forth through the ages and to take a measure of the broad sweep of history.

HOLLYWOOD NONFICTION
Tinsel Town Laid Bare

Described by Hollywood producer Joe Roth as "the most observant, knowledgeable and intuitive screenwriter in the business today," two-time Academy Award winner William Goldman has written such classic films as *All the President's Men*, *Butch Cassidy and the Sundance Kid* and *Marathon Man*. After forty-plus years of swimming with the showbiz sharks — and living to tell about it — Goldman wittily summed up his impressions of Hollywood in three words: "Nobody knows anything." So begins his 1983 memoir *Adventures in the Screen Trade*, which has become essential reading for wannabe scribes or anyone trying to make sense of the fear, arrogance and confusion endemic to Tinsel Town, where sure-fire properties often tank at the box office and Teflon-coated executives fail upwards while others crash and burn.

Here are twelve must-reads, listed alphabetically, which give readers the insider scoop on life and work in the Dream Factory, where, as the saying goes, "You're only as good as your last picture."

1. **Adventures in the Screen Trade: A Personal View of Hollywood and Screenwriting** by William Goldman, 1983 – Goldman's collection of essays, reminiscences and screenwriting tips is a bracingly funny and whip-smart book that spawned an equally good sequel, ***Which Lie Did I Tell? More Adventures in the Screen Trade***.

2. **Bright Boulevards, Bold Dreams: The Story of Black Hollywood** by Donald Bogle, 2005 – The author of ***Toms, Coons, Mulattoes, Mammies and Bucks: An Interpretive History of Blacks in American Films***, Bogle brings his laserlike

116

focus to this eye-opening and much-needed history of African-Americans working before and behind the cameras from the silent era through the sixties.

3. **City of Nets: A Portrait of Hollywood in the 1940s** by Otto Friedrich, 1986 – A monumental social history of Hollywood that reads like a vivid, epic novel. Although the film industry is covered extensively in Friedrich's book, he widens his gaze to write about everything from the zoot suit riots to mobster Bugsy Siegel.

EXCERPT: CITY OF NETS:

[Errol] Flynn's search for enjoyment consisted of endless drinking and fornicating, plus a certain indulgence in drugs. On the crest of a hill on Mulholland Drive, he designed and built a $125,000 house that embodied all the sensual fantasies of that time and place, from glass cases filled with guns to a cockfighting arena in the stable to bedrooms outfitted with black silk hangings, sable bed coverings, and two-way mirrors in the walls and ceilings, so that guests could watch the other guests at play.

4. **The Devil's Candy: The Anatomy of a Hollywood Fiasco** by Julie Salamon, 1991 – No doubt filmmaker Brian De Palma still rues the day he agreed to let *The Wall Street Journal* reporter Julie Salamon shadow him 24/7 during the making of *The Bonfire of the Vanities*. What was supposed to be De Palma's masterpiece turned out to be a colossal bomb. In Salamon's lively and fascinating account of how *not* to make a hit film, only Tom Hanks emerges unscathed from the wreckage of *The Bonfire of the Vanities*.

5. **Easy Riders, Raging Bulls: How the Sex-Drugs-and- Rock 'N' Roll Generation Changed Hollywood** by Peter Biskind, 1998 – Truth is far stranger than fiction in Biskind's jaw-dropping overview of Hollywood in the seventies, when wunderkinds Francis Ford Coppola, Martin Scorsese and Steven Spielberg forever transformed the movie business. While it's packed with juicy, often embarrassing anecdotes about stars and filmmakers running wild, *Easy Riders, Raging Bulls* is an informative and insightful analysis of an industry in crisis.

6. **An Empire of Their Own: How the Jews Invented Hollywood by** Neal Gabler, 1990 – In his vigorously written and thoroughly researched book about the early movie moguls, Gabler examines the cultural and political forces that inspired Harry Cohn, Louis B. Mayer and Samuel Goldwyn, among others, to find their niche in Hollywood.

7. **Final Cut: Art, Money and Ego in the Making of Heaven's Gate, The Film That Sank United Artists** by Stephen Bach, 1985 – Given creative and financial carte blanche after the success of *The Deer Hunter*, director Michael Cimino let his bloated ego get the better of him —and everyone involved in the making of his dream project, *Heaven's Gate*. One of the biggest disasters in Hollywood history, *Heaven's Gate*

effectively rendered Cimino persona non grata in Hollywood and forced United Artists to close. A United Artists executive at the time, Bach chronicles the film's ill-fated production in this book veteran producer David Brown called "compulsively readable."

8. **Hit & Run: How Jon Peters and Peter Guber Took Sony for a Ride in Hollywood** by Nancy Griffin and Kim Masters, 1996 – Über-schmoozers Jon Peters and Peter Guber took over the reins of Sony in the eighties — and went on a spending spree until the studio coffers nearly ran dry. How these two shameless self-promoters snookered Hollywood bigwigs and Sony's Japanese executives makes for diverting reading in this terrific book from Griffin and Masters.

9. **The Men Who Would Be King: An Almost Epic Tale of Moguls, Movies, and a Company Called DreamWorks** by Nicole LaPorte, 2010 – This up-close story of Hollywood power focuses on three charismatic personalities who transformed the business landscape by forming a studio: Steven Spielberg, David Geffen and Jeffery Katzenberg. LaPorte provides an intimate look at the business of moviemaking, and the ways these power players broke the rules to create both phenomenal successes and monumental disasters.

10. **Picture** by Lillian Ross, 1952 – A regular contributor to *The New Yorker*, Ross got permission from director John Huston to watch him direct *The Red Badge of Courage* in 1950. First published in serial form in *The New Yorker*, *Picture* is widely considered the best book ever written about Hollywood: a revealing, warts-and-all portrait of movie studio politics, hubris and Machiavellian intrigue.

11. **The Studio** by John Gregory Dunne, 1969 – Granted unlimited access to observe the corporate and production divisions of Twentieth Century Fox for one year in 1967, Dunne wrote this meticulously detailed and wonderfully engaging account of glitzy excess, bad behavior and ego-driven studio politics that's a classic of Hollywood journalism.

12. **Tales From Development Hell: The Greatest Movies Never Made?** by David Hughes, updated 2012 – Hughes takes readers behind the glamour of moviemaking to the place where scripts are written and actors hired for movies that are often never produced. Learn why big-budget projects, with marquee stars attached, end up as studio write-offs well into production, after millions have been spent, and why some of the best scripts ever written have never made it to the screen.

HOLOCAUST FICTION
Never Forget

The saying "Never forget" is both a lament and a vow regarding the estimated six million victims of the Holocaust. Nearly seventy years after the end of World War II, the unspeakable atrocities perpetrated by Nazi Germany under the aegis of Hitler's "Final Solution" defy rationality: How could this happen? It's a question that's obsessed writers since the full magnitude of the horrific genocide became public knowledge.

With piercing insight, harrowing detail and occasional mordant wit, the following books listed alphabetically, represent some of the most unforgettable works of fiction written about the Holocaust.

1. **The Emperor of Lies** by Steve Sem-Sandberg, 2011 – A critical and commercial triumph in Sweden, Sem-Sandberg's gripping and thought-provoking novel is based on the true story of Mordechai Chaim Rumkowksi, a Jewish elder who effectively "ruled" the Jewish ghetto in Lodz with the proverbial iron fist. To write *The Emperor of Lies*, Sem-Sandberg drew from the Ghetto Chronicle, a 3,000-page archive that Rumkowski created in 1940.

2. **Fatelessness** by Imre Kertesz, 1975 – Masterful, shattering novel from Kertesz, the 2002 Nobel Prize winner. Reportedly autobiographical, *Fatelessness* immerses the reader in the grueling concentration camp experiences of the narrator, a fourteen-year-old Hungarian Jewish boy.

3. **If Not Now, When?** by Primo Levi, 1982 – Levi's only novel is a stunner about a group of Jewish Soviet partisans fighting their way across war-torn Eastern Europe in hopes of reaching Palestine.

4. **King of the Jews** by Leslie Epstein, 1979 – Appointed the head of the Judenrat in the Jewish ghetto of Lodz, Poland, an unscrupulous, charismatic doctor treats the ghetto like his personal fiefdom in Epstein's marvelous and complex novel.

5. **Mila 18** by Leon Uris, 1961 – Assigned to Warsaw, circa 1943, an Italian-American reporter joins the Jewish ghetto uprising in this gripping and prodigiously researched novel from Uris, the author of *Exodus* and *Battle Cry*.

6. **The Painted Bird** by Jerzy Kosinski, 1965 – Not for the faint-hearted, Kosinski's graphically violent novel about a war orphan suffering undue cruelty at the hands of Eastern European peasants is nonetheless a remarkable achievement.

7. **Sarah's Key** by Tatiana de Rosnay, 2006 – A fixture on the bestseller lists, de Rosnay's novel seamlessly blends two narratives, set in contemporary and World War II-era Paris, respectively. Buying an apartment in Paris, American journalist Julia Jarmond discovers that it was once home to a Jewish family who'd been rounded up by the Nazis. She sets out to discover what happened to the family's daughter Sarah, whose grueling story of survival and loss will move you to tears.

8. **Schindler's List** by Thomas Keneally, 1982 – Winner of the Booker Prize, Keneally's seamless blend of fact and fiction tells the incredible story of an unlikely savior: womanizing, boozing playboy businessman Oscar Schindler, who saved the lives of a thousand Polish Jews in World War II.

9. **The Shawl** by Cynthia Ozick, 1989 – Comprised of a short story and a novella, *The Shawl* is a brilliant character study about an elderly Holocaust survivor, living in embittered retirement in Florida, who lost her sense of self in the camps.

10. **Sophie's Choice** by William Styron, 1979 – Styron's masterpiece unfolds through the eyes of Southern born-writer "Stingo," whose life is forever changed by his relationship with the beautiful, tormented concentration camp survivor, Sophie Zawistowski.

EXCERPT: SOPHIE'S CHOICE:

Sophie paused for a few moments and locked her eyelids shut as if in savage meditation, then gazed once more out onto the baffling distances. "So there is one thing that is still a mystery to me. And that is why, since I know all this and I know the Nazis turned me into a sick animal like all the rest, I should feel so much guilt over all the things I done there. And over just being alive. This guilt is something I cannot get rid of and I think I never will."

11. **This Way for the Gas, Ladies and Gentlemen** by Tadeusz Borowski, 1947 – Unflinching, matter-of-fact stories of concentration camp life narrated by the author's fictional alter ego, Tadeusz. A major influence on Imre Kertesz, Borowski committed suicide in 1951, reportedly bereft over the brutality of the Communist regime in Poland.

12. **Wartime Lies** by Louis Begley, 1991 – As Warsaw falls to Nazi Germany in 1939, a young Polish Jew escapes with his cunning and beautiful aunt to live by their wits, changing identities and forging papers, in Begley's wonderful picaresque novel.

HOLOCAUST MEMOIRS
Bearing Witness to the Unthinkable

Anne Frank wrote in her diary: "I still believe, in spite of everything, that people are still truly good at heart." She kept that treasured diary faithfully for the two years she and her family hid from the Nazis in the attic of an Amsterdam warehouse. Published two years after the end of World War II, *The Diary of a Young Girl* is an extraordinary testament to the generosity of spirit and wisdom of Frank, whose resilience in the looming face of despair continues to inspire generations of readers worldwide.

The most widely read and beloved of Holocaust memoirs, Frank's *The Diary of a Young Girl* moved Eleanor Roosevelt to call it "one of the wisest and most moving commentaries on war and its impact on human beings that I have ever read." It's one of twelve astonishing, and at times heart-wrenching, true stories of survival during one of the darkest times in history, which are listed below alphabetically.

1. **All But My Life** by Gerda Weissman Klein, 1995 – Beautifully written memoir by a woman who seemingly lost everything during her time in the concentration camps, yet somehow held onto her humanity in the midst of horrific suffering.

2. **The Diary of a Young Girl** by Anne Frank, 1947 – The 1993 edition of the diary gives the reader a more rounded version of Frank, thanks to the restoration of passages her father deleted from the original version.

3. **Europa, Europa** by Solomon Perel, 1989 – One of the oddest survival stories in all of Holocaust literature. A young Polish Jew so successfully passes for Aryan that the Germans send him to a prestigious training school for Hitler Youth (!).

4. **The Girl in the Green Sweater: A Life in Holocaust's Shadow** by Krystyna Chiger and Daniel Paisner, 2008 – Made into the powerful motion picture *In Darkness* by acclaimed Polish director Agnieszka Holland (who also made the film of *Europa, Europa*), this gripping memoir recounts the struggle of a group of Polish Jews who survive the Nazi liquidation of the Lvov ghetto by escaping into the city's sewer system. Aided by a Catholic sewer worker named Leopold Socha, whose humanity ultimately supersedes his greed, Chiger and her fellow refugees endure a hellish, fourteen-month battle to stay alive that ends with hope for human redemption.

EXCERPT: THE GIRL IN THE GREEN SWEATER:

In June 1941, almost two years after the Germans cut short their approach into Lvov, we heard those Messerschmitt planes flying once again overhead. My parents did not talk about it, but they must have known this would happen. Once again we heard the bombs, and once again we retreated to my grandparents' basement. This time, too, I helped with the pushing of Pawel's stroller, laden with some of our worldly possessions. This time we expected the worst, and on June 29, 1941, when the Wehrmacht marched into the city, my parents were terrified. There was a big panic. The nonaggression pact was no more. The Russians had fled. The Jews were afraid to come out of their apartments. And the Ukrainians were dancing in the streets. This was one of the most disturbing aspects of the German occupation, the collaboration of the Ukrainians. You see, the Germans had promised the Ukrainians a free Ukraine, which was why they were so overjoyed at being liberated from Russian rule. They welcomed the Germans with flowers. The German soldiers paraded through the streets with their motorcycles, with their helmets and their boots and their black leather coats, and the Ukrainian women would walk out among the motorcade and greet the German men with hugs and kisses. We watched from our balcony. My father, he was very upset. Once again, he said, "This is the end for us."

5. <u>**I Will Bear Witness: 1942-1945: A Diary of the Nazi Years**</u> by Victor Klemperer, 2000 – The second volume in a trilogy of diaries kept by Klemperer, a Jewish university professor whose marriage to a Christian woman saved his life. That said, he still endured great hardship, as this fascinating and insightful diary so memorably demonstrates.

6. <u>**A Lucky Child: A Memoir of Surviving Auschwitz as a Young Boy**</u> by Thomas Buergenthal, 2010 – It's a lucky ten-year-old indeed who survives Auschwitz — where the vast majority of children were immediately sent to the gas chambers — to eventually become a judge in the International Court of Justice in The Hague. Separated from his parents, the young Buergenthal manages to make it through the war and eventually reunite with his mother in a story that Elie Wiesel said "strikes us by its need to seek out strains of humanity, even in the very depths of hell."

7. <u>**Memoirs of a Warsaw Ghetto Fighter**</u> by Kazik, 1994 – Dramatic, nerve-fraying account of the month-long Warsaw Uprising by one of the outnumbered and untrained freedom fighters.

8. <u>**The Men With the Pink Triangle: The True Life-and-Death Story of Homosexuals in the Nazi Death Camps**</u> by Heinz Heger, 1994 – Arrested in 1939 for being a "degenerate," Heger spent the next six years in a concentration camp. An invaluable record of the Nazi persecution of homosexuals.

9. <u>**Night**</u> by Elie Wiesel, 1958 – Wiesel's memoir of his concentration camp experiences hits you like a punch to the gut. If you can bear it, however, *Night* is truly an unforgettable and important book that's a classic of the genre.

10. <u>**The Pianist: The Extraordinary True Story of One Man's Survival in Warsaw, 1939-1945**</u> by Wladyslaw Szpilman, 1945 – Understated, gracefully written memoir by Szpilman, whose story was later adapted for the screen by Roman Polanski.

11. <u>**Playing for Time**</u> by Fania Fenelon, 1977 – A Parisian cabaret singer relies on her musical gifts to survive concentration camp life in Fenelon's grueling but uplifting memoir.

12. <u>**Survival in Auschwitz: If This Is a Man**</u> by Primo Levi, 1959 – A stark, straightforward account of the ten months Levi spent in Auschwitz in 1943. The author's clinical description of the atrocities he witnessed renders *Survival in Auschwitz* all the more disturbing.

IRAQ BOOKS
Essential Titles

Although the American occupation of Iraq lasted from 2003 to 2011, the Middle Eastern country's long history and cultural traditions nonetheless remain somewhat of a mystery to many people. To foster greater understanding of both the country and the current situation, the Washington, D.C.-based human rights group EPIC (Education for Peace in Iraq Center) compiled this list of ten essential titles about Iraq. Covering everything from women's lives to the war to Saddam Hussein's brutal dictatorship, here are EPIC's choices, per its rankings, plus two more recent titles.

1. **A Soldier's Story: From Ottoman Rule to Independent Iraq – The Memoirs of Jafar Pasha al-Askari** by Jafar Pasha al-Askari, 2004 – Al-Askari's memoir is an unusually vivid and forcefully told chronicle of his experiences fighting the Turks in 1916 and building the Iraqi Army.

2. **The Waiting List: An Iraqi Woman's Tales of Alienation** by Daisy Al-Amir, 1995 – A powerful collection of short stories that "intimately reflect women's experiences in the chaotic world … of Saddam Hussein," per EPIC.

3. **Squandered Victory: The American Occupation and the Bungled Effort to Bring Democracy to Iraq** by Larry Diamond, 2005 – At the behest of his former Stanford colleague, Secretary of State Condoleezza Rice, Diamond went to Iraq in 2003 to serve as an advisor to the Coalition Provisional Authority. *Squandered Victory* chronicles his frustrating tenure in Iraq, working alongside Paul Bremer. EPIC called Diamond's book a "sobering and critical assessment of America's effort to implant democracy."

4. **Iraq's Future: The Aftermath of Regime Change** by Toby Dodge, 2005 – In what EPIC calls "a short, highly informed read," Dodge probes the immense difficulties of regime change in Iraq, and the forces and ideologies that shaped the exponential growth of the insurgency.

5. **Iraq Since 1958: From Revolution to Dictatorship** by Marion Farouk-Sluglett and Peter Sluglett, 1987 – The ideology of the Ba'athist regime, tribalism and Hussein's dictatorship are just some of the topics covered in this enlightening book.

6. **The Modern History of Iraq** by Phebe Marr, 2003 – First published in 1984, Marr's revised second edition spans eighty-odd years in the turbulent history of Iraq, from the twenties through the 2003 U.S-led invasion of the country. EPIC hailed Marr's book as "an absolute thrill to read."

7. **Guests of the Sheik: An Ethnography of an Iraqi Village** by Elizabeth Warnock Fernea, 1965 – Praised by EPIC as "fascinating and deeply revealing," Fernea's memoir of the two years she spent living as a harem woman in southern Iraq in

the fifties is essential reading for anyone interested in the sheltered lives of Middle Eastern women.

8. **The Marsh Arabs** by Wilfred Thesiger, 1964 – A lively and evocative memoir of Thesiger's eight year-stint living among the Ma'dan people in the lowlands of south Iraq. According to EPIC, *The Marsh Arabs* is "a classic book that underscores the tragedy of what has been lost, and the hopes of what can be restored."

9. **Faith at War: A Journey on the Frontlines of Islam, from Baghdad to Timbuktu** by Yaroslav Trofimov, 2005 – The many permutations of Islamic culture are covered in fascinating, engaging detail by Trofimov, a *Wall Street Journal* correspondent, in his political travelogue.

10. **Waging Peace: A Special Occupations Team's Battle to Rebuild Iraq** by Rob Schultheis, 2005 – For six months, Schultheis watched the men and women of the U.S. Civil Affairs Team A-13 risk their lives to provide necessary healthcare, education and sanitation services to Iraqis. Both inspiring and alarming, *Waging Peace* is "a powerful wake-up call," according to EPIC.

CONTEMPORARY TITLES

11. **The Long Walk: A Story of War and the Life That Follows** by Brian Castner, 2012 – On his two tours of duty in Iraq, the author commanded a team responsible for finding and disarming the IEDs (improvised explosive devices) that have killed or maimed so many American soldiers. But this powerful book is not just about "the long walk" a soldier must sometimes take to disarm a live bomb — it's also about the long journey back to civilian life once he or she returns home.

12. **The Snake Eaters: An Unlikely Band of Brothers and the Battle for the Soul of Iraq** by Owen West, 2012 – As told by a third-generation U.S. Marine, this remarkable Iraq war story centers on twelve American army reservists tasked with helping an Iraqi battalion, the "Snake Eaters," crush a ferocious insurgency in the small city of Khalidiya, Iraq. Through extraordinary perseverance and pluck, this ragtag group of Americans eventually manages to earn the respect of its Iraqi charges and turn an impossible assignment into an unexpected success.

EXCERPT: THE SNAKE EATERS:

This time, Boiko was no longer a spectator. He grasped the hand wheel that swiveled the heavy machine gun, cranking like a yachtsman turning the winch on his sail. The wheel's teeth bit into the turret base ring, shifting the half-ton steel doughnut fluidly to let Boiko's barrel sweep over one car after the other as Iraqi drivers peeled off the road to let the three trucks of jundis and the Humvee pass.

As the up-gunner, the Humvee's only defense, Boiko figured he had about two seconds to decide to open fire if one of the hundreds of erratic Iraqi motorists suddenly sped directly at the Humvee. He pointed the jiggling front sight post of his gun at one car, then another, and slightly depressed an imaginary trigger finger for the fifth — or was it the fiftieth?—time.

IRISH NOVELS
Noteworthy Fiction from the Emerald Isle

Legend has it that if you kiss the famous Blarney Stone just outside Cork in southwest Ireland, you'll be rewarded with the gift of eloquence. Whether or not any of Ireland's illustrious literary figures have literally bent over backwards to plant their lips on this stone is not known, but the Emerald Isle has certainly produced some of the most dazzling and inventive wordsmiths of all time. In the eighteenth century, Jonathan Swift and Laurence Sterne put Ireland on the world's literary map with ___Gulliver's Travels___ and ___The Life and Opinions of Tristram Shandy, Gentleman___, respectively. And in the twenties, Dublin-born James Joyce revolutionized fiction with his colossal, modernist, stream-of- conscious epic ___Ulysses___. Spanning one day in the life of Leopold Bloom, this protean, densely allusive and often bawdy book was named the twentieth century's greatest English-language novel by Modern Library in 1999.

Taking up the mantle from Joyce, Flann O'Brien and Samuel Beckett, among others, contemporary Irish writers like John Banville, Roddy Doyle and Colm Toibin continue to explore life in Eire in fiction blessed with Blarney Stone eloquence. Here are twelve notable books, listed alphabetically, by Irish writers past and present.

1. **At Swim, Two Boys** by Jamie O'Neill, 2002 – Written over the course of ten years, O'Neill's stream-of-conscious novel about two teenaged boys falling in love against the backdrop of the impending 1916 Easter Rebellion is a literary tour de force.

2. **The Blackwater Lightship** by Colm Toibin, 2001 – Estranged for years, three generations of women from a dysfunctional family attempt to make peace when a gay sibling is stricken with AIDS. Rigorously unsentimental, Toibin's novel is intensely moving.

3. **City of Bohane** by Kevin Barry, 2011 – An accomplished short story writer (___There Are Little Kingdoms___), Barry won raves for his first novel. Set in in a crime-plagued Irish city circa 2053, *City of Bohane* depicts the escalating battle between two longtime adversaries, a gang leader and former crime boss, over a woman. Lyrical, funny and punctuated by scenes of brutal violence, *City of Bohane* was called "the best novel to come out of Ireland since *Ulysses*" by ___Trainspotting___ author Irvine Welsh.

4. **The Country Girls** by Edna O'Brien, 1960 – Leaving behind their strict convent upbringing to revel in their newfound freedom in London, O'Brien's naïve heroines Kate and Baba try to maintain their friendship amid numerous

distractions — namely men. Controversial when published, *The Country Girls* is the first novel in O'Brien's trilogy (the others are **_Girl with Green Eyes_** and **_Girls in Their Married Bliss_**) charting the roller coaster friendships of her heroines.

5. **Dubliners** by James Joyce, 1914 – Far more accessible than either *Ulysses* or **_Finnegans Wake_**, Joyce's short story collection wittily satirizes the Irish middle class living in and around Dublin during an era of rising political tensions.

6. **Fools of Fortune** by William Trevor, 1983 – Hailed by Irish novelist Frank Delaney as one of the "great books that deals with the Irish question," Trevor's Whitbread Prize winner depicts the psychological fallout of the Anglo-Irish War on a wealthy man and his mother, the sole survivors of a brutal attack on their estate.

7. **The Ginger Man** by J. P. Donleavy, 1955 – One of the Modern Library's hundred best novels of the twentieth century, Donleavy's jaunty and ribald comic novel chronicles an Irish-American's academic's drunken, womanizing exploits through the pubs of Dublin.

8. **The Last September** by Elizabeth Bowen, 1929 – In the midst of the bloody tumult of the IRA's war against the British government in Ireland, an idealistic young woman of privilege rejects her aristocratic family's values to find her identity, in Bowen's most famous novel.

9. **The Lonely Passion of Judith Hearne** by Brian Moore, 1955 – Moore's first novel is almost unbearably sad. A repressed, aging spinster in a Belfast boarding house is shattered when she falls prey to the charms of a n'er-do-well, who only sees her as a potential investor in a business.

10. **Paddy Clarke Ha Ha Ha** by Roddy Doyle, 1993 – The author of **_The Commitments_** won England's Booker Prize for this rollicking coming-of-age yarn about a working class ten- year-old on the hunt for adventure in the streets of Barrytown. Doyle's feel for the colorful vernacular of his street urchin title character lends *Paddy Clarke Ha Ha Ha* a raucous immediacy.

11. **The Sea** by John Banville, 2005 – Grieving the recent death of his wife, a middle-aged man retreats to the Irish seaside village where he spent his summers during childhood. Flashing back and forth between the past and present, Banville's Booker Prize-winning character study is an elegiac, beautifully written novel.

EXCERPT: THE SEA:

We seemed to spend, Chloe and Myles and I, the most part of our days in the sea. We swam in sunshine and in rain; we swam in the morning, when the sea was sluggish as soup, we swam at night, the water flowing over our arms like undulations of black satin; one afternoon we stayed in the water during a thunderstorm, and a fork of lightning struck the surface of the sea so close to us we heard the crackle of it and smelt the burnt air.

12. **The Secret Scripture** by Sebastian Barry, 2008 — Masterfully blending two narratives, Barry's captivating novel depicts the efforts of a hundred-year-old mental patient to write her autobiography — and a therapist's attempts to discover why she was committed decades ago. Set in rural west Ireland, *The Secret Scripture* paints a vivid and often disturbing portrait of the country's civil war and the Catholic Church's views on women's sexuality.

JEWISH-AMERICAN NOVELS
From Sholem Aleichem to Michael Chabon

He was known as the "Jewish Mark Twain." An estimated 100,000 mourners attended his Brooklyn funeral in 1916. And his tragicomic stories about Tevye the milkman in Czarist Russia inspired *Fiddler on the Roof*, one of Broadway's longest-running musicals. Yet while the great Yiddish humorist/writer Sholem Aleichem may not be as widely read today, he certainly helped pave the way for Saul Bellow, Philip Roth and other Jewish-American novelists too numerous to list who've flourished in post-World War II-era America.

Although Jewish-American writers have achieved preeminence in all literary genres — from science fiction (Isaac Asimov) to poetry (Stanley Kunitz) to children's literature (Maurice Sendak), to name three — the following twelve novels, listed alphabetically, specifically address the Jewish-American experience in its many permutations, past and present.

1. **The Adventures of Augie March** by Saul Bellow, 1953 - Eulogized by Roth as part of the "backbone of twentieth century American literature," Bellow won the first of his three National Book Awards for this superb picaresque about the title character's rough-and-tumble coming of age in Depression-era Chicago. Both Martin Amis and Salman Rushdie regard *The Adventures of Augie March* as "the great American novel."

2. **Adventures of Mottel: The Cantor's Son** by Sholem Aleichem, 1953 — Unfinished at the time of Aleichem's death in 1916, this boisterously funny novel about poor Russian immigrants in turn-of-the-century America was published sans ending in English in 1953.

3. **The Amazing Adventures of Kavalier and Clay** by Michael Chabon, 2000 - Chabon's Pulitzer Prize-winning novel is a dazzling tour de force about two Jewish cousins turned comic book innovators in World War II-era America.

4. **American Pastoral** by Philip Roth, 1997 — One of Roth's novels featuring his alter ego, Nathan Zuckerman, *American Pastoral* depicts the impact of the sixties-era social unrest on Seymour "Swede" Levov, a golden boy with a beauty queen wife, whose daughter becomes a radical fugitive. Richly imagined and

brilliantly written, *American Pastoral* won the 1998 Pulitzer Prize and was named one of the best American novels published between 1980 and 2005 by the *New York Times Book Review* in 2006.

EXCERPT: AMERICAN PASTORAL:

The Swede. During the war years, when I was still a grade school boy, this was a magical name in our Newark neighborhood, even to adults just a generation removed from the city's old Prince Street ghetto and not yet so flawlessly Americanized as to be bowled over by the prowess of a high school athlete. The name was magical; so was the anomalous face. Of the few fair-complexioned Jewish students in our preponderantly Jewish public high school, none possessed anything remotely like the steep-jawed, insentient Viking mask of this blue-eyed blond born into our tribe as Seymour Irving Levov.

5. **The Book of Daniel** by E. L. Doctorow, 1971 - Doctorow's fictionalized retelling of the notorious Ethel and Julius Rosenberg espionage case is a profoundly affecting novel that ranks among the author's very best.

6. **Call it Sleep** by Henry Roth, 1934 - Overlooked when first published, Roth's stream-of-consciousness novel about a Jewish immigrant growing up in New York's Lower East Side is now considered one of the greatest books of twentieth century American literature.

7. **The Chosen** by Chaim Potok, 1967 - A heartwarming story of two boys — a Modern Orthodox Jew and the son of a Hasidic rebe — and their struggles with their fathers in forties-era Brooklyn.

8. **Enemies: A Love Story** by Isaac Bashevis Singer, 1972 - Winner of the 1978 Nobel Prize for Literature, Singer wrote short stories, children's books, memoirs and novels in a career spanning sixty-odd years. In this tragicomic novel, a Holocaust survivor living in New York City, circa 1949, finds himself torn between three very different women.

9. **The Instructions** by Adam Levin, 2010 – Clocking in at 1,030 pages, Levin's ambitious, overstuffed, heartwarming and wildly funny first novel depicts four raucous days in the life of Gurion Maccabee, a rebellious, prodigiously intelligent ten-year-old Chicago schoolboy obsessed with Philip Roth and Jewish theology.

10. **Kaaterskill Falls** by Allegra Goodman, 1998 – A National Book Award finalist, Goodman's wonderful first novel takes place in a small upstate New York town where a close-knit Orthodox Jewish community spends the summer, circa 1976. Skillfully depicting the interwoven lives of three families, *Kaaterskill Falls* is an observant and sensitively written novel brimming with wit and charm.

11. **The Middlesteins** by Jami Attenberg, 2012 – After thirty years of marriage, Richard Middlestein leaves his wife Edie, whose compulsive overeating has

packed 350 pounds on her frame. Blissfully ignoring the warnings of her children and daughter-in-law, who's busily planning her twins' b'nai mitzvah party, Edie continues eating her way toward an early grave in Attenberg's wonderful novel, which *Kirkus Reviews* hailed as a "sharp-tongued, sweet-natured masterpiece of Jewish family life."

12. **The Puttermesser Papers** by Cynthia Ozick, 1997 - Ozick's National Book Award finalist is a witty and shrewdly observed blend of mysticism and character study about Ruth Puttermesser, a middle-aged Jewish lawyer in New York City.

LATINO NOVELS
Viva la Literatura!

In 1990, Cuban-American Oscar Hijuelos became the first Latino writer to win the Pulitzer Prize for his second novel, *The Mambo Kings Play Songs of Love*. This elegiac, jazzily atmospheric story of two Cuban brothers/musicians fleeing Havana for fifties-era New York effectively jump-started the boom in Latino literature. Although several, notable works of Latino-themed fiction had preceded *The Mambo Kings*, none of them had ever caught on with the general public quite like Hijuelos' acclaimed bestseller, which was later turned into a popular film starring Antonio Banderas.

Today, with the Latino population in the United States estimated at fifty million and counting, the market for Latino fiction will only continue to grow. Spanning genres from historical fiction to salsa-flavored "chick lit" to coming-of-age stories, here are twelve notable Latino-themed novels, listed alphabetically.

1. **The Barbarian Nurseries** by Hector Tobar, 2011 – Tobar earned comparisons to Charles Dickens and Tom Wolfe for *The Barbarian Nurseries*, which captures the melting pot that is contemporary Los Angeles with insight and honesty. When her affluent employers disappear, inexplicably leaving their two young sons in her care, a Mexican maid begins a search for the boys' grandfather that will take her and the boys on an extraordinary, life-changing journey.

2. **Bless Me, Ultima** by Rudolfo Anaya, 1973 – In forties-era New Mexico, a seven-year-old Chicano boy finds an unlikely mentor in his aged aunt, a mystical healer, who comes to live with the family. Under her benevolent influence, he gradually comes to terms with his parents' divergent expectations and his cultural identity. Anaya's coming-of-age novel won the Premio Quinto Sol, the national Chicano literary award.

3. **Bodega Dreams** by Ernesto Quinonez, 2000 – Steeped in the vernacular and street customs of Spanish Harlem, Quinonez's debut novel practically boils over with raw energy and ebullient wit. Chino, the streetwise hero, is torn between his love

for an ultra-religious classmate and the lure of quick money offered by Willie Bodega, a local gangster.

4. **The Brief Wondrous Life of Oscar Wao** by Junot Diaz, 2007 – The winner of both the National Book Critics Circle Award and the Pulitzer Prize, Diaz's sensational debut novel is a tragicomic tour de force. Laden with footnotes, comic book references and science fiction and fantasy allusions, it depicts both the coming of age of the title character — an overweight, sci-fi loving Dominican teenager in New Jersey — and his family's experiences during the brutal reign of the Dominican dictator Raoul Trujillo.

5. **Conquistadora** by Esmeralda Santiago, 2011 – When eighteen-year-old Spanish beauty Ana marries and moves to Puerto Rico in 1844, the demands of running a sugar plantation destroy her romantic illusions about life on the Caribbean island. Yet despite the loneliness and physical hardship of plantation life, she gradually comes to love her new life — and will do anything to protect it in Santiago's beautifully realized and enthralling novel.

6. **Dreaming in Cuban** by Cristina Garcia, 1992 – A 1992 National Book Award finalist, Garcia's arresting family saga blends otherworldly imagery and political upheaval as it portrays the lives of three generations of Cuban women.

7. **The Guardians** by Ana Castillo, 2007 – The winner of the American Book Award for ***The Mixquiahuala Letters***, Castillo writes with unflinching honesty and empathy about the plight of illegal immigrants in this gripping novel set in a U.S.-Mexico border town. When her brother vanishes while crossing the border, a fiftysomething widow sets out to discover his fate, accompanied by her deeply religious nephew, a divorced high school teacher and his chatty grandfather, two gangbangers and a priest.

8. **The House on Mango Street** by Sandra Cisneros, 1984 – Growing up in rough, inner city Latino neighborhood in Chicago, sensitive, bookish Esperanza Cordero finds solace in writing poetry and short stories. A captivating and moving debut novel from Mexican-American poet/novelist Cisneros, author of ***Caramelo***.

EXCERPT: THE HOUSE ON MANGO STREET:

Your abuelito is dead, Papa says early one morning in my room. Esta muerto, and then as if he just heard the news himself, crumples like a coat and cries, my brave Papa cries. I have never seen my Papa cry and don't know what to do.

I know he will have to go away, that he will take a plane to Mexico, all the uncles and aunts will be there, and they will have a black-and-white photo taken in front of the tomb with flowers shaped like spears in a white vase because this is how they send the dead away in that country.

9. **Hot Tamara** by Mary Castillo, 2005 – A specialist in "chica lit," Castillo (***In Between Men***), spins an engaging romantic yarn about twenty-six-year-old

Tamara Contreras, who shocks her family by turning down a marriage proposal to strike out on her own in Los Angeles. Yet Tamara can't quite escape her past — not that she'd want to — when she bumps into her high school crush, a sexy fireman whose "bad boy" reputation makes him all the more irresistible.

10. **The Hummingbird's Daughter** by Luis Alberto Urrea, 2005 – Urrea reportedly spent twenty years researching and writing this marvelous historical epic based on the life of his great Aunt Teresita, the "Saint of Cabora" a political lightning rod denounced by the Catholic Church and embraced by Mexico's indigenous people.

11. **The Mambo Kings Play Songs of Love** by Oscar Hijuelos, 1989 – Visions of music stardom in their eyes, brothers Nestor and Cesar Castillo leave Cuba in 1949 for New York, where they encounter triumph and tragedy as the "Mambo Kings."

12. **The Ordinary Seaman** by Francisco Goldman, 1997 – Goldman's second novel couldn't be more timely — or wrenching. Promised work on a freighter, fifteen Central American illegal immigrants find themselves trapped on a derelict ship moored at a Brooklyn pier. Based on a true story, *The Ordinary Seaman* is a stunning novel by the author of *The Long Night of White Chickens*.

LETTERS
Great Collections from the Past

One of the most entertaining and surprising ways to get to know the people of the past is to read the letters they sent one another. There are a wealth of collections of the letters of great writers from Jane Austen to J. R. R. Tolkien — see if you can find any by your favorite author the next time you're at the bookstore or library. Some novels are even written completely in the form of letters, like Montesquieu's eighteenth-century *Persian Letters*, in which Persian travelers visit the exotic land of Europe. What follows is an alphabetical list of collections of real-life letters that will let you peek into the lives of some of the world's greatest observers, lovers, and wits. Reading them just might make you decide, in this age of e-mail and texting, to pen some spirited snail mail yourself!

1. **The Adams-Jefferson Letters: The Complete Correspondence Between Thomas Jefferson and Abigail and John Adams** edited by Lester J. Cappon, 1988 – Friends and rivals who took part in the birth of our nation and died on the same day (exactly fifty years after the Declaration of Independence), John Adams and Thomas Jefferson left a remarkable legacy of correspondence on politics, philosophy, and daily life, in which John Adams's perceptive wife Abigail Adams also took part.

2. **Dear Professor Einstein: Albert Einstein's Letters To and From Children** edited by Alice Calaprice, 2002 – Touching, insightful, and often hilarious correspondence

between one of mankind's most highly developed minds and the inquisitive young.

3. **Lawrence of Arabia: The Selected Letters** edited by Malcolm Brown, 2005 – A glimpse into the private world of the legendary T.E. Lawrence, soldier, leader, archaeologist, and writer.

4. **Letters from Africa, 1914–1931** by Isak Dinesen, edited by Frans Lasson, translated by Anne Born, 1982 – Before Dinesen wrote ***Out of Africa***, the memoir of her life as a struggling farmer in British East Africa, she described many of her experiences in these fascinating letters.

5. **Letters from Russia** by Astolphe De Custine, edited by Anka Muhlstein, 2002 – In 1839, a French writer called the Marquis de Custine visited Russia, where he met the Tzar, attended balls, and spent time in the impoverished countryside. His letters vividly portray life in nineteenth-century Russia, and some think his political critiques are still relevant today.

6. **The Letters of Abelard and Héloise** by Peter Abelard, Héloise, edited by Michael Clanchy, translated by Betty Radice, 2004 – The passionate correspondence between the tragic medieval lovers, a Parisian scholar and his student who continued to write to each other even after they became a monk and an abbess.

7. **The Letters of the Younger Pliny** by Pliny the Younger; translated by Betty Radice, 1963 – From a firsthand account of the eruption of Mt. Vesuvius to sophisticated chitchat, this collection of letters by a Roman lawyer and public figure gives an intimate portrait of life under the emperor Trajan.

8. **The Poems of Exile: Tristia and the Black Sea Letters** by Ovid, translated by Peter Green, 2005 – Late in his life, the author of ***Metamorphoses*** was banished by the Roman emperor Augustus to a distant fishing village on the Black Sea. We don't know why he was exiled, but we do have these letters in verse, some of them quite beautiful, pleading (unsuccessfully, alas) to be allowed back to Rome.

9. **Selected Letters** by Madame de Sévigné, edited by Leonard Tancock, 1982 – Politics, culture, and everyday concerns in Louis XIV's France come to life in the letters of this court lady, mother, and friend to the likes of the great aphorist La Rochefoucauld.

10. **Women's Letters: America from the Revolutionary War to the Present** edited by Lisa Grunwald and Stephen J. Adler, 2005 – The letters in this absorbing and at times heartbreaking collection show you a slave writing to her husband after their forced separation; frontier women describing the hardships of their lives; society ladies negotiating friendships and politics; Emily Dickinson asking a respected author for his opinion of her work, and much more.

EXCERPT: WOMEN'S LETTERS:

I hear by Captn Wm Riley news that makes me very Sorry for he Says you proved a Grand Coward when the fight was at Bunkers hill. . . . If you are afraid

pray own the truth & come home & take care of our Children & I will be Glad to Come & take your place, & never will be Called a Coward, neither will I throw away one Cartridge but exert myself bravely in so good a Cause.
—*Abigail Grant to her husband*
August 19, 1776

MEDITATIVE LITERATURE
Writings on Solitude

Our means of communication are amazing — cell phones, e-mail, televisions set into the walls of elevators, and who knows what will be next — but they can make it hard to get a moment's peace. Sometimes we can use a little time completely alone to balance all that interconnectedness. Silence, solitude, and reflection, especially in a natural setting, can teach us valuable lessons about our lives and provide a wordless peace. For inspiration, here are some books by people who committed to making time for reflection, listed alphabetically.

1. **Blue Nights** by Joan Didion, 2011 – Didion confronts loss, illness and mortality in this moving memoir written shortly after the death of her daughter Quintana Roo. Coming so soon after the death of Didion's novelist husband John Gregory Dunne, this poignant book is a searing recitation of grief, regret, fear, and unanswerable questions.

EXCERPT: BLUE NIGHTS:

In certain latitudes there comes a span of time approaching and following the summer solstice, some weeks in all, when the twilights turn long and blue. This period of the blue nights does not occur in subtropical California, where I lived for much of the time I will be talking about here and where the end of daylight is fast and lost in the blaze of the dropping sun, but it does occur in New York, where I now live. You notice it first as April ends and May begins, a change in the season, not exactly a warming—in fact not at all a warming—yet suddenly summer seems near, a possibility, even a promise. You pass a window, you walk to Central Park, you find yourself swimming in the color blue: the actual light is blue, and over the course of an hour or so this blue deepens, becomes more intense even as it darkens and fades, approximates finally the blue of the glass on a clear day at Chartres, or that of the Cerenkov radiation thrown off by the fuel rods in the pools of nuclear reactors. The French called this time of day "l'heure bleue." To the English it was "the gloaming." The very word "gloaming" reverberates, echoes— the gloaming, the glimmer, the glitter, the glisten, the glamour—carrying in its consonants the images of houses shuttering, gardens darkening, grass-lined rivers slipping through the shadows.

2. **Fifty Days of Solitude** by Doris Grumbach, 1994 – With her companion away for over a month, the author, in her seventies, spends the time alone in their home in coastal Maine, occasionally visiting town but avoiding speaking to anyone. "A strong wind had disconnected the antenna to the television set," she writes; at home, she focuses on her books, her mail, and her thoughts. It is a hushed but not always easy time.

3. **Gift from the Sea** by Anne Morrow Lindbergh, 1955 – During a brief sojourn by the ocean, Lindbergh meditates on the rhythms of nature and the lovely shells that wash up on the beach, using the peaceful interlude to restore her spirit and gain insight into her busy life. "The sea does not reward those who are too anxious, too greedy, or too impatient," she writes. "…Patience, patience, patience is what the sea teaches."

4. **Society and Solitude** by Ralph Waldo Emerson, 1870 – The title essay (originally lecture) in this collection discusses the necessity and difficulty of being alone in order to create works of genius. Emerson, one of America's greatest philosophers, believes that it is possible for us to fulfill our highest potentials "if we keep our independence, yet do not lose our sympathy."

5. **Thoughts in Solitude** by Thomas Merton, 1956 – The author was a Trappist monk, but his thoughts on the importance of solitude to our spiritual and ethical lives has at least at much relevance — perhaps more — for those of us who live in the modern world.

6. **Walden** by Henry David Thoreau, 1854 – Thoreau built himself a small house in the woods by Walden Pond in order to live in an uncomplicated and unfettered way. He wasn't in solitude all the time; people came to visit his little cabin, and he often visited Concord. But he seems to have been far enough away from the mentality of Main Street to make it a fruitful experiment.

7. **Winter Journal** by Paul Auster, 2012 – In this, his second memoir — his first was his acclaimed writing debut *The Invention of Solitude* — Auster contemplates aging and mortality. Inspired by his mother's death and his awareness of time passing as he enters his mid-sixties, the writer is both frank and moving as he describes the effects of accumulated time on his body and mind.

MEMOIRS
Celebrity Kiss & Tell-Alls

Dropping names and her drawers with tireless frequency, the late, blowsy character actress Shelley Winters dished the dirt with gossipy relish about her sexual exploits with Hollywood stars in her bestselling 1980 autobiography, *Shelley: Also Known as Shirley*. And while few stars have divulged as many "intimate" details about their Tinsel Town affairs as the four-time married Winters, others have written frankly about their struggles with mental illness, alcoholism and drug abuse. Due in part to the increasing "tabloidization" of the media, where nothing is off-limits and paparazzi launch surprise attacks on celebrities, it's become the norm for stars to 'fess up to scandals, addictions and other indiscretions in juicy autobiographies. Here are twelve celebrity tell-alls, listed alphabetically, that give readers the inside scoop on Hollywood, from its golden age to today.

1. **Bossypants** by Tina Fey, 2011 – A tight, rippingly funny collection of anecdotes, aphorisms and deep thoughts exploring the life and times of this *Saturday Night Live* alum and star of television's *30 Rock*. Readers responded to Fey's inimitable ability to use humor as a subtle instrument of feminist power, and *Bossypants* topped the *New York Times* best seller list for five weeks.

EXCERPT: BOSSYPANTS:

My whole life, people who ask about my scar within one week of knowing me have invariably turned out to be egomaniacs of average intelligence or less. And egomaniacs of average intelligence or less often end up in the field of TV journalism. So, you see, if I tell the whole story here, then I will be asked about it over and over by the hosts of Access Movietown *and* Entertainment Forever *for the rest of my short-lived career.*

2. **Dean and Me (A Love Story)** by Jerry Lewis with James Kaplan, 2005 – With surprising candor and more than a touch of regret, Lewis probes his volatile, love-hate relationship with former partner, Dean Martin, in this even-handed memoir.

3. **Dropped Names: Famous Men and Women as I Knew Them** by Frank Langella, 2012 – The Tony Award-winning actor and Oscar nominee (*Frost/Nixon*) dishes with good-humored relish about his encounters with the famous (and infamous) over his decades-spanning career. Yet there's more to Langella's memoirs than simply a collection of juicy anecdotes. He also writes perceptively about the ups and downs of being an actor and the price of fame in a memoir *The New Yorker* pronounced "splendid."

4. **The Kid Stays in the Picture** by Robert Evans, 1994 – Discovered by Norma Shearer poolside at the Beverly Hills Hotel, Evans acted in a few films before finding his unlikely niche as a studio mogul. In his funny, warts-and-all chronicle

of his rollercoaster professional and personal life, Evans gives readers their money's worth of Hollywood dirt.

5. **The Million Dollar Mermaid** by Esther Williams with Digby Diehl, 1999 – Memorably dissed by Fanny Brice, who said of her, "Wet she's a star; dry she ain't," the MGM bathing beauty leaves the pool to share revealing anecdotes about her co-stars, stormy marriage to Fernando Lamas and affair with cross-dressing he-man Jeff Chandler.

6. **My Wicked, Wicked Ways** by Errol Flynn, 1959 – A scandal magnet for much of his film career, the dashingly handsome swashbuckler burned the proverbial candle at both ends, drinking, womanizing and carousing his way into an early grave at age 50. Published just months after his death, *My Wicked, Wicked Ways* vividly demonstrates what it meant to be "In like Flynn."

7. **A Paper Life** by Tatum O'Neal, 2004 – Although Ryan O'Neal publicly disputed many of his daughter's most shocking claims in this headline-making book, *A Paper Life* is a Hollywood cautionary tale that tracks the fallen child star's decline into heroin addiction, following a combative marriage to tennis player John McEnroe. In 2011, O'Neal published a sequel, ***Found: A Daughter's Journey Home***.

8. **Shelley: Also Known as Shirley** by Shelley Winters, 1980 – Although she refrains from sharing graphic details about her torrid affairs with Marlon Brando, William Holden and Burt Lancaster, to name three, Winters otherwise lets it all hang out, in an autobiography that spawned a sequel, ***Shelley II: The Middle of My Century***.

9. **Tab Hunter Confidential: The Making of a Movie Star** by Tab Hunter with Eddie Muller, 2005 – Under the predatory sway of notorious Hollywood agent Henry Willson, Arthur Gelien became fifties-era heartthrob Tab Hunter — a blonde, blue-eyed All-American boy whose homosexuality was a carefully guarded secret. Now happily out of the closet, Hunter writes about his checkered career and long-term affair with Anthony Perkins in his frank autobiography.

10. **Then Again** by Diane Keaton, 2011 – Named one of the best books of the year by the *New York Times*, *People* and *Vogue*, this Academy Award-winning actress' memoir does more than just reveal details of her relationships with Hollywood heavyweights like Warren Beatty, Al Pacino and Woody Allen. It's also a moving — and well-written — tribute to her maxim-loving, multifaceted mother, and an incisive meditation on the value of friends and family.

11. **What Falls Away** by Mia Farrow, 1997 – "Hell hath no fury" like Farrow scorned, as the actress proves in her autobiography, which spews ample venom at her ex-lover, Woody Allen. A true child of Hollywood privilege, Farrow also paints a starry portrait of her life, career and marriages to Frank Sinatra and Andre Previn.

12. **You'll Never Eat Lunch in this Town Again** by Julia Phillips, 1991 – The first female producer to win a Best Picture Oscar (for 1973's *The Sting*), Phillips eventually crashed and burned, due to a raging cocaine problem that left her a broke and embittered pariah. Sparing no one, least of all herself, Phillips writes of seventies-era Hollywood excess in a memoir full of nasty swipes at such Hollywood luminaries as Warren Beatty, Goldie Hawn and Steven Spielberg.

MEMOIRS
Childhoods Interrupted

If you think you had it rough growing up, odds are that Frank McCourt probably had it worse — a lot worse. In his phenomenally popular memoir *Angela's Ashes*, McCourt writes movingly of the extreme hardship he endured as poverty-stricken Irish Catholic boy in the slums of thirties-era Limerick. What little money McCourt's alcoholic wastrel of a father managed to scrap together usually went towards his pub tab, rather than the family, despite the best efforts of McCourt's mother, Angela. Yet there's not a whiff of self-pity in McCourt's lively, colorful memoir of childhood interrupted.

Thanks in large part to *Angela Ashes*, the memoir has become a staple on the nonfiction bestseller list. While some memoirs of rampant dysfunction and abuse paint dark, nightmarish portraits of family life in explicit, borderline exploitative detail, the following memoirs, listed alphabetically, brook that unfortunate literary trend towards melodramatic freak show tell-alls. With unsparing honesty, rueful humor and keen insight, these books reveal the joys and sorrows of childhood — and how these authors found the tools to survive, often under extraordinary duress.

1. **All Over But the Shoutin'** by Rick Bragg, 1997 – To describe Bragg's childhood in rural northern Alabama as "hardscrabble" would be an understatement. Deserted by her husband, an alcoholic, psychologically traumatized Korean War veteran, Bragg's dirt-poor mother worked 24/7 to provide for him and his two brothers. In this richly evocative memoir, the *New York Times* reporter pays tribute to his remarkable mother.

2. **Angela's Ashes** by Frank McCourt, 1996 – The proverbial luck of the Irish did not shine on the embattled, tragedy-prone McCourt clan, who returned to Ireland from New York in search of a better life, only to sink deeper into poverty. Yet in the midst of all this suffering, there is ample wit and warmth in McCourt's Pulitzer Prize-winning bestseller.

3. **Borrowed Finery** by Paula Fox, 2001 – The unwanted daughter of alcoholic screenwriters who barely acknowledged her existence, except with thinly veiled contempt, Fox took refuge in literature at an early age. In her highly acclaimed

memoir, the Newberry Award-winning novelist depicts her abandonment with admirable restraint that makes it all the more poignant.

4. **Don't Let's Go to the Dogs Tonight: An African Childhood** by Alexandra Fuller, 2001 – The daughter of white, gun-wielding farmers, Fuller grew up in seventies-era Rhodesia (now Zimbabwe), when racial tensions regularly exploded into violence. In plainspoken yet intensely felt prose, Fuller describes a childhood composed of equal parts wonder and anxiety. Fuller delves deeper into her parents' marriage in the equally riveting ***Cocktail Hour Under the Tree of Forgetfulness***.

5. **The Glass Castle** by Jeannette Walls, 2005 – Although she's the very image of the sleek, urban sophisticate, New York gossip columnist Walls still bears the scars of a poor, itinerant childhood that took her from Arizona to West Virginia. Her parents were brilliant, loving eccentrics spectacularly ill-equipped to feed and clothe Walls and her siblings on a regular basis. Utterly devoid of self-pity, *The Glass Castle* is an emotionally powerful memoir that's unforgettable.

6. **I Know Why the Caged Bird Sings** by Maya Angelou, 1969 – A landmark autobiography from one of America's most beloved poets, *I Know Why the Caged Bird Sings* is a stunning work, at once lyrical and brutally honest. Spanning Angelou's childhood and adolescence, *I Know Why the Caged Bird Sings* addresses the racism Angelou faced growing up in Depression-era Arkansas.

7. **The Liar's Club** by Mary Karr, 1995 – Born into a "terrific family of liars and drunks" in a tiny, East Texas refinery town, Karr mines literary gold in this compelling tragicomic saga that packs an emotional wallop. Two equally mesmerizing sequels, ***Cherry*** and ***Lit,*** followed in 2000 and 2009, respectively.

EXCERPT: THE LIAR'S CLUB:

She changed the tire and must have made some note of his raw good looks. He was some part Indian — we never figured out which tribe-black-haired and sharp-featured. His jug-eared grin reminded her of Clark Gable's. Since she fancied herself a sort of Bohemian Scarlett O'Hara, the attraction was deep and sudden. I should also note that Mother was prone to conversion experiences of various kinds, and had entered a fervent Marxist stage. She toted Das Kapital *around in her purse for years. Daddy was active in the Oil Chemical and Atomic Workers Union. Whenever they renegotiated a contract-every two years, he was known as an able picket-line brawler. He was, in short, a Texas working man, with a smattering of Indian blood and with personality traits that she had begun to consider heroic.*

8. **A Prisoner of Tehran: One Woman's Story of Survival Inside an Iranian Prison** by Marina Nemat, 2007 – This gut-wrenching memoir details a girlhood lost to the

Ayatollah Khomeini's Islamic Revolution. Just sixteen, Nemat was imprisoned, tortured and sentenced to death. She would be subsequently saved — and betrayed — by the man who fell in love with her. Brutal, shocking, and elegantly rendered, this memoir will not be forgotten.

9. **Running With Scissors** by Augusten Burroughs, 2002 – Given the sheer insanity of Burroughs' childhood, it's a miracle he can still form sentences, much less write such a morbidly hilarious memoir that leaves you shaking — with shocked laughter, that is.

10. **A Stolen Life: A Memoir** by Jaycee Dugard, 2011 – This ripped-from-the-headlines chronicle avoids feeling voyeuristic or exploitative by virtue of its being written by the person who experienced it, without aid from a ghostwriter. In spare and simple terms, Dugard describes how she was kidnapped from a normal American childhood and thrust into an abusive hell that lasted eighteen years. Now a mother, Dugard refuses to see herself as a victim and offers her story as one of hope and inspiration.

11. **Them: A Memoir of Parents** by Francine du Plessix Gray, 2005 – The novelist and Marquis de Sade biographer explores the emotional turmoil lurking beneath the glittering surface of her childhood in forties-era Manhattan, where her parents ran in the most exclusive circles. Although Gray's Russian émigré mother displayed all the maternal instincts of a snake, *Them* is no ***Mommie Dearest,*** but an elegant and surprisingly even-handed memoir.

12. **This Boy's Life: A Memoir** by Tobias Wolff, 1989 – Criss-crossing the country with his divorced mother, Wolf learns survival skills at an early age, thanks to his mother's knack for getting involved with abusive men. When she rashly marries a macho control freak in the Pacific Northwest, Wolff locks horns with his bully of a stepfather in this gritty, emotionally resonant memoir laced with mordant wit.

MEMOIRS
Curious Careers

Have you ever wondered what it's really like to be an astronaut? A chef at a fine restaurant? An FBI agent posing as a jewel thief? A *real* jewel thief? Not to worry if these careers are beyond your reach (or beyond your wishes) — you can learn all about them from the safety and peace of a comfortable armchair. These twelve memoirs, listed alphabetically, offer plenty of excitement, little-known facts about mysterious corners of society, and insights into the minds of people in unusual circumstances.

1. **Blood, Bones & Butter: The Inadvertent Education of a Reluctant Chef** by Gabrielle Hamilton, 2011 – In this *New York Times* bestseller and the winner of a 2012

James Beard Book Award, the celebrated owner of a groundbreaking eatery recounts how her devotion to cooking, developed during a childhood riven by divorce, was the one constant in her life through more than twenty years of troubled searching for meaning and purpose. Viscerally transcending the sunny tropes of similar chef stories, this memoir is about family every bit as much as about food.

2. **Blowing My Cover: My Life as a CIA Spy** by Lindsay Moran, 2005 – A recent Harvard graduate, the author joined the Central Intelligence Agency in her late twenties. Her career with the CIA (working undercover in Macedonia) was brief but challenging. She writes about the intensive training process, the difficulties of remembering all the details of her fake life, and the strains of being unable to communicate freely with some of the people most important to her.

3. **Carrying the Fire: An Astronaut's Journeys** by Michael Collins, 1974 – During his career as an astronaut, Collins traveled into space on three different missions — of them the famous Apollo 11 flight, for which he piloted the command module while Neil Armstrong and Buzz Aldrin explored the surface of the moon. He describes the moving and peculiar experience of being completely alone in orbit around the moon, as well as the unique perspective on our own planet that he gained in his travels.

4. **Catch Me If You Can: The True Story of a Real Fake** by Frank W. Abagnale with Stan Redding, 1980 – As a young man, Frank Abagnale was a brazen and frighteningly successful liar. He spent millions of dollars that he didn't have, traveled internationally free of charge by pretending to be a pilot, and conned people into placing him in several other positions of responsibility for which he was vastly unqualified. Now an expert in fraud prevention, Abagnale may not win your admiration, but his story will astonish you (and convince you of the value of thorough background checks).

5. **Confessions of a Master Jewel Thief** by Bill Mason and Lee Gruenfeld, 2004 – This is the story of another resourceful but less-than-stellar character — a family man with a secret criminal career. Bill Mason describes his carefully planned thefts of jewels from Phyllis Diller, a mafia boss, and various others.

6. **Confessions of a Tax Collector: One Man's Tour of Duty Inside the IRS** by Richard Yancey, 2004 – This memoir is a testament to life's unpredictability. When Richard Yancey went to work for the Internal Revenue Service, he had no idea how it would change him. Over time, his personality and even his physique were transformed, and his quest to bring tax evaders to account is actually exciting.

EXCERPT: CONFESSIONS OF A TAX COLLECTOR:

I had begun to shut down mentally: too much information had been thrown at me in six hours to absorb it all. The only things I had clear by this point were

Inspection was probably something bad, the Union was probably something good, and thirty minutes for lunch was definitely something unreasonable.

7. **Donnie Brasco: My Undercover Life in the Mafia** by Joseph D. Pistone, 1988 – Pistone, an FBI agent, spent about half a decade working undercover among criminals, pretending to be a jewel thief named Donnie Brasco. Here he shares what he learned about the Mafia lifestyle and describes the challenges of his dangerous (and ultimately disorienting) jobs.

8. **Jumping Fire: A Smokejumper's Memoir of Fighting Wildfire** by Murray A. Taylor, 2000 – For over a quarter century, Taylor spent his summers parachuting out of airplanes into remote areas of the rugged, beautiful Alaskan landscape to battle wildfires. This memoir mainly focuses on 1991, a particularly fiery year. Courage, strength, and a strong sense of humor are all job requirements — and Taylor is also a wonderful storyteller.

9. **Kitchen Confidential: Adventures In the Culinary Underbelly** by Anthony Bourdain, 2000 – There is often a wide gulf between the people who consume the food at the world's better restaurants and the people who create that food. Bourdain, an accomplished chef, swings the kitchen doors wide open for curious gourmands. You might not want to see everything he reveals, but you're sure to be a better-informed customer, and it's an entertaining read.

10. **Memoirs of a Sword Swallower** by Daniel P. Mannix,1996 – Mannix explains how he came to be a fire-eater and sword-swallower, some tricks of the trade to keep the entertainment from becoming fatal, and what carnival life is really like, writing with sympathy about his fellow special talents and "freaks."

11. **My Korean Deli: Risking It All for a Convenience Store** by Ben Ryder Howe, 2011 – A WASPy *Paris Review* editor with genteel visions of shop keeping and his lawyer wife, the daughter of Korean immigrants, get in over their heads after buying a rough-and-tumble convenience store in Brooklyn. Populated with strange, *Newhart*-esque characters, this witty fish-out-of-water tale demonstrates an appreciation for the survival instincts and values of hardworking immigrants, for the importance of family and for the tender core of even the most outsized personality.

12. **Spy Handler: Memoir of a KGB Officer** by Victor Cherkashin and Gregory Feifer, 2005 – A unique Russian perspective on cold war-era espionage, this is the story of the KGB agent who recruited CIA men Aldrich Ames and Robert Hanssen as double agents for the Soviet Union. It's a thoughtful but unnerving exposé of deception, blackmail, and treason.

MEMOIRS
Inspirational Stories of Overcoming Disabilities

Throughout our history and in all areas of our culture, disabled people have been among the greats — think of Homer, Milton, Goya, Beethoven, Dostoyevsky, Franklin D. Roosevelt, Stephen Hawking, and Helen Keller, to name just a few. Many others, of course, have led more ordinary lives, but without the luxury of taking for granted some of the things that nondisabled people do. The stories of the challenges disabled people face — and their responses to them — encompass not only suffering and loss but also resilience, ingenuity, and joy. This list of memoirs includes works by authors with a range of mental and physical disabilities. They describe lives that are rich despite their disabilities, and sometimes even because of them.

1. **Breathing for a Living** by Laura Rothenberg, 2003 – When she was just a few days old, Rothenberg was diagnosed with cystic fibrosis, a disease that prevents the lungs from functioning normally. Her condition worsened when she was a student at Brown University, and she decided to document her experiences in this collection of e-mails, journal entries, poetry, and other materials. The result is an affecting account of her battles with the disease, her complex and engaging personality, and the emotional ups and downs of a lung transplant that was ultimately unsuccessful.

2. **The Diving Bell and the Butterfly** by Jean-Dominique Bauby, 2008 – In 1995 at age forty-three, Jean-Dominique Bauby, editor-in-chief of *Elle* magazine in France, suffered a massive stroke that left him almost completely paralyzed. Made into a moving film directed by artist Julian Schnabel, Bauby's story is a celebration of the human spirit, even when his only link to the world is the ability to blink one eye. Bauby died two days after his book was published, but his joie de vivre lives on.

3. **House of Prayer No. 2: A Writer's Journey Home** by Mark Richard, 2011 – *The New Yorker* magazine described this book as "so varied, dramatic, and, at times, incredible that it is bound to leave almost every reader with the feeling that they haven't lived at all." Mark Richard was born in the sixties-era South with hip deformities so severe that he faced spending his adulthood in a wheelchair. Determined to live as fully as possible before he can no longer walk, he embarks on a life rife with love affairs, odd jobs, and criminal behavior, experiences which eventually coalesce in the making of a gifted writer.

EXCERPT: HOUSE OF PRAYER NO.2:

Say you have a "special child," which in the South means one between Down's and dyslexic. Birth him with his father away on Army maneuvers along East Texas bayous. Give him his only visitor in the military hospital his father's father,

a sometime railroad man, sometime hired gun for Huey Long with a Louisiana Special Police badge. Take the infant to Manhattan, Kansas, in winter, where the only visitor is a Chinese Peeping Tom, little yellow face in the windows during the cold nights. Further frighten the mother, age twenty, with
child's convulsions. There's something "different" about this child, the doctors say.

4. **Limbo: A Memoir b**y A. Manette Ansay, 2001 – It's common for budding concert pianists to have to deal with physical pain as a result of their demanding practice, but the author, dedicated to music from her childhood, found herself coping with pain and muscular dysfunction that seemed to have another cause. Her exact illness has never been diagnosed, but it eventually put her in a wheelchair and made her give up her dream of becoming a musician. Instead, she put her gifted "ear" and imagination to use as a novelist, and they're also evident in this thoughtful and lovely memoir.

5. **Over My Head: A Doctor's Own Story of Head Injury from the Inside Looking Out** by Claudia L. Osborn, 1998 – Right at the beginning of the book, readers get a vivid picture of what the author's life was like after her brain was damaged — she shares her three-hour odyssey to get out of her friend's apartment in New York City and to an appointment just two-and-a-half miles away. With humor and precision, Osborn recounts what it was like to be an often-bewildered patient instead of the doctor she had been at the time of her fateful bicycle accident, and takes us through the process of her recovery.

6. **The Quiet Room: A Journey Out of the Torment of Madness** by Lori Schiller and Amanda Bennett, 1994 – As a seventeen-year-old girl with schizo-affective disorder, Schiller didn't know what was happening to her when she began to hear ominous voices inside her head. For several years she battled her illness on her own, and she spent much of her twenties in and out of mental hospitals. Then she started taking a newly developed medication that helped her turn her life around.

7. **The Story of My Life** by Helen Keller, 1903 – Helen Keller's story is familiar — scarlet fever destroyed both her vision and hearing when she was not yet two years old, but a dedicated teacher helped her learn to read and write — but it's well worth reading in her own words. She describes her earliest memories; the frustrations (and joys) of the years when she had almost no way to communicate with the people around her, or even the words to express reality to herself in thought; the elation of realizing what her new teacher was signing into her hand; and the exciting and difficult years that followed. The book is a testament to the transformative power of knowledge.

8. **Thinking in Pictures: And Other Reports from My Life with Autism** by Temple Grandin, 1995 – This book does a wonderful job of communicating what it's like to be autistic. Grandin is a scientist whose unique way of experiencing the world

has helped her develop widely used systems and equipment for humane livestock handling. She offers an astonishing glimpse of the world through the eyes of a sensitive, intelligent, and inventive woman.

9.   **An Unquiet Mind: A Memoir of Moods and Madness** by Kay Redfield Jamison, 1995 – Bipolar disorder, or manic depression, is often associated with brilliant creativity, but it can also cause anguish and destruction in the lives of those who suffer from it. Jamison's understanding of the disease is both professional (she's a psychiatrist) and personal (she is bipolar herself). This is her life story — a tale of unusual highs and lows and unusual insights.

10. **Waist-High in the World: A Life among the Non-Disabled** by Nancy Mairs, 1997 – Essayist and poet Nancy Mairs gives a sharp-witted and humorous account of her life as a woman confined to a wheelchair by multiple sclerosis. She discusses the joys and sorrows of her family life, our culture's stereotypes about crippled people, and even her stint as an undercover agent. It's a lively, thought-provoking book.

MEMOIRS
Medical Stories

Doctors are so notoriously busy, it's a wonder that they ever have time to write about their experiences. But some of them manage it, and they have fascinating stories to tell. These ten books, listed alphabetically, describe grueling years of study, life-and-death decisions made at a frenetic pace, the marvels of modern science, and the still greater marvels of the human body and spirit.

1.   **Complications: A Surgeon's Notes on an Imperfect Science** by Atul Gawande, 2002 – This book probes the scientific and ethical difficulties of medicine in the modern age, from the effectiveness of stomach stapling for weight loss to dealing with the nightmare of flesh-eating bacteria in a young patient's leg. A masterfully written, National Book Award finalist.

EXCERPT: COMPLICATIONS:

When you are in the operating room for the first time and see the surgeon press his scalpel to someone's body, you either shudder in horror or gape in awe. I gaped. It wasn't the blood and guts that enthralled me. It was the idea that a mere person would ever have the confidence to wield that scalpel. I wondered how the surgeon knew that all the steps would go as planned, that bleeding would be controlled and organs would not be injured. He didn't, but still he cut.

Later, I was allowed to make an incision myself. The surgeon drew a six-inch dotted line across the patient's abdomen and then, to my surprise, had the nurse hand me the knife. It was, I remember, still warm. I put the blade to the skin and cut. The experience was odd and addictive, mixing exhilaration, anxiety, a righteous faith that operating was somehow beneficial, and the slightly nauseating discovery that it took more force than I realized. The moment made me want to be a surgeon — someone with the assurance to proceed as if cutting were routine.

2. **Doctor Confidential: Secrets behind the Veil** by Richard Sheff, 2011 – Dr. Richard Sheff has more than three decades of experience practicing medicine, not only as a family physician but also as a hospital administrator and healthcare entrepreneur. In this series of autobiographical tales that reveal the various stages of his medical training, Dr. Sheff recounts his riveting and moving journey from doctor to healer — a man who understands the unique bond between the sick and those charged with making them well.

3. **God's Hotel: A Doctor, a Hospital and a Pilgrimage to the Heart of Medicine** by Victoria Sweet, 2012 – Dr. Victoria Sweet spent twenty years at San Francisco's Laguna Honda Hospital, a place of last resort for destitute people needing long-term care. Eventually, the hospital — "God's Hotel" — helps answer a question that has haunted Sweet ever since her first autopsy – what is it that makes the human body more than just a machine?

4. **Hot Lights, Cold Steel: Life, Death and Sleepless Nights in a Surgeon's First Years** by Michael J. Collins, 2005 – Heartwarming human connections, the gradual development of confidence, and some terrifying moments along the way in a surgeon's residency at the Mayo Clinic.

5. **The Intern Blues: The Timeless Classic About the Making of a Doctor** by Robert Marion, 1989 – This discussion of medical internship is based on the diaries kept by three young pediatric doctors whom the author advised during their yearlong internships at a busy, sometimes chaotic New York hospital.

6. **Love, Medicine and Miracles: Lessons Learned about Self-Healing from a Surgeon's Experience with Exceptional Patients** by Bernie S. Siegel, 1990 – A modern classic on the mind-body connection, this is a surgeon's account of the cancer-fighting power of optimism, love, and acceptance.

7. **My Stroke of Insight: A Brain Scientist's Personal Journey** by Jill Bolte Taylor, Ph.D., 2007 – When she suffered a devastating stroke that left her unable to talk, walk, read or write, Taylor was a thirty-seven-year-old brain scientist on track for a brilliant career. Over the course of her eight-year recovery, Taylor gradually realized that the key to inner peace lay in tapping into her right side of her brain, where she experienced a sense of euphoria and well-being — even as the left side of her brain was basically "nonfunctional."

8. **On Call: A Doctor's Days and Nights in Residency** by Emily R. Transue, 2004 – A compassionate recounting of the author's experiences with all kinds of patients over the course of three exhausting but emotionally rich years.

9. **Singular Intimacies : Becoming a Doctor at Bellevue** by Danielle Ofri, 2004 – From bewildered novice to experienced physician, Ofri chronicles her experiences at an inner-city hospital. She also examines her relationships with her colleagues and a close friend with a fatal medical condition.

10. **When the Air Hits Your Brain** by Frank T. Vertosick, 1996 – Neurosurgery is one of the most delicate and demanding specialties in medicine. This is a figurative look inside the mind of someone who has *literally* looked inside into the minds of many people, in a noble effort to save them from gunshot wounds, cancer, and other disasters.

MEMOIRS
Political Lives

Politicians — we see them on television holding press conferences and giving speeches, but it's often devilishly hard to get a sense of their inner lives. Luckily, many of the most influential politicians and political operatives have written autobiographies. Given the nature of the beast, we have to read them skeptically. In many cases, even a retired politician will succumb to the impulse for "spinning" the truth that helped him or her rise to prominence. Even so, these are fascinating reads about some of history's most interesting characters and what really goes on behind the scenes in high places.

1. **All Too Human: A Political Education** by George Stephanopoulos, 1999 – The author managed Bill Clinton's bumpy presidential campaign and served as a senior (albeit very young) advisor during Clinton's first term in office. He writes insightfully about Bill, Hillary, the vice president, and the other major players; the administration's internal rivalries; and the extreme stress of his crash course in high and low politics.

EXCERPT: ALL TOO HUMAN:

In the House, the personal is political and the political is personal. To know the House, you have to know the members—their home districts, their pet projects, their big contributors. You have to know what votes they'll throw away and which lines they'll never cross. You have to listen for the message in a throwaway line and laugh at the joke you've heard a thousand times. A personal feud might persist for decades, or an alliance could shift in a moment. The most fascinating part of the job was following those patterns, figuring out who held the key votes or which amendment would lock in a majority, watching the coalitions form, crack apart, and come together again.

2. **Decision Points** by George W. Bush, 2010 – Characteristically promising, as reported by the Associated Press, "an authoritarian [sic] voice saying exactly what happened" during his administration, Bush presents a terse, yet insightful memoir that captures the heat of presidential decision-making — split-second, life-or-death choices that almost always come bundled with incomplete information.

3. **Gandhi, An Autobiography: The Story of My Experiments With Truth** by Mohandas Karamchand Gandhi, 1927–1929 – Gandhi wrote this book two decades before India won its independence from Britain. It is not an exhaustive account of his political activities, but rather describes the development of the ethical ideas that led him to devote himself to justice by way of *satyagraha*, nonviolent resistance — the basis for his remarkable political achievements.

4. **Inside the Third Reich: Memoirs** by Albert Speer, 1970 – An architect and friend of Adolf Hitler, Speer held important positions in Hitler's government in the thirties and forties. It is still debated how much he knew about the regime's most heinous crimes (he himself served twenty years in prison after the Nuremburg tribunal), but this is a valuable firsthand look at the personality of the dictator and the inner workings of his totalitarian system.

5. **Long Walk to Freedom: The Autobiography of Nelson Mandela** by Nelson Mandela, 1994 Mandela helped form the African National Congress Youth League as a young man and went on to make immense sacrifices for the cause of ending apartheid. Learn about his long struggle against both the brutal and the subtle aspects of South Africa's racist system.

6. **Memoirs of the Second World War** by Winston S. Churchill, 1959 – If you don't have time for Churchill's six-volume *The Second World War*, read this abridgment. It describes the most dramatic conflict of the twentieth century from the perspective of the man who warned rallied his countrymen (along with international allies) for victory.

7. **My Life** by Bill Clinton, 2004 – Very little of Clinton's life and presidency seems to be left out of this detailed and energetic account. He describes his troubled but lively youth in Arkansas, the formation of his political ideas, and what it was really like to spend eight years in the Oval Office during an accomplished but scandal-ridden presidency.

8. **My Life: An Attempt at an Autobiography** by Leon Trotsky, 1930 – One of the early leaders of the Communist movement in Russia, Trotsky was later exiled by Stalin and ultimately murdered. Trotsky's intelligence and the drama of his story (two escapes from banishment in Siberia, negotiating Russia's separate peace at the

end of World War I, organizing the Red Army, and more) make this an extraordinary read.

9. **RN: The Memoirs of Richard Nixon** by Richard Milhous Nixon, 1978 – It's hard to think of Nixon without thinking of Watergate, but there was much more to his career than the scandal that brought his presidency down. His memoirs discuss the Alger Hiss controversy, the end of the Vietnam War, his administration's other diplomatic activities abroad, and the great scandal itself.

10. **True Compass: A Memoir** by Edward M. Kennedy, 2009 – The theme of this memoir, movingly demonstrated time and again, is that preserving your convictions, your "true compass," and working hard are the essence of a successful, and, if you're fortunate, transcendental life. Achingly frank about some of his most painful — and public — experiences, Kennedy tells a story of steely determination in a way no one else can.

MEMOIRS
Political Revolution Chronicles

Some of the most dramatic (and harrowing) passages in human history have taken place during times of political revolution. The United States owes its democracy to one such revolution, but many of them have not met with such success. In all too many cases, legitimate grievances have led to the overthrow of one oppressive regime, only to replace it with chaos or new forms of oppression. This alphabetical list comprises some firsthand accounts of life in revolutionary times — some by people who were more or less obscure, others by prominent people. By definition, of course, the subject matter of these memoirs is divisive; we can't claim all the authors are free from bias of one sort or another. But they all offer insight into very unusual times.

1. **An American Family in the Mexican Revolution** by Robert Woodmansee Herr; edited by Richard Herr, 1999 – Based on family documents, this is the story of American silver miners in Mexico during a period of tumultuous national politics, beginning during the presidency of Porfirio Díaz and continuing through several revolts and coups from 1911 into the twenties.

2. **Blessed by Thunder: Memoir of a Cuban Girlhood** by Flor Fernández Barrios, 1998 – The author was a small child when the Cuban revolution took place, but its repercussions affected her entire youth. Her father had political troubles — first for being suspected of pro-Castro sympathies, later for considering leaving the country after Castro's takeover — and she herself spent two years harvesting tobacco and sugar at a work camp while still a young girl.

3. **How We Survived Communism and Even Laughed** by Slavenka Drakulić, 1992 – A Croatian woman describes daily life before, during, and just after the 1989–90 revolution in Zagreb, prior to the ensuing civil war. It's an intelligent and sensitive look at the legacy of decades of Communism.

4. **Iran Awakening: A Memoir of Revolution and Hope** by Shirin Ebadi and Azadeh Moaveni, 2006 – A winner of the Nobel Peace Prize, Ebadi was Iran's first female judge. She originally had high hopes for the revolution that overthrew the unpopular shah in 1979, but found herself demoted by the theocratic regime because of her gender. However, she went on to become a prominent human rights attorney. This is a fascinating inside view of the Islamic revolution in Iran and its aftermath.

EXCERPT: IRAN AWAKENING:

The head-scarf "invitation" was the first warning that this revolution might eat its sisters, which was what women called one another while agitating for the shah's overthrow. Imagine the scene, just days after the revolution's victory. A man named Fathollah Bani-Sadr was appointed provisional overseer of the Ministry of Justice. Still flush with pride, a group of us chose a clear, breezy afternoon to descend on his office and congratulate him. We filed into the room, and many warm greetings and flowery congratulations were exchanged. Then Bani-Sadr's eyes fell on me. I expected he might thank me, or express how much it meant to him that a committed female judge such as myself had stood with the revolution.

Instead, he said, "Don't you think that out of respect for our beloved Imam Khomeini, who has graced Iran with his return, it would be better if you covered your hair?" I was shaken. Here we were, in the Ministry of Justice, after a great popular revolt had replaced an antique monarchy with a modern republic, and the new overseer of justice was talking about hair. Hair!

5. **Life and Death in Shanghai** by Nien Cheng, 1987 – When Mao Zedong's Cultural Revolution sent China into upheaval, the author became a target of persecution because she worked for a foreign company and was prosperous. While people all around her were intimidated into making false confessions (and accusations), she stood her ground. She spent several years in jail; after her release, she discovered that her daughter had died in custody. Although later freed, the author continued

to be harassed and was even knocked down in front of a bus. Throughout it all she maintained her sense of truth and dignity.

6. **Love and Struggle: My Life in SDS, the Weather Underground, and Beyond** by David Gilbert, 2011 – As a college student, Gilbert founded the Columbia University chapter of Students for a Democratic Society (SDS), then upped the ante on his political activities when he joined the Weather Underground, an organization dedicated to revolution. Written from behind prison bars where Gilbert has spent thirty years for his part in a botched 1981 Brinks armored-car robbery that resulted in the deaths of two police officers and a security guard, this riveting memoir is a forthright tale of one young man's immersion in radical politics during the turbulent sixties.

7. **The Memoirs of Madame Roland: A Heroine of the French Revolution** by Jeanne-Marie Roland de la Platière, 1795 – Madame Roland and her husband were prominent members of the Girondin Party during the French Revolution — a revolution that destroyed many of its own leaders. She ended up going to the guillotine, famously saying on the way, "O Liberty, what crimes are committed in thy name!" She wrote her memoirs during the months she spent in prison before her execution; they recount both her early life and her revolutionary years.

8. **Memoirs of a Revolutionary** by Victor Serge, 1951 – A remarkable writer, Serge shares the equally remarkable story of his political experiences in the first half of the twentieth century in Europe. He was an anarchist who originally supported the Russian Revolution but lived to see it turn into a brutal dictatorship. The book brings his turbulent times to life with great immediacy.

9. **The Revolutionary War Memoirs of General Henry Lee** by Henry Lee, 1812 – The father of Robert E. Lee, General Henry "Light-Horse Harry" Lee was an important military leader and politician — he was friends with George Washington and helped win the political battle for Virginia to ratify the Constitution. In 1808 and 1809 he was imprisoned for debts, and made good use of the time by writing this book.

10. **Tamil Tigress: My Story as a Child Soldier in Sri Lanka's Bloody Civil War** by Niromi de Soyza, 2012 – When she was a middle-class Tamil teenager, de Soyza joined the Tamil Tigers, the militant group that waged war in Sri Lanka for over three decades in an ultimately unsuccessful fight to create a separate nation for the Tamil people. In frank and clear-eyed prose, de Soyza describes her radicalization, her experience fighting with the Tigers in the Sri Lankan jungle and her eventual break from the group.

METAMORPHOSES
Startling Transformations in Classic Prose and Verse

One of the great delights of the literary arts is their ability to give form to dreams and fantasies. There is no limit to a writer's imagination, and a skillful writer can make the strangest things seem quite natural. A compelling theme in literature is that of transformation, or metamorphosis. One of the most famous tales of metamorphosis is Franz Kafka's novella by that name, but there are many others. Why do we like reading about these things, pleasant or unpleasant? Partly because they tickle our fancies, no doubt, and partly because we can identify with them on some level, even if most of the transformations we undergo are less dramatic. Here are five works of fiction, listed alphabetically, that depict some of the most amazing metamorphoses in prose and verse.

1. **Alice's Adventures in Wonderland** by Lewis Carroll, 1865 – A mushroom that makes you grow or shrink, courtiers who turn into a pack of playing cards, a fussy baby who turns into a pig, a queen who turns into a sheep — Carroll's beloved classic and its equally charming sequel, ***Through the Looking Glass***, are full of fantastical transformations. For full immersion in this world where precise logic mingles freely with utter nonsense, read the editions with the original illustrations by Sir John Tenniel.

EXCERPT: ALICE'S ADVENTURES IN WONDERLAND:

"What a curious feeling!" said Alice. "I must be shutting up like a telescope!" And so it was indeed: she was now only ten inches high, and her face brightened up at the thought that she was now the right size for going through the little door into that lovely garden. First, however, she waited for a few minutes to see if she was going to shrink any further: she felt a little nervous about this; "for it might end, you know," said Alice to herself, "in my going out altogether, like a candle. I wonder what I should be like then?" And she tried to fancy what the flame of a candle looks like after the candle is blown out, for she could not remember ever having seen such a thing.

2. **Don Quixote** by Miguel de Cervantes, 1605 and 1615 – In this Spanish masterpiece many people and things are transformed — windmills become threatening giants and an earthy peasant girl becomes a fine lady named Dulcinea —strictly in the hero's mind, of course, as he bravely acts upon his deluded convictions.

3. **Just So Stories** by Rudyard Kipling, 1902 – These imaginative tales of origins explain how the world changed from primordial times and became what it is today, with alphabets and wondrous beasts. For example, find out how a

misadventure on the banks of the "great grey-green, greasy Limpopo River" gave the elephant his long trunk.

4. **Metamorphoses** by Ovid, circa 8 AD – This beautiful collection of myths by one of Rome's great poets concerns "bodies changed to various forms." A girl fleeing the embraces of a god turns into a laurel tree; a nymph becomes fused with the boy she is amorously attacking, creating the hermaphrodite; a beloved sculpture, in the tale of Pygmalion, comes to life under its creator's caresses. The strange stories are told with such vividness that they have inspired centuries of artwork and literature.

5. **Orlando: A Biography** by Virginia Woolf, 1928 – Inspired by Woolf's friend Vita Sackville-West, this unusual novel follows the title character from Elizabethan England to the modern world of the twenties. The peculiarly long lifespan is not the only supernatural element in the book; Orlando begins as a male, but in his thirtieth year turns into a woman after a weeklong trance.

MUCKRAKING CLASSICS
Exposés Past and Present

Never at a loss to turn a colorful phrase, Teddy Roosevelt contributed such choice terms as "lunatic fringe" and "bully pulpit," among many others, to the American vernacular during his two terms as the twenty-sixth president of the United States. One of his most enduring terms — "muckraker," i.e., a man who rakes dung — was originally intended as a put-down of crusading investigative journalists like Ida Tarbell, whose exposé of the Standard Oil Company monopoly eventually led to the break-up of John D. Rockefeller's industrial giant. Over time, however, the term "muckraker" has become a term of honor for investigative journalists, much to the chagrin of the U.S. government and big business. Here are twelve classic exposés, listed alphabetically, from muckrakers past and present.

1. **All the President's Men** by Bob Woodward and Carl Bernstein, 1974 – Rightly called *the* political exposé of the twentieth century, *All the President's Men* is a thrilling account by the two *Washington Post* reporters who broke the Watergate scandal that forced President Nixon's resignation.

2. **The American Way of Death** by Jessica Mitford, 1963 – Prior to her death in 1996, Mitford revised and updated her mordantly funny exposé of the exploitative and greedy practices driving the United States funeral industry. Not for the squeamish — Mitford goes into grisly detail about embalming processes.

3. **A Century of Dishonor: The Classic Exposé of the Plight of the Native Americans** by Helen Hunt Jackson, 1881 – Disgusted by the U.S. government's callous mistreatment of Native Americans stretching back to the Revolutionary War,

Jackson poured her anger into this book, which she wrote while gravely ill. Initially ignored by Congress, *A Century of Dishonor* later helped spur the creation of the Indian Rights Association.

4. **Chain of Command: The Road from 9/11 to Abu Ghraib** by Seymour Hersh, 2004 – A blistering critique of the Bush administration's "War on Terror" from the veteran journalist, who reveals the intelligence failures and foreign policy decisions behind the U.S.-led invasion of Iraq.

5. **The Deal from Hell: How Moguls and Wall Street Plundered Great American Newspapers** by James O'Shea, 2011 – The slow death of print newspapers can be largely attributed to a series of misguided high-level decisions starting in the year 2000. That's the opinion of *Los Angeles Times* editor James O'Shea, who presents a behind-the-scenes look at the way senior executives brought down the very papers they were trying to save.

6. **Fast Food Nation** by Eric Schlosser, 2001 – The insidious grip of the fast food industry on Americans' wallets and waistlines is the all-too-timely subject of Schlosser's powerful and disturbing book that's been compared to *The Jungle*.

7. **The History of the Standard Oil Company: Briefer Version** by Ida Tarbell, 1904, edited by David M. Chalmers, 1993 – A condensed version of Tarbell's monumental, two-volume exposé that forever tarnished John D. Rockefeller's reputation and changed big business.

8. **How the Other Half Lives: Studies Among the Tenements of New York** by Jacob A. Riis, 1890 – This impassioned plea for social reform captures the squalor and despair of slum life for poverty-stricken immigrants in striking prose and photographs.

9. **The Jungle** by Upton Sinclair, 1906 – Sinclair's fictionalized exposé of the meat-packing industry depicts a Lithuanian immigrant's horrific experiences in a turn-of-the-century Chicago stockyard. Sinclair's graphic, stomach-churning novel led to the passage of the Meat Inspection Act and the Pure Food and Drug Act.

10. **Nickel and Dimed: On (Not) Getting By in America** by Barbara Ehrenreich, 2001 – Going undercover as one of the "working poor" for a few months, Ehrenreich gets a firsthand look at the struggles of unskilled labors to survive in today's economy.

11. **Reckless Endangerment: How Outsized Ambition, Greed, and Corruption Created the Worst Financial Crisis of Our Time** by Gretchen Morgenson and Joshua Rosner, 2011 – Pulitzer Prize-winning *New York Times* columnist Gretchen Morgenson, with co-author Joshua Rosner, presents her views on the causes of the 2007 economic meltdown, which she attributes to a perfect storm of Wall Street and Washington corruption and incompetence. The people trusted to safeguard the economy, she writes, were the ones who helped the collapse to occur.

As 2004 dawned, therefore, it had become more and more evident that the mortgage lending machine was sputtering. By midyear, Citigroup, Bear Stearns, and Morgan Stanley had all reported serious declines in their mortgage-backed securities deals. Lehman's volumes had fallen 35 percent from the previous year while Goldman Sachs's had plummeted by more than 70 percent. But instead of serving as a warning to the banks, this hiccup in loan origination only made them redouble their efforts in the subprime arena.

It was a moment of truth for Wall Street, an industry not known for veracity. The firms that had made so much money on the American dream of homeownership were faced with a decision. Recognizing that the easy money days were over, the firms knew that continuing down the path of big mortgage profits was going to require a more concerted effort, greater creativity. Wall Street, always at the ready for such duty, concocted new types of loans to be offered to borrowers as well as new entities that would buy them.

12. **Unsafe at Any Speed: The Designed-In Dangers of the American Automobile** by Ralph Nader, 1965 – The book that launched Nader's career as America's most influential consumer advocate provoked the wrath of General Motors for Nader's queries regarding car safety.

NATURE WRITING
At Home in the World

Save for either the ongoing strife in the Middle East or the economy, no issue probably generates more ink — or controversy — than the threat of global warming. If temperatures continue to rise unchecked, the environmental consequences could be very dire. Although there is considerable, often vehement disagreement in both the scientific and political communities as to the climate change worst-case scenarios, few, if any, would argue against the need to protect the environment and conserve resources.

In light of skyrocketing energy prices, plummeting clean air standards, and other ecological woes, perhaps it's time to return to the writings of naturalist/philosopher Henry David Thoreau, whose memoir *Walden; or, Life in the Woods* stresses the utmost importance of living in harmony with nature. An early classic of American nature writing, *Walden* has lost none of its relevance for contemporary readers. In a 2001 poll of readers conducted by The World at Home, a website devoted to promoting "ecological literacy," *Walden* came in second on the list of the ten best books about nature writing. Here is the list, per the website ranking, plus two recent titles deserving of mention.

1. **Desert Solitaire** by Edward Abbey, 1968 – Reviled and revered by environmentalists, Abbey is best known for his novel ***The Monkey Wrench Gang***, the purported inspiration for the militant Earth First! Organization. *Desert Solitaire* is Abbey's provocative and heartfelt meditation on the desolate beauty of Arches National Monument near Moab, Utah, where he worked for three years as a park ranger in the late fifties.

2. **Walden; or, Life in the Woods** by Henry David Thoreau, 1854 – Thoreau's memoir of the two years, two months, and two days he spent living alone in a cabin on Walden Pond outside Concord, Massachusetts is a landmark of nineteenth-century American letters.

3. **A Sand County Almanac** by Aldo Leopold, 1949 – A seminal text in the environmental movement, Leopold's illustrated collection of personal essays reveals how his work for the U.S. Forest Service informed his pro-conservation stance.

4. **Pilgrim at Tinker Creek** by Annie Dillard, 1974 – Winner of the 1975 Pulitzer Prize, Dillard's exquisitely written study of the everyday wonders of the natural world is a must-read. Keenly observed and spiritually satisfying, *Pilgrim at Tinker Creek* urges the reader to experience nature in all its amazing and sometimes terrible beauty.

5. **Silent Spring** by Rachel Carson, 1962 – A polarizing book to this day, Carson's influential best-seller sent a shock wave through the scientific and industrial community with its claims about the harmful effects of pesticides.

6. **Arctic Dreams: Imagination and Desire in a Northern Landscape** by Barry Lopez, 1986 – During a five-year period, Lopez made several trips into the farthest reaches of the Arctic to study the wildlife and Eskimo culture. The result is a magnificent book of grace and sensitivity that deservedly won the National Book Award.

7. **Refuge: An Unnatural History of Family and Place** by Terry Tempest Williams, 1991 – In elegiac and deeply moving prose, Utah writer/activist Williams draws a haunting parallel between the decline of bird populations around the Great Salt Lake, and her mother's and grandmother's death from cancer, which may have been caused by radioactive fallout from nuclear testing in the fifties and sixties.

8. **New and Selected Poems: Volume One** by Mary Oliver, 1992 – Luminous poems celebrating nature from Oliver, who won the National Book Award for this astonishing collection of her work, much of it inspired by the flora and fauna of Cape Cod.

9. **The Solace of Open Spaces** by Gretel Ehrlich, 1985 – Leaving the city for the vastness of Wyoming, poet/naturalist Ehrlich found emotional and spiritual succor in ranch life, which she describes in this radiant memoir.

10. **The Outermost House: A Year of Life on the Great Beach of Cape Cod** by Henry Beston, 1928 – As invigorating as a blast of Atlantic sea air, Beston's utterly captivating and transcendently beautiful memoir is one of the most beloved works of nature writing in American literary history.

CONTEMPORARY TITLES

11. **Cabin Fever: A Suburban Father's Search for the Wild** by Tom Montgomery Fate, 2011 – Clearly influenced by Henry David Thoreau's *Walden* — but with a modern-day, minivan-driving, text-messaging twist — the author of this collection of essays, a professor, husband, and father of three, searches for "a more deliberate life" than he has in suburban Chicago by living part-time in a cabin tucked into the Michigan woods. Directed at suburbanites, these essays provide lyrical insights into our relationships with nature, technology, and each other.

12. **Fire Season: Field Notes from a Wilderness Lookout** by Philip Connors, 2011 – Connors walked away from an editing job at *The Wall Street Journal* to work as one of the few remaining fire lookouts in America, spending six months in a tower overlooking remote New Mexico forests. Following in the footsteps of poet Gary Snyder, environmental advocate Edward Abbey and beat novelist Jack Kerouac, all of whom undertook similar stints watching for signs of smoke, this book is a compact and frequently poetic meditation on solitude and the austere beauty of the wilderness. Winner of the 2011 National Outdoor Book Award.

EXCERPT: FIRE SEASON:

It is a world of extremes. Having spent each fire season for nearly a decade in my little glass-walled perch, I've become acquainted with the look and feel of the border highlands each week of each month, from April through August: the brutal gales of spring, when a roar off the desert gusts over seventy miles an hour and the occasional snow squall turns my peak white; the dawning of summer in late May, when the wind abates and the aphids hatch and ladybugs emerge in great clouds from their hibernation; the fires of June, when dry lightning connects with the hills, sparking smokes that fill the air with the sweet smell of burning pine; the tremendous storms of July, when the thunder makes me flinch as if from the threat of a punch; and the blessed indolence of August, when the meadows bloom with wildflowers and the creeks run again, the rains having turned my world a dozen different shades of green. I've seen fires burn so hot they made their own weather; I've watched deer and elk frolic in the meadow below me and pine trees explode in a blue ball of smoke. If there's a better job anywhere on the planet, I'd like to know about it.

NEW YORK CITY BOOKS
New York Times' Ten Best about the Big Apple

On February 5, 1995, Sam Roberts published an article in the *New York Times* introducing a suggested "canon" of books about New York City. With apparent pride in New Yorkers' opinionated and individualistic spirit, he admitted that residents are certain to take issue with the list. In any case, each of the ten selections will help you understand one facet of the lively, contradictory, creative metropolis that is one of history's great cities. Here they are, per his ranking, plus two more recent titles worthy of mention.

1. **The Power Broker: Robert Moses and the Fall of New York** by Robert A. Caro, 1975 – This is a biography of "master builder" of New York City, who managed to transform the political and physical landscape of the city, despite the objections of the city's residents and even its leaders.

2. **The Bonfire of the Vanities** by Tom Wolfe, 1987 – A classic satire of yuppie-era New York, when greed and conspicuous consumption ran amok, Wolfe's novel follows a wealthy stockbroker's descent from his own world of entitlement and complacency into scandal and disgrace.

3. **Beyond the Melting Pot: The Negroes, Puerto Ricans, Jews, Italians, and Irish of New York City** by Nathan Glazer and Daniel P. Moynihan, 1963 – This is an analysis of the power of ethnicity in New York politics and daily life, arguing against the idea that immigrants to the city quickly assimilate into a homogeneous whole.

4. **The WPA Guide to New York City: The Federal Writers' Project Guide to 1930s New York** by the Federal Writers Project, 1939 – Much in the city has changed since the *Works Progress Administration Guide* was originally published, but it's still a wonderfully evocative source of information about the diversions, institutions, and atmosphere of the city in the thirties.

5. **Manchild in the Promised Land** by Claude Brown, 1965 – The autobiography of a young black man describes his childhood in Harlem and how he survived the destructive forces all around him.

6. **The Great School Wars: New York City: A History of the New York City Public Schools** by Diane Ravitch, 1974 – There is a long history of conflicts between the people running the public school system in New York and the families it serves. Ravitch's book is a thoughtful account of these "wars" and the reasons behind them.

7. **Down These Mean Streets** by Piri Thomas, 1967 – Based on the author's youth in East Harlem, *Down These Mean Streets* paints a picture of the hardships and joys of life in the Hispanic ghetto.

8. **World of Our Fathers: The Journey of the East European Jews to America and the Life They Found and Made** by Irving Howe, 1976 – From Eastern Europe to the New World, from immigrant to first-generation offspring, and from city to suburbs, the Jewish New Yorkers Howe writes about have undergone sometimes difficult transformations in this city of constant change. Called a "marvelous narrative" by the *New York Times Book Review*, *World of Our Fathers* received the National Book Award.

9. **Time and Again** by Jack Finney, 1970 – Part novel, part charming picture book, this is the story of a modern New Yorker who travels back in time to the nineteenth century and explores his home city anew.

10. **Here Is New York** by E.B. White, 1949 – The man who wrote so movingly of the delights of being a pig in a quiet, cozy barn in **Charlotte's Web** writes equally movingly here of the noisy, crowded, passionate island of Manhattan.

CONTEMPORARY TITLES

11. **Just Kids** by Patti Smith, 2010 – Smith's National Book Award winner is a love story and memoir of her relationship with the late photographer Robert Mapplethorpe, forged when she was just twenty-one. The delightful and moving tale that the punk goddess weaves is not merely about a young couple in the big city, but about New York itself and the art, literary, and music scenes there during a golden epoch, when it felt like it was possible to stumble onto something magical on the boardwalk at Coney Island, in the lobby of the Chelsea Hotel or onstage at Max's Kansas City or CBGB.

EXCERPT: JUST KIDS:

I had often come to this area of the Bowery to visit William Burroughs, who lived a few blocks south of the club, in a place called the Bunker. It was the street of winos and they would often have fires going in large cylindrical trash cans to keep warm, to cook, or light their cigarettes. You could look down the Bowery and see these fires glowing right to William's door, just as we did on that chilly but beautiful Easter night.

CBGB was a deep and narrow room with a bar along the right side, lit by overhanging neon signs advertising various brands of beer. The stage was low, on the left-hand side, flanked by photographic murals of turn-of-the-century bathing belles. Past the stage was a pool table, and in back was a greasy kitchen and a room where the owner, Hilly Krystal, worked and slept with his saluki, Jonathan.

12. **Lush Life** by Richard Price, 2008 – A bartender's murder is the jumping off point for a gripping portrait of a world in flux. Housing projects still dot the Lower East Side, but the neighborhood that was once primarily the home of working-class immigrant families has gentrified at a terrifying rate to become the playground for well-off hipsters. These disparate groups collide in Price's closely observed novel, which is less about crime that it is about social upheaval in New York at the dawn of a new century. "It's ***The Bonfire of the Vanities*** 2.0," wrote Kyle Smith in *The Wall Street Journal*.

THE NEW YORKER
CONTRIBUTORS' BOOKS
Books by Parker, Thurber & Co.

In 1925, *The New Yorker* magazine founder/editor Harold Ross summed up his vision for the fledgling magazine in the following, oft-quoted prospectus: "*The New Yorker* will be a reflection in word and picture of metropolitan life … It is not edited for the old lady in Dubuque." To realize his dream of publishing a sophisticated, urbane weekly dedicated to culture and current events, Ross hired many charter members of the legendary Algonquin Round Table as contributors. While Dorothy Parker, S. J. Perelman and James Thurber brought their wit to the pages of *The New Yorker*, journalists and essayists like Joseph Mitchell and E. B. White regularly contributed articles on the unique flavor and idiosyncratic characters of the Big Apple. Later, during World War II, *The New Yorker* would gain international renown for its war reportage; Ross devoted an entire issue to John Hersey's *Hiroshima*.

Today, nearly ninety years after Ross incurred the wrath of little old ladies in Dubuque, the pages of *The New Yorker* now feature the essays and articles of such literary lights as Woody Allen, Susan Orlean (***The Orchid Thief***) and David Sedaris. Here are twelve books, listed alphabetically, by some of the most famous of *The New Yorker* contributors.

1. **Here at The New Yorker** by Brendan Gill, 1997 – No tell-all, Gill's affectionate yet irreverent memoir of his sixty years at *The New Yorker* is a treasure trove of colorful anecdotes about the magazine and some of its most famous contributors.

2. **Hiroshima** by John Hersey, 1946 – Ross devoted an entire issue of *The New Yorker* to Hersey's stunning, four-part account of the atomic bomb blast that decimated this Japanese city.

3. **The Insanity Defense: The Complete Prose** by Woody Allen, 2007 — A compendium of Allen's bestselling works: ***Getting Even***, ***Without Feathers*** and

Side Effects. Allen waxes witty on everything from death to dribble glasses. A must-have for any fan of the neurotic comedy genius.

EXCERPT: THE INSANITY DEFENSE: "THE METTERLING LISTS":

Venal & Sons has at last published the long-awaited first volume of Metterling's laundry lists (The Collected Laundry Lists of Hans Metterling, Vol. I, 437 pp., plus xxxii-page introduction; indexed; $18.75), with an erudite commentary by the noted Metterling scholar Gunther Eisenbud. The decision to publish this work separately, before the completion of the immense four-volume oeuvre, is both welcome and intelligent, for this obdurate and sparkling book will instantly lay to rest the unpleasant rumors that Venal & Sons, having reaped rich rewards from the Metterling novels, play, and notebooks, diaries, and letters, was merely in search of continued profits from the same lode. How wrong the whisperers have been!

4. **Joe Gould's Secret** by Joseph Mitchell, 1965 – A compassionate, haunting portrait of an eccentric, downtrodden Greenwich village character, whose claims of writing the definitive oral history of New York turned out to be bogus.

5. **Higher Gossip: Essays and Criticism** by John Updike, 2012 — When Updike died in 2009, he left behind this collection of nonfiction pieces whose subjects range from religion and faith to *Peanuts* comics. The writer worried he might have been losing his power, but his writing proves as compelling as ever.

6. **Most of the Most of S.J. Perelman** by S. J. Perelman, 2000 – A side-splittingly funny collection of Perelman's writings from 1930 to 1958. When not penning essays for *The New Yorker*, Perelman wrote screenplays for the Marx Brothers.

7. **One Man's Meat** by E. B. White, 1941– Best known for his classic children's books ***Charlotte's Web*** and ***Stuart Little,*** White also wrote some of *The New Yorker's* most memorable essays. *One Man's Meat* is a witty and sharply observed collection of essays about life at a Maine saltwater farm.

8. **Paris Was Yesterday, 1925 -1939** by Janet Flanner, 1972 – For fifty years, Flanner wrote *The New Yorker's* "Letter from Paris" feature. This collection of her articles takes the reader on a glittering tour of the City of Lights, with frequent stops to the watering holes and salons of the "Lost Generation."

9. **A Piece of My Mind: Reflections at Sixty** by Edmund Wilson, 1956 – The literary critic writes brilliantly about everything from religion to Communism to evolution in this provocative book.

10. **The Portable Dorothy Parker** by Dorothy Parker, 2006 – More "fresh hell" from the endlessly quotable Algonquin Round Table wit, whose verse, short stories and essays crackle with wit and gimlet-eyed intelligence in this updated edition.

11. **The Road Back to Paris** by A. J. Liebling, 1944 – Wartime dispatches from England, France, and North Africa from the masterful journalist.
12. **The Thurber Carnival** by James Thurber, 1945 – A priceless collection of Thurber's essays, short stories and sketches for *The New Yorker*.

NINETEENTH CENTURY NOVELS
Joanna Trollope's Favorites

Both a literary and *literal* descendent of the great Victorian-era novelist Anthony Trollope, English author Joanna Trollope typically focuses on the everyday lives of middle-class English families in such novels as **The Rector's Wife** and **Next of Kin**. Her frequent choice of subject matter mirrors her passion for the realistic classics of nineteenth century literature like George Eliot's *Middlemarch*, which weaves together the disparate stories of several English villagers into a brilliantly nuanced epic narrative. Famously hailed by Virginia Woolf as "one of the few English novels written for grown up people," *Middlemarch* is truly a monumental achievement in literary realism that Trollope named her favorite nineteenth century novel. Here are Trollope's ten favorites, as she ranked them for the British newspaper *The Guardian*.

1. **Middlemarch** by George Eliot, 1871 – Trapped in a loveless marriage to a pompous clergyman, an intelligent and passionate young woman struggles to find happiness in the provincial village of Middlemarch. Eliot skillfully juxtaposes the heroine's search for true love against the experiences of friends and family in what Trollope calls "a marvelous portrait of nineteenth century provincial life."
2. **The Last Chronicle of Barset** by Anthony Trollope, 1867 – Trollope concluded his renowned **Chronicles of Barsetshire** literary sextet with this remarkably even-handed portrait of a proud and mercurial curate whose mounting debts bring him and his family to the brink of ruin. Joanna Trollope pronounces *The Last Chronicle of Barset* "a masterpiece."
3. **Persuasion** by Jane Austen, 1818 - The ubiquitous Austen's last novel, published two years after her untimely death at the age of forty-two-years-old, is another gem of love story about a woman pining for the man she rejected seven years earlier. Trollope calls *Persuasion* as "a subtle and elegiac novel — more heartfelt than some of her earlier romances."

EXCERPT: PERSUASION:
A few years before, Anne Elliot had been a very pretty girl, but her bloom had vanished early; and as even in its height, her father had found little to admire in her, (so totally different were her delicate features and mild dark eyes from his

own), there could be nothing in them, now that she was faded and thin, to excite his esteem.

4. **Vanity Fair** by William Makepeace Thackeray, 1848 – With cunning, guile and bewitching charm, Becky Sharp claws her way into the rarefied world of English society during the Napoleonic Wars era. Subtitled "A Novel Without a Hero," *Vanity Fair* skewers the snobbery and hypocrisy endemic to English society in a sprawling narrative that Trollope praises as "sharp, brilliant, touching, clever and cruel."

5. **The Mayor of Casterbridge** by Thomas Hardy, 1886 – A fatalist with a singularly gloomy perspective, Hardy set this novel and many others in the fictitious county of Wessex, England. In this emotionally wrenching story — "a tale of true tragedy," per Trollope — the title character's alcoholism hastens his downfall.

6. **The Moonstone** by Wilkie Collins, 1868 – A young woman inherits a fabled Indian diamond, the Moonstone, which is stolen the night of her eighteenth birthday in Collins' epistolary novel. Most critics point to this convoluted yarn with multiple narrators and ample red herrings as the first modern English detective novel. As for Trollope, she calls *The Moonstone* "a great, bold, theatrical mystery."

7. **Bleak House** by Charles Dickens, 1852-1853 – First published in serial form, Dickens' sweeping novel depicts an epic legal battle that ensnarls the lives of a cast of characters in a book that Trollope says "has everything — joy, grief, success, failure, wealth, poverty, comedy, tragedy."

8. **North and South** by Elizabeth Gaskell, 1854 – Championed by Dickens, Gaskell wrote ghost stories, a biography of Charlotte Brontë and novels set in the industrialized north of England. In *North and South*, Gaskell examines the plight of the working class in what Trollope describes as "a really remarkable picture of the reality…of northern industrial life."

9. **The Portrait of a Lady** by Henry James, 1881 – The sole book by an American author on Trollope's list, *The Portrait of a Lady* follows an independent-minded American heiress encountering her "destiny" abroad, where she falls prey to the scheming of fellow expatriates. Alluding to James' psychologically astute use of interior monologue, Trollope finds *The Portrait of a Lady* "subtle and sophisticated."

10. **Rob Roy** by Sir Walter Scott, 1818 – The literary antithesis of *The Portrait of a Lady, Rob Roy* is a grand, larger-than-life yarn loosely based on the eighteenth century Scottish folk hero Rob Roy MacGregor. While not a critical darling like the other books on her list, *Rob Roy* earns Trollope's admiration as "a true adventure story."

PEN NAMES
Famous Noms de Plume

Les Krantz, the publisher of this book, once wrote a book, *Light Your House with Potatoes*, under the name Jay Kaye. In fact, you might be surprised by how many of the items on the shelves of your local bookstore are credited to people who technically don't exist. There are lots of reasons for writers to use pseudonyms, or pen names: to exchange an unwieldy name for something snappier; to evade prejudice by disguising ethnicity or gender; or to express controversial opinions from the safety of anonymity. *Noms de plume* are a rich tradition in literature and politics. *The Federalist Papers* (1787–1788) were originally published in New York newspapers under the dignified pseudonym Publius; its real authors were Alexander Hamilton, James Madison, and John Jay.

Listed alphabetically by pen name, here are twelve writers whose real names don't appear on book covers.

1. **Lewis Carroll** – The real name of the author of *Alice's Adventures in Wonderland* (1865) was Charles Lutwidge Dodgson.
2. **Joseph Conrad** – The author of *Heart of Darkness* (1902) and *Lord Jim* (1900) was born Jozef Teodor Konrad Nalecz Korzeniowski.
3. **George Eliot** – The pen name is very masculine, but the author of *The Mill on the Floss* (1860) and *Middlemarch* (1872) was really Mary Ann Evans.
4. **Pablo Neruda** – The author of *Twenty Love Poems and a Song of Despair* (1924, translated 1969), the great Chilean poet was really named Ricardo Eliecer Neftalí Reyes Basoalto.
5. **George Orwell** – The real name of the author of *Homage to Catalonia* (1938), *Animal Farm* (1945), and *1984* (1949) was Eric Arthur Blair.
6. **J. D. Robb** – Romance novelist Nora Roberts took this pseudonym for her "In Death" crime series, which includes *Portrait in Death* (2003) and *Promises in Death* (2009).
7. **George Sand** – The author of *Indiana* (1832) and *Lelia* (1833) and lover of both the writer Alfred de Musset and the composer Frédéric Chopin was actually named Amandine-Aurore-Lucile Dupin. In addition to using a male pseudonym, she shocked society by dressing as a man.
8. **Dr. Seuss** – The whimsical writer and illustrator of *The Cat in the Hat* (1957), *The Sneetches and Other Stories* (1961) and *Oh, the Places You'll Go!* (1990) was *Mr.* Theodor Seuss Geisel in everyday life.
9. **Mark Twain** – The real name of the man who spun the great American yarns *The Adventures of Tom Sawyer* (1876) and *The Adventures of Huckleberry Finn* (1884) was Samuel Langhorne Clemens.

10. **Barbara Vine** – The prolific British crime writer Ruth Rendell has written such novels as *__A Dark Adapted Eye__* (1986) and *__The Child's Child__* (2012) under this pseudonym.
11. **Voltaire** – The single-word name is very grand, but the author of the novel *__Candide__* (1759) and various plays and philosophical treatises was named François-Marie Arouet in real life.
12. **Nathanael West** – The true name of the author of *__The Day of the Locust__* (1939) was Nathan Wallenstein Weinstein.

PHOTOGRAPHY COLLECTIONS
Capturing the World for Posterity

Photography revolutionized the way we see the world. The "mechanical eye" has allowed us to share visual reality (or some version of it) with people thousands of miles away, recording great moments in human history, fleeting moments of light over a seascape, and every wrinkle of a single person's face for posterity. Whether you are an amateur photographer looking for inspiration or you just want something fascinating for your coffee table, these twelve books, listed alphabetically, provide a wealth of stunning images to contemplate.

1. __100 Photographs That Changed the World__ by the editors of *Life Magazine*, 2003 – This collection brings together indelible images in four categories: "The Arts," "Society," "War and Peace," and "Science and Nature." From wartime Normandy and Iwo Jima to the Beatles arriving in the United States, these remarkable — sometimes shocking — photos will grab your attention.
2. __The American Wilderness__ by Ansel Adams, edited by Andrea Stillman, 1990 – Ansel Adams produced awe-inspiring landscapes, capturing the grandeur of mountains and clouds and the shimmering beauty of trees in leaf. This volume offers large, fine reproductions of his work, along with some of the artist's writings on conservation.
3. __Believing is Seeing: Observations on the Mysteries of Photography__ by Errol Morris, 2011 – Selected by the *New York Times Book Review* as a Notable Book of the Year, this collection, selected by the Academy Award-winning documentarian, explores the nature of truth and deception in photography. Each essay poses a question and asks the reader to reflect upon a photograph — depicting events as disparate as the Crimean War and the Israeli bombing of a Lebanese apartment building — and the reality it supposedly represents. Philosophical and provocative, this book is intelligent reading in an age of Photoshop.
4. __Earth from Above__ by Yann Arthus-Bertrand, 2002 – Unless you have your own private helicopter, you'd be unlikely to see any of these amazing sights on your

own. The complex interactions of land, sea, plants, animals, and humans are spread out in front of your eyes in rich and vivid color.

5. **Golden States of Grace: Prayers of the Disinherited** by Rick Nahmias, 2010 – An acclaimed social documentarian, Nahmias (***The Migrant Project: Contemporary California Farmworkers***) turn his compassionate lens on eleven marginalized religious communities in California. His haunting black-and-white photographs capture everything from a transsexual gospel choir to rural Pentecostal congregations to a Buddhist community in San Quentin.

6. **L'Amour Fou: Photography and Surrealism** by Rosalind Krauss, Dawn Ades, and Jane Livingston, 1985 – Long before digital cameras gave amateurs the ability to manipulate their pictures at will, the surrealists of the twenties and thirties were creating strange and dreamlike images that blended eroticism and the bizarre. This relatively small volume with its photos by Brassaï, Man Ray, Salvador Dalí, and others provide a field day for a Freudian analyst — or for a photography lover interested in the outer boundaries of the form.

7. **The Photography Book** by the editors of Phaidon Press, 1997 – This impressive book provides a sort of survey course (though not in chronological order) on the history of photography. Five hundred photographers are each represented by one work, with a net effect of stunning diversity and endless surprises.

8. **Richard Avedon Portraits** by Richard Avedon, Mia Fineman, Maria Morris Hambourg and Philippe de Montebello, 2002 – Half a century of portraits of creators and celebrities, from painters to movie stars, are brought together in this stylish book. Whether you are interested in the personalities or in the artistic medium, you will find this an absorbing collection.

9. **Through the Lens: National Geographic Greatest Photographs** edited by Leah Bendavid-Val, 2003 – Pick up any issue of *National Geographic* magazine and you're likely to find several photographs that wow you. Here are 250 of the very best of the renowned magazine's images, running the gamut from breathtaking outer space photographs to the iconic portrait of a young Afghan refugee with piercing green eyes.

10. **Vivian Maier: Out of the Shadows** edited by Richard Cahan and Michael Williams, 2012 – A professional nanny, Maier took more than 100,000 photographs of street life, primarily in Chicago, from the fifties through the nineties. Yet no one knew of her work until 2007, when a Chicago historian purchased a box of her negatives at an auction house. Although Maier died in 2009, she is now regarded as one of the all-time great street photographers. *Vivian Maier: Out of the Shadows* features 300 of her most striking images, along with fascinating biographical information about the intensely private photographer.

11. **Women** by Annie Leibovitz and Susan Sontag, 1999 – Leibovitz is a famed celebrity photographer, but this book is not restricted to portraits of the stars. It

also depicts ordinary women in a remarkable variety of roles, ranging from coal miner to school teacher.

12. **A Year in Photography: Magnum Archive** by the editors of Magnum Photos, 2010 – Created by an international photography cooperative, this book contains 365 photos — hence the title — taken by seventy of the world's greatest photojournalists, both living and dead. All corners of the planet receive attention, as do events both large and small over a seventy-year span of time. Demonstrating curiosity about and a compassion for the human condition, each photo is accompanied by reflections, dates and notes.

POET LAUREATES
Library of Congress Appointees, 2000 – Present

Each year, the Library of Congress appoints a notable poet to the position of Poet Laureate Consultant in Poetry. Each poet laureate gives an annual lecture and reading and create events and programs to bring poetry to a wider public. Robert Pinsky, for example, created the "Favorite Poem Project," soliciting readers all across the country for their favorite poems and collecting them into an anthology. Here is a list of our poet laureates since 2000, along with some collections of their works.

2000–2001: Stanley Kunitz - Collections include *Selected Poems 1928–1958* (1958), *The Testing-Tree* (1971), and *Passing Through: The Later Poems, New and Selected* (1985).

2001–2003: Billy Collins - Collections include *The Art of Drowning* (1995), *Picnic, Lightning* (1998), and *Sailing Alone Around the Room: New ad Selected Poems* (2001).

2003–2004: Louise Glück - Collections include *Firstborn* (1968), *Descending Figure* (1980), and *The Wild Iris* (1992).

2004–2005: Ted Kooser - Collections include *Sure Signs* (1980), *One World at a Time* (1985), and *Delights and Shadows* (2004).

2006-2007: Donald Hall - Collections include *The Old Life* (1996), *The Painted Bed* (2002) and *The Back Chamber* (2011).

2007-2008: Charles Simic – Collections include *The World Doesn't End: Prose Poems* (1990 Pulitzer Prize for Poetry), *The Voice at 3:00 A.M.: Selected Late and New Poems* (2006) and *Master of Disguises* (2010).

2008-2010: Kay Ryan – Collections include *Flamingo Watching* (1994), *Say Uncle* (2000) and *The Best of It: New and Selected Poems* (2010).

2010-2011: W. S. Merwin - Collections include *Present Company* (2005), *Migration: New and Selected Poems* (2007 National Book Award) and *The Shadow of Sirius* (2009 Pulitzer Prize for Poetry).

2011-2012: Philip Levine - Collections include ***What Work Is*** (1991 National Book Award) ***The Simple Truth*** *(*1995 Pulitzer Prize for Poetry*)* and ***The Mercy*** *(*1999).
2012-2013: **Natasha Trethewey** – Collections include ***Domestic Work*** (2000), ***Native Guard: Poems*** (2007 Pulitzer Prize for Poetry) and ***Thrall*** (2012).

POLITICAL NOVELS
Corruption, Conspiracies and Cronyism

Drawing upon a seemingly bottomless well of cynicism, H.L. Mencken, aka the "Sage of Baltimore," passed scathing judgment on all facets of American culture in essays and reviews that cut to the marrow. Turning his jaundiced gaze on the American political landscape, he famously quipped, "Democracy is the art and science of running the circus from the monkey-cage."

Mencken's withering assessment of politics certainly resonates in many of the following novels, listed alphabetically, which depict the American political system on the local and national level as rife with corruption, conspiracies and cronyism. It's enough to put the "Founding Fathers" on the spin cycle in their graves!

1. **Advise and Consent** by Allan Drury, 1959 – To ease cold war tensions with the Soviet Union, a sickly U.S. president nominates a former Communist party official to be the Secretary of State. Drury's Pulitzer Prize-winning classic was inspired by the experiences of Alger Hiss, the U.S. Department of State official accused of being a Communist spy in 1948.

2. **All the King's Men** by Robert Penn Warren, 1946 – Warren's monumental account of the rise and dizzying fall of charismatic Louisiana governor Willie Stark draws brilliantly from the real-life story of populist legend Governor Huey Long, aka "The Kingfisher."

3. **American Wife** by Curtis Sittenfeld, 2008 – Often called "the Laura Bush book," Sittenfeld's not-so-thinly veiled portrait of the former First Lady was alternately praised and panned by critics and Bush supporters, respectively.

4. **Democracy: An American Novel** by Henry Adams, 1880 – A lively and caustically observed satire that skewers the rich and power-hungry who scheme and claw their way to the top of the political food chain.

5. **Echo House** by Ward Just, 1997 – A finalist for the National Book Award, *Echo House* is a masterfully drawn, century-spanning family saga about three generations of political dynasty.

EXCERPT: ECHO HOUSE:
They've got him now, Willy said. They've got his actual language, the language of a race-baiting roughneck. And that will become the issue. He's finished. Washington cannot abide the common speech, the words that people actually use,

the petty evasions and nuance and exaggeration and resentment and hatred of the other. They want all Presidents to talk like Lincoln or FDR. They want words you can chisel in marble. He's let them down, you see. Just as they knew he always would. Poor bastard; they'll ride him out of town on a rail. It's a matter of revenge, Willy said. So they can think better of themselves.

6. **The Last Hurrah** by Edwin O'Connor, 1956 – Determined to go out with a bang, not a whimper, wily Boston Mayor Frank Skeffington launches his final reelection bid in O'Connor's compelling novel about the Irish political machine in Beantown.

7. **The Manchurian Candidate** by Richard Condon, 1959 – A doozy of a cold war-era conspiracy thriller about a brainwashed assassin targeting a presidential candidate.

8. **Primary Colors** by Anonymous, 1996 – Barely veiled roman à clef about Bill Clinton's 1992 presidential campaign is a sophisticated, witty and penetrating novel from "Anonymous," aka Joe Klein, a longtime Washington, D.C. journalist.

9. **Protect and Defend** by Richard North Patterson, 2000 – Taking a break from legal thrillers, Patterson tackles the hot-button topic of abortion in this gripping, densely plotted novel about a recently elected president facing the political fight of his career.

10. **Wag the Dog** by Larry Beinhart, 1995 – Uproariously funny, razor-edged political satire about the *extreme* lengths spin doctors will go to when a president is caught in a very compromising situation.

11. **Washington, D.C.: A Novel** by Gore Vidal, 1967 – Vidal concludes his six-volume Narratives of Empire series of novels with this acutely observed, unsparing overview of the American political scene from the Depression through World War II.

12. **Watergate** by Thomas Mallon, 2012 – Mallon's ambitious and darkly funny reimagining of the biggest American political scandal of all time was hailed by the *New York Times* as "a stealth bulls-eye of a political novel."

POLITICAL SCIENCE BOOKS
The Globalization Debate

More than at any other time in history, our world is interconnected — in terms of security, the economy, climate, and culture — and this raises all kinds of difficult issues. Can liberal democracy succeed in traditionally authoritarian countries? Are the West and the Muslim worlds doomed to endless conflict? How will rapid advances in communications affect the economy? Should we take responsibility for preventing atrocities in other nations? Here are eleven books, listed alphabetically, that tackle these questions and more, illuminating the dangers and opportunities of the contemporary world.

1. **The Clash of Civilizations and the Remaking of World Order** by Samuel P. Huntington, 1996 – The author argues that the religious, ethnic, and cultural sentiments of a few distinct civilizations will replace ideological concerns (such as capitalism vs. socialism) as the main source of international conflict in the post–cold war era.

2. **The End of History and the Last Man** by Francis Fukuyama, 1992 – Fukuyama argues that capitalist democracy will take hold in most of the world's countries, spreading prosperity and stability and eliminating many of the sources of international conflict. While 9/11 and its aftermath have made his thesis seem less convincing now than in 1992, the yearning for democracy remains a major force even in the most troubled parts of the world.

3. **The Future of Freedom: Illiberal Democracy at Home and Abroad** by Fareed Zakaria, 2003 – Why have some democracies self-destructed, while others remain stable and free? Zakaria argues that democracy rarely survives without the development of liberal institutions such as free markets and the rule of law — and sometimes these institutions have to come first.

4. **Getting Better: Why Global Development is Succeeding—And How We Can Improve the World Even More** by Charles Kenny, 2011 – Despite increasing wealth disparities, globalization has, for the most part, improved the quality of life in even the most depressed corners of the planet, Written by a senior economist at the World Bank, *Getting Better* makes its case by critically surveying the purported causes of economic growth.

5. **Globalization and Its Discontents** by Joseph E. Stiglitz, 2002 – A Nobel Prize winner in Economics, Stiglitz shares his views of how the institutions of globalization, the World Bank and the IMF, need to change in order to help developing nations join the world economy.

6. **In Defense of Globalization** by Jagdish Bhagwati, 2004 – In this short and witty book, the renowned economist counters claims that globalization has failed to benefit developing nations and explains how they can make the most of its opportunities.

7. **Jihad vs. McWorld**: How Globalism and Tribalism Are Reshaping the World by Benjamin R. Barber, 1995 – Barber explores the uneasy coexistence, competition, and interdependence of the forces of consumerism and fundamentalism across the world.

8. **Power and Plenty: Trade, War, and the World Economy in the Second Millennium** by Ronald Findlay and Kevin H. O'Rourke, 2009 – Contrary to

169

popular belief, globalization isn't a brand-new phenomenon. Tracing consecutive waves of globalization and retrenchment in the past 1,000 years, Findlay and O'Rourke offer a sweeping historical survey of the world economy and the ever-changing geopolitical concerns that shape it.

9. **A Problem from Hell: America and the Age of Genocide** by Samantha Power, 2002 – A number of genocides and "ethnic cleansings" have taken place in the last century. As a matter of basic human values, the author argues, the U.S. needs to be much more willing to intervene in such cases.

EXCERPT: A PROBLEM FROM HELL:

When word of the gas attacks began spreading to other villages, terrified Kurds began fleeing even ahead of the arrival of Iraqi air force bombers. Al-Majid's forces were fairly predictable. Jets began by dropping cluster bombs or chemical cocktails on the targeted villages. Surviving inhabitants fled. When they reached the main roads, Iraqi soldiers and security police rounded them up. They then often looted and firebombed the villages so they could never be reoccupied. Some women and children were sent to their deaths; others were moved to holding pens "where many died of starvation and disease. The men were often spirited away and never heard from again. In the zones that Hussein had outlawed, Kurdish life was simply extinct.

10. **The World is Flat: A Brief History of the Twenty-First Century** by Thomas L. Friedman, 2005 – The *New York Times* columnist followed up on his previous book on globalization, ***The Lexus and the Olive Tree***, with a survey of how telecommunications are revolutionizing the global economy and increasing competition. Toward the end of the book, he also discusses some of the economic aspects of international Islamic fundamentalism.

11. **World On Fire: How Exporting Free Market Democracy Breeds Ethnic Hatred and Global Instability** by Amy Chua, 2003 – This startling and cautionary book shows how the shift to free market democracies in countries can lead to violent upheavals by economically empowering ethnic minorities while politically empowering poorer ethnic majorities.

POLITICAL THRILLERS
Page-Turning Stories of International Intrigue

Like your stories complicated and chock-full of international intrigue, terrorists with secret new weapons and disillusioned government agents and military officers? Do you prefer your heroes to be smart, nervy and physically tough enough to wrestle the bad guy while figuring out the secret formula in their heads? Then these eight novels, listed alphabetically by author, will give you the page-turning thrills that are the hallmarks of the best political thrillers.

1. **The Hunt for Red October** by Tom Clancy, 1984 – With this underwater techno-thriller, Clancy established his credentials as a master of complex tales involving spies, conspiracies and technological miracles (or monstrosities.) What always sets a Clancy novel apart is his scrupulous concern for detailed accuracy. Jack Ryan, the naval historian/free-lance CIA operative hero of *The Hunt for Red October* and its seven sequels, which include ***Patriot Games*** and ***The Sum of All Fears***, is more Sherlock Holmes than James Bond.

2. **Raise the Titanic!** by Clive Cussler, 1976 – Cussler's brash hero, Dirk Pitt, made his debut in ***The Mediterranean Caper***, but this below-the-sea adventure jump-started the franchise. Pitt has since chewed up the scenery in twenty more books; seventeen in a row have reached the *New York Times* best-seller list. Cussler's novels don't feature the meticulous plotting of Frederick Forsyth or technical savvy of Tom Clancy. It's all about thrills and chills and slap-you-back-in-your-chair action in Cussler's sometimes far-fetched but always entertaining page-turners.

3. **Wild Fire** by Nelson DeMille, 2006 – DeMille has written mysteries about mobsters and murderers, but if you're hunting one in the Clancy/Ludlum political thriller mode, look for his series featuring John Corey, a former New York Police detective who now heads a government anti-terrorist task force. *Wild Fire* is one of the best of the series, which also includes ***Night Fall***, ***The Lion*** and ***The Panther***.

4. **Transfer of Power** by Vince Flynn, 1999 – This is the first in the ongoing series featuring tough CIA operative Mitch Rapp (even his name is tough), a specialist in counter-terrorism. Rapp is a loose cannon in the 007 mode who hates routine and paperwork and doesn't mind taking extreme measures when terrorists invade the White House.

5. **Eye of the Needle** by Ken Follett, 1978 – This is one of Follett's most famous political thrillers, along with ***The Key to Rebecca*** and ***The Man from St. Petersburg***. In this rattling good yarn set in World War II-era England, a ruthless Nazi spy meets his surprising match in a lonely English woman on an isolated island.

6. **The Day of the Jackal** by Frederick Forsyth, 1971 – It has been said that Forsyth's novels more closely resemble investigative journalism more traditional spy/thriller fiction. Called a "masterpiece tour de force of crisp, sharp, suspenseful writing" by *The Wall Street Journal, The Day of the Jackal* is a nail-

biter about the hunt for the "jackal" — an English assassin hired to kill the president of France, Charles De Gaulle.

7. **The Bourne Identity** by Robert Ludlum, 1980 – No matter which of the many Ludlum political thrillers you choose to read, you're going to find smart, tough good guys slugging it out in the world of international secrets and adventure with really, really bad guys. *The Bourne Identity* introduces his best-known character, government agent Jason Bourne, who's pulled barely alive from the Mediterranean with no clue as to who he is — or why he's been marked for death by some of the world's deadliest assassins.

8. **Full Black** by Brad Thor, 2011 – One of the most popular and acclaimed writers working in the political thriller genre today, Thor is best known for his series featuring former Navy Seal turned covert counterterrorism operative Scot Harvath. Thor's 2005 Harvath novel, **Blowback,** was voted one of the "100 Top Killer Thrillers of All Time" by NPR listeners. In *Full Black*, which won the International Thriller Writers' Award for Best Novel of 2011, Harvath goes after terrorists intent on triggering the collapse of the United States.

EXCERPT: FULL BLACK:

He was reflecting on whether it would be a good idea to bring Mansoor to the actual safe house or find somewhere else for him to hide temporarily when the Skype icon on his laptop bounced.

He had been sent a message from the man whom he served – the Sheikh from Qatar.

Everything is in place? asked the Sheikh.

Everything is in place, typed Karami.

POST-WORLD WAR II NOVELS
Gore Vidal's "Useful" Picks

Essayist, novelist, playwright and full-time provocateur, Gore Vidal was known as much for his vitriolic tongue as his literary talents. Over the course of his decades-spanning career, Vidal famously tangled with everyone from William F. Buckley to Truman Capote to his macho nemesis, Norman Mailer. In 1971, Vidal compared Mailer to Charles Manson — and got head-butted by Mailer in reply.

But if Vidal was notorious for his withering dismissal of some writers, he was also a surprisingly passionate and generous champion of others, like Dawn Powell, whom he pronounced "a comic writer as good as Evelyn Waugh and better than Clemens" in a 1981 issue of the *Antioch Review*. Powell, whose satirical novels about the Manhattan literary and bohemian scenes were then out of print, eventually enjoyed a posthumous renaissance, due in large part to Vidal's effusive praise for her work. One of her fifteen novels, *The Golden Spur*, comes in fourth on Vidal's 1999 Salon.com list of five "useful" novels published since World War II.

1. **Doctor Faustus** by Thomas Mann, 1948 – Topping Vidal's list is this staggeringly complex masterwork by the 1929 Nobel Prize winner for Literature. Mann's protagonist is a musical prodigy who forges a Faustian pact that seals his downfall, which mirrors Germany's intellectual and moral collapse with Hitler's rise to power. An ambitious, demanding novel that Vidal succinctly describes as a "powerful metaphor, great novel."

2. **Good as Gold** by Joseph Heller, 1979 – Never one to toe the party line, Vidal bypasses Heller's *Catch-22* in favor of this tragicomic novel about a frustrated middle-aged college professor reinventing himself as a Washington political broker. To that end, protagonist Bruce Gold ditches his loudly dysfunctional family and reclaims his Jewish heritage, solely for political expediency. Vidal calls Heller "a superb comic novelist with an eye and ear for American idiocies."

3. **Cosmicomics** by Italo Calvino, 1965 – Wrapping your mind around Calvino's densely layered, self-reflexive prose can be daunting for even the most adventurous reader. That said, if your tastes run to Franz Kafka, Jorge Luis Borges and Umberto Eco, you'll probably share Vidal's admiration for Calvino's heady work, like this 1965 collection of short stories, inspired by various scientific facts and theories, and narrated by a being known as Qfwfq. "Total fireworks," according to Vidal.

EXCERPT: COSMICOMICS:

How well I know! — old Qfwfq cried,– the rest of you can't remember, but I can. We had her on top of us all the time, that enormous Moon: when she was full — nights as bright as day, but with a butter-colored light — it looked as if she were going to crush us; when she was new, she rolled around the sky like a black umbrella blown by the wind; and when she was waxing, she came forward with her horns so low she seemed about to stick into the peak of a promontory and get caught there. But the whole business of the Moon's phases worked in a different way then: because the distances from the Sun were different, and the orbits, and the angle of something or other, I forget what; as for eclipses, with Earth and Moon stuck together the way they were, why, we had eclipses every minute: naturally, those two big monsters managed to put each other in the shade constantly, first one, then the other.

4. **The Golden Spur** by Dawn Powell, 1962 – One of Powell's last novels, *The Golden Spur* follows an impressionable young man from the suburbs stumbling

173

his way into the Greenwich Village art scene, where he hopes to find his long-lost father. For Vidal, *The Golden Spur* may be "*the* New York novel."

5. **Creation** by Gore Vidal, 1981 – Modesty in any form was never one of Vidal's virtues, so it should come as no surprise that he picked one of his own books to round out the list. In *Creation*, a fifth century BC Persian diplomat embarks on a tour of the ancient world's political and religious systems; en route he has pivotal meetings with such figures as Socrates, Buddha, Confucius and Zoroaster. Vidal includes *Creation* on his list because it "tells us things we ought to know but don't."

REAL-LIFE DISASTERS
From Krakatoa to 9/11

Ever since Pliny the Younger wrote his eyewitness account of the cataclysmic eruption of Mount Vesuvius in 79 AD, historians have chronicled the world's worst disasters, often in harrowing, graphic detail. There's something morbidly irresistible about catastrophes, both natural and man-made, that draw readers back to certain events like moths to the proverbial flame. Case in point: the 1912 sinking of the legendary luxury liner *Titanic* has spawned a publishing cottage industry, with *hundreds* of books devoted to that tragic April night, when over 1,500 passengers went down with the supposedly "unsinkable" ship in the freezing waters of the North Atlantic. Given the staggering number of books about the ill-fated luxury liner, you'd think that there'd be nothing further to add about history's most famous maritime disaster, yet the centennial of the ship's sinking in 2012 brought even more books.

The sinking of the *Titanic* is just one of the disasters historians have tackled in the following, critically lauded books, listed in alphabetical order, that cover everything from earthquakes to hurricanes to 9/11.

1. **102 Minutes: The Untold Story of the Fight to Survive Inside the Twin Towers** by Jim Dwyer and Kevin Flynn, 2005 – A finalist for the 2005 National Book Award for nonfiction, this suspenseful and emotionally shattering book reconstructs the final moments inside the World Trade Center towers, that terrible September morning in 2001.

2. **The Circus Fire: A True Story of an American Tragedy** by Stewart O'Nan, 2001 – Faint-hearted readers be warned: O'Nan's engrossing recreation of the horrific, 1944 Ringling Brothers Barnum & Bailey Circus fire is gruesomely detailed. But if you have the stomach for it, *The Circus Fire* is well worth a look, thanks to O'Nan's immensely readable prose style and the wealth of fascinating information.

EXCERPT: THE CIRCUS FIRE:

High up, the guyropes parted, the rigging gave way, and the poles by the northeast corner slumped inward, then the center of the canvas. The tent sagged-- slowly, not all at once, the flags on top bending almost horizontal--and then with a hissing, swishing sound, the big top collapsed on itself, the heavy centerpoles falling one after another, smashing the animal cages, crushing people. The quarters--thick as phone poles--banged into the grandstands, denting the railings.

Robert Onorato caught it on film, shooting from atop an embankment at the east end. Slowed down on video, the fire licks up the visible tip of the eastmost centerpole and wraps the flag. The flag catches and drops as if it's melting, falls, and immediately the tent collapses, softly, belling like a ball gown when its wearer curtsies, like a sail emptied of wind.

3. **A Crack in the Edge of the World: America and the Great California Earthquake of 1906** by Simon Winchester, 2005 – The seemingly tireless British author/journalist turns his attention to the quake and its fiery aftermath that reduced San Francisco to smoke and rubble. While some critics fault Winchester for his overly digressive approach, he nonetheless cranks out one compelling, albeit tangent-laden book after another — *A Crack in the Edge of the World* is no exception.

4. **Five Past Midnight in Bhopal: The Epic Story of the World's Worst Industrial Disaster** by Dominique Lapierre and Javier Moros, 2002 – The heartbreaking and infuriating story of the deadly gas leak that killed thousands of poor Indian villagers in Bhopal comes tragically to life in this profoundly haunting book.

5. **The Great Chicago Fire and the Myth of Mrs. O'Leary's Cow** by Richard F. Bales, 2002 — Finally, Mrs. O'Leary and her cow can rest in peace. This exhaustively researched exploration of the fire that destroyed three square miles and killed 300 people debunks the urban legend, drawing instead from primary sources and witness testimonies to construct a new theory. A fascinating read for those who want the true story.

6. **In Harm's Way: The Sinking Of The U.S.S. Indianapolis And The Extraordinary Story Of Its Survivors** by Doug Stanton, 2002 — In this account of the worst naval disaster in American history, Stanton reconstructs the sinking of the *U.S.S. Indianapolis* and the horrifying aftermath through the personal stories of her crew. In the process, he offers a new theory of the disaster that largely exonerates Captain Charles McVay, who was court-martialed for his part in the sinking. Even skeptics will be persuaded by Stanton's authoritative narrative.

7. **Isaac's Storm: A Man, A Time and the Deadliest Hurricane in History** by Erik Larson, 1999 – For the people of Galveston, Texas, the twentieth century got off to a devastating start, when a hurricane laid waste to this Gulf of Mexico community. In Larson's vivid book, meteorologist Isaac Cline emerges as the

175

prototypical tragic hero: a short-sighted yet courageous man whose pregnant wife was among the hurricane's estimated 10,000 fatalities.

8. **The Johnstown Flood** by David McCullough, 1968 – Before he won Pulitzer Prizes for his comprehensive biographies of presidents Harry S. Truman and John Adams, America's most honored living historian wrote this riveting book about the terrible flood that killed over 2,000 people in Johnstown, Pennsylvania in 1889. With his customary blend of erudite prose and extensive research, McCullough examines the disaster from a variety of angles.

9. **Krakatoa: The Day the World Exploded: August 27, 1883** by Simon Winchester, 2003 – The book's subtitle is only a slight exaggeration. When the Indonesian volcano Krakatoa erupted in apocalyptic fury, it spewed more than six cubic miles of rock, ash and pumice into the atmosphere and killed over 36,000 people. Ranging far and wide on geology, Indonesian politics and survivor stories, Winchester's book makes for lively, intellectually stimulating reading.

10. **The Last Days of St. Pierre: The Volcano Disaster That Claimed 30,000 Lives** by Ernest Zebrowksi, 2002 – Zebrowski's thorough account of the 1902 eruption of Mt. Pelée in Martinique is a briskly-paced, highly entertaining page-turner that's also a stinging indictment of the Caribbean island's French colonial authorities. Their policies, according to Zebrowski, contributed to the catastrophic loss of life.

11. **A Night to Remember** by Walter Lord, 1955 – Obsessed with the *Titanic* since childhood, Lord pored over archival information and interviewed more than sixty survivors to write what many regard as the definitive account of the sinking. Thirty-one years after *A Night to Remember* became a bestseller, Lord wrote a well-received sequel, ***The Night Lives On: The Untold Stories and Secrets of the Sinking of the "Unsinkable" Ship — Titanic***.

12. **Triangle: The Fire That Changed America** by David Von Drehle, 2003 – Von Drehle examines the sociopolitical factors that precipitated the deadly fire at the Triangle Shirtwaist Factory in 1911. One hundred and forty-six factory workers, most of them poor, immigrant women, died when flames engulfed this sweatshop. Famed *Washington Post* journalist Bob Woodward hailed *Triangle* as "a riveting history written with flare and precision."

REVOLUTIONARY WAR NONFICTION
All About Our Founding Fathers

Called "a one-man historical machine" by fellow Revolutionary War scholar Gordon S. Wood, historian Joseph J. Ellis has maintained a regular berth on the nonfiction bestseller list, thanks to such critical and commercial favorites as *Founding Brothers: The Revolutionary Generation* and ***First Family: Abigail and John Adams***. Ellis, along with *John Adams* biographer David McCullough, deserves the lion's share of the credit for whetting the general public's appetite for serious yet accessible nonfiction books about the Revolutionary War. Although Ellis came under fire in 2001 for lying about serving in the Vietnam War — the very same year he won a Pulitzer Prize for *Founding Brothers* — he weathered the scandal with his reputation for top-notch scholarship intact. Whatever his personal failings, there's never been a question raised about the veracity of any of his prize-winning Revolutionary War histories, two of which appear on the following, alphabetical list of nonfiction titles about the founding of the United States.

1. **1776** by David McCullough, 2005 – Confining his focus to a pivotal year in the Revolutionary War, McCullough crafts another impeccably researched and compelling book that sheds light on both George Washington and his nemesis across the pond, King George III.

2. **Alexander Hamilton** by Ron Chernow, 2004 — In this comprehensive biography, Chernow aims to set the record straight about the controversial figure often dismissed as a self-interested aristocrat. Painting Hamilton in a nuanced, sympathetic light, Chernow argues that it was Hamilton, not Washington and Jefferson, who shaped the course of American capitalism.

3. **American Creation: Triumphs and Tragedies at the Founding of the Republic** by Joseph Ellis, 2008 — Pulitzer Prize-winning historian Joseph Ellis examines this precarious moment in American history through six stories, each illuminating a particular creative success or failure that shaped the war — and the country it created.

EXCERPT: AMERICAN CREATION:

If permitted the historical license to stretch the definition of a year, then the fifteen months between the shots fired at Lexington and Concord in April of 1775 and the adoption of the Declaration of Independence in July of 1776 can justifiably claim to be both the most consequential and the strangest year in American history. It was consequential because the rationale for American independence and the political agenda for an independent American republic first became explicit at this time. It was strange because while men were dying, whole towns being burned to the ground, women being raped, captured spies and traitors being executed, the official posture of what called itself "The United Colonies of North America" remained abiding loyalty to the British Crown.

4. **Benjamin Franklin: An American Life** by Walter Isaacson, 2003 – A marvelously erudite and entertaining biography of the charming, witty and brilliant Franklin. The inventor/humorist/statesman/diplomat and all-around bon vivant comes alive in the pages of Isaacson's bestseller, but this is no fawning hagiography; Isaacson skillfully reveals Franklin's idiosyncrasies and character flaws.

5. **Founding Brothers: The Revolutionary Generation** by Joseph J. Ellis, 2000 – Ellis struck literary gold again with his Pulitzer Prize-winning examination of six key moments in the lives of the "Founding Fathers." Wonderfully concise — Ellis covers a lot of historical ground in just over 300 pages — *Founding Brothers: The Revolutionary Generation* was pronounced "lively and illuminating" by the *New York Times*.

6. **John Adams** by David McCullough, 2001– Long overshadowed by Washington and Jefferson, Adams has finally been recognized for the vital role he played in the creation of the United States of America, thanks to this magnificent biography by McCullough that topped the bestseller list for a year.

7. **The Radicalism of the American Revolution** by Gordon S. Wood, 1991– With tremendous clarity, Wood gives readers an illuminating overview of the social and ideological forces that enabled the thirteen colonies to form a united front against the British. Winner of the 1992 Pulitzer Prize.

8. **Samuel Adams: Father of the American Revolution** by Mark Puls, 2006 – Many people today only know Adams as a brand of beer, but he was a fierce patriot and gifted organizer whose contemporaries regarded him as one of the key architects of the American Revolution. Although Adams reportedly destroyed much of his correspondence, Puls nevertheless draws upon extensive research to paint a full portrait of an overlooked "Founding Father."

9. **Saratoga: Turning Point of America's Revolutionary War** by Richard M. Ketchum, 1997– Engrossing, scrupulously researched account of the battle in which the Americans stopped the supposedly "invincible" British forces dead in their tracks. No less an authority than David McCullough praised Ketchum's book as "superbly researched, full-scale narrative history at its best."

10. **Thomas Jefferson: The Art of Power** by Jon Meacham, 2012 – Meacham brings a novelist's flair for narrative to his masterful biography of one of the most complex figures in all of American history. A prodigiously talented man committed to liberty yet ambivalent about slavery, Jefferson comes across as a man of strong convictions and many contradictions in *Thomas Jefferson: The Art of Power*, which Pulitzer Prize-winning historian Gordon S. Wood hailed as "probably the best single-volume biography of Jefferson ever written."

11. **The Traitor and the Spy: Benedict Arnold and John Andre** by James Thomas Flexner, 1953 – One of America's foremost historians, Flexner separates fact from fiction regarding the infamous Benedict Arnold in this absorbing book, as dramatic as any novel.

12. **Washington's Crossing (Pivotal Moments in American History)** by David Hackett Fisher, 2004 – The 2005 winner of the Pulitzer Prize, *Washington's Crossing* is a wonderfully thorough and smartly-paced account of Washington leading his men to decisive victories at Trenton and Princeton.

REVOLUTIONARY WAR NONFICTION
Essential Nonfiction about George Washington

To commemorate the 200th anniversary of the death of George Washington in 1999, the Mount Vernon Ladies' Association teamed up with the Organization of American Historians to poll more than 250 professional historians for their favorite books on America's first president. Here are the top ten vote-getters, listed per their ranking, plus two contemporary titles worth reading.

1. **Washington: The Indispensable Man** by James Thomas Flexner, 1969 - One of the most respected Washington scholars, Flexner condenses his four-volume biography of the "great and good man" who was the father of our country into one readable and compelling volume.

2. **George Washington: Man and Monument** by Marcus Cunliffe, 1958 - This brief biography reveals how Washington transcended his individuality to become one of the most powerful and enduring symbols of America.

3. **The Genius of George Washington** by Edmund S. Morgan, 1980 - Using Washington's letters and other sources, Morgan demonstrates how the general and president's understanding of the nature of power helped to create the United States of America.

4. **Washington** by Douglas Freeman, abridged by Richard Harwell (1948, abridged in 1968) - This abridgment of Freeman's Pulitzer-Prize-winning seven-volume biography gives the reader a vivid sense of Washington as an imperfect but great individual.

5. **George Washington and the American Military Tradition** by Don Higginbotham, 1985 – Derived from a series of engaging lectures, this book shows how many of Washington's decisions were informed by his dual experience of military and sociopolitical concerns.

6. **The Presidency of George Washington** by Forrest McDonald, 1974 – A brief but compelling analysis of Washington's presidency, when he faced such issues as war debts, regional factionalism and European political strife.

7. **The Papers of George Washington** edited by W.W. Abbot and Dorothy Twohig, 1983-1995 - If you like to learn about history from letters, military reports and other primary documents, this edited compilation of Washington's papers is a treasure trove.

8. **George Washington: A Biography** by John R. Alden, 1984 - Alden covers Washington's life from his first days in the countryside of Virginia and his

entrance into the military after working as a surveyor to his role as a leader of the emerging nation.

9. **The Meaning of Independence: John Adams, George Washington, Thomas Jefferson** by Edmund S. Morgan, 1976 - We sometimes take the revolutionary fervor of the first generation of independent Americans for granted. But an enormous shift of public opinion, brought about in part by the convictions of a few leaders (Washington among them), was required to make the revolution a reality. Morgan brings this dramatic story to life.

10. **George Washington's Diaries: An Abridgment** edited by Donald Jackson and Dorothy Twohig, 1976-1979 - Here is a view of Washington's daily life from the man himself, chronicling his travels, social activities, interest in horticulture and other elements of his life both mundane and unexpected.

CONTEMPORARY TITLES

11. **His Excellency: George Washington** by Joseph Ellis, 2004 – One of America's most revered historians, Ellis goes beyond the myth of Washington to reveal his complex personality by focusing on three periods in his life: the French-Indian War, the Revolutionary War and his presidential tenure.

12. **Washington: A Life** by Ron Chernow, 2010 – Critics repeatedly used the word "magnificent" to describe Chernow's enlightening biography of our first president, an intensely private man who kept his emotions in rigorous check as he rose to the heights of power. The winner of both the Pulitzer Prize for History and the American History Book Prize.

EXCERPT: WASHINGTON:

Around noon on April 14, 1789, Washington flung open the door at Mount Vernon and greeted his visitor with a cordial embrace. Once in the privacy of the mansion, he and Thomson conducted a stiff verbal minuet, each man reading from a prepared statement. Thomson began by declaring, "I am honored with the commands of the Senate to wait upon your Excellency with the information of your being elected to the office of President of the United States of America" by a unanimous vote. He read aloud a letter from Senator John Langdon of New Hampshire, the president pro tempore. "Suffer me, sir, to indulge the hope that so auspicious a mark of public confidence will meet your approbation and be considered as a sure pledge of the affection and support you are to expect from a free and enlightened people." There was something deferential, even slightly servile, in Langdon's tone, as if he feared that Washington might renege on his promise and refuse to take the job. Thus was greatness once again thrust upon George Washington.

ROAD TRIPS
Into the Great Unknown

Suffering a bout of wanderlust, but don't want to leave the comforts of home for the uncertainty of the open road? Or endure fresh pain at the pump? Relax — you only need to go as far as your bookshelf to experience the glory of the great outdoors, albeit vicariously, in the pages of the following novels and memoirs about getting away from it all. By turns meditative, witty, elegiac and philosophical, these chronicles of epic, life-changing road trips — some taken on foot —should quench your desire for adventure as you nestle deeper into your Barcalounger. Featuring books by everyone from Charles Kuralt to John Steinbeck, here are twelve literary road trips, listed alphabetically.

1. **Blue Highways: A Journey into America** by William Least-Heat Moon, 1982 – Fired from his job and ditched by his wife on the same day, Least-Heat Moon decides to take stock of his life by driving cross-country on America's back roads. A delightful and unexpectedly moving book.

2. **In Search of Captain Zero: A Surfer's Road Trip Beyond the End of the Road** by Allan Weisbecker, 2002 — In 1996, the middle-aged author packed up all his belongings, including his surfboard, and set out to find a friend who had gone missing somewhere in Central America. A story that might otherwise sink into a trite account of midlife crisis stays afloat with its unflinching honesty, vivid imagery and lively humor.

3. **On the Road with Charles Kuralt** by Charles Kuralt, 1985 – Inspiring collection of human-interest stories culled from Kuralt's long-running series of reports on Americana for *CBS Sunday Morning*.

4. **Road Angels: Searching for Home Down America's Coast of Dreams** by Kent Nerburn, 2001– Longing to revisit the West Coast where he spent his twenties, Nerburn leaves frozen Minnesota for an extended trip down memory lane in this poetic, beautifully written journey of self-discovery.

5. **Road Fever** by Tim Cahill, 1991 – Talk about your crazy ideas! Cahill and a professional long-distance driver drove from Chile to Alaska in 23 ½ days — and lived to tell about it. *Road Fever* is a funny and engaging account of their wild and woolly misadventures en route.

6. **Route 66: The Mother Road** by Michael Wallis, 1990 – You'll get your kicks from *Route 66: The Mother Road*, Wallis' lively and fact-filled history of America's most famous highway.

7. **A Thousand Mile-Walk to The Gulf** by John Muir, 1916 – The founder of the Sierra Club left his Indiana home in 1867 to wind his way across the post-Civil War South, sketching plants that caught his eye and recording his impressions of the people he met en route to the Gulf of Mexico. Published two years after Muir's

death in 1914, *A Thousand Mile-Walk to the Gulf* is an exhilarating memoir of his trek.

8. **Travels With Charley in Search of America** by John Steinbeck, 1962– With his standard poodle Charley for company, Steinbeck drove a camper all over America for three months in 1960. His memoir of that trip succeeds as both a charming travelogue and a profound assessment of the American character.

9. **A Walk Across America** by Peter Jenkins, 1979 – His ideals tarnished by the Vietnam War and Watergate, a twenty-two year-old college graduate decides to walk from New York City to New Orleans. *A Walk Across America* is the touching memoir of the people and places Jenkins met over the course of his nearly two-year journey.

10. **A Walk in the Woods: Rediscovering America on the Appalachian Trail** by Bill Bryson, 2006 – Irresistibly witty account of Bryson hiking the Appalachian Trail with his equally out-of-shape middle-aged buddy.

11. **Wild: From Lost to Found on the Pacific Crest Trail** by Cheryl Strayed, 2012 — This Oprah Book Club 2.0 selection chronicles the distances the author went to — literally — to put her life back together after the death of her mother and her own divorce. With no experience as a long-distance hiker, Strayed hiked from California to Washington, embarking on an emotional odyssey that included its share of wilderness adventure. Strayed's confident prose make this an engaging read.

EXCERPT: WILD:

My solo three-month hike on the Pacific Crest Trail had many beginnings. There was the first, flip decision to do it, followed by the second, more serious decision to actually do it, and then the long third beginning, composed of weeks of shopping and packing and preparing to do it. There was the quitting my job as a waitress and finalizing my divorce and selling almost everything I owned and saying goodbye to my friends and visiting my mother's grave one last time. There was the driving across the country from Minneapolis to Portland, Oregon, and, a few days later, catching a flight to Los Angeles and a ride to the town of Mojave and another ride to the place where the PCT crossed a highway.

At which point, at long last, there was the actual doing it, quickly followed by the grim realization of what it meant to do it, followed by the decision to quit doing it because doing it was absurd and pointless and ridiculously difficult and far more than I expected doing it would be and I was profoundly unprepared to do it.

And then there was the real live truly doing it.

12. **Zen and the Art of Motorcycle Maintenance: An Inquiry Into Values** by Robert M. Pirsig, 1974 - A literary phenomenon in the seventies, Pirsig's challenging

mixture of travel narrative and philosophical quest ponders notions of reality from a metaphysical perspective.

ROMAN EMPIRE NONFICTION
Historians at the Gates

Contrary to the ancient proverb, all roads do not lead to Rome — at least not the Rome of today, a gorgeous, bustling urban monument to its imperial past, when the city on the banks of the Tiber River was the center of the known world. Although the exact date of its founding remains a mystery cloaked in myth, the history and culture of ancient Rome has emerged in sharp relief for contemporary readers, thanks to the writings of historians from antiquity to today. Towering above all other histories of ancient Rome is Edward Gibbon's four-volume masterpiece, *The Decline and Fall of the Roman Empire*, which begins in the second century AD and ends with the fall of Constantinople in 1453. A colossal but invaluable undertaking, Gibbon's epic account of Rome's slow and steady fall to the barbarians at the gates is one of twelve nonfiction books, listed alphabetically, about ancient Rome that focus on everything from the conquest of Gaul to cuisine to carnal pleasures.

1. **Ancient Rome** by William E. Dunstan, 2010 – Covering hundreds of years in the life of the empire, Dunstan's book tells a human story populated by a who's who of famous personalities, including Hannibal, Julius Caesar, Cleopatra, Cicero, Hadrian, Nero and more. To bring his characters to life, Dunstan illuminates every corner of Roman society, from marriage and divorce to slavery, sex, religion and art. This tour de force is a must-read for anyone seeking a basic knowledge of what was not the world's first empire, but its greatest.

2. **The Annals of Imperial Rome** by Tacitus, 109 AD – A mesmerizing and unflinchingly critical year-by-year account of Rome that begins with the death of Augustus and ends with Nero.

3. **The Assassination of Julius Caesar: A People's History of Ancient Rome** by Michael Parenti, 2003 – A fresh take on a familiar subject, Parenti's fascinating book examines the savage murder of Julius Caesar in the context of the rigid class system that governed the Roman republic.

4. **The Decline and Fall of the Roman Empire** by Edward Gibbon, 1776-1788 – The sheer bulk of Gibbon's massive tome may be intimidating, but once you dive into it, you'll be engrossed, thanks to the clarity of Gibbon's erudite but never stuffy prose. For an excellent abridged version of Gibbon's masterwork, check out the **Penguin Classics edition**.

Trajan was ambitious of fame; and as long as mankind shall continue to bestow more liberal applause on their destroyers than on their benefactors, the thirst of military glory will ever be the vice of the most exalted characters. The praises of Alexander, transmitted by a succession of poets and historians, had kindled a dangerous emulation in the mind of Trajan. Like him, the Roman emperor undertook an expedition against the nations of the east, but he lamented with a sigh that his advanced age scarcely left him any hopes of equaling the renown of the son of Philip. Yet the success of Trajan, however transient, was rapid and specious. The degenerate Parthians, broken by intestine discord, fled before his arms. He descended the river Tigris in triumph, from the mountains of Armenia to the Persian Gulf. He enjoyed the honour of being the first, as he was the last, of the Roman generals, who ever navigated that remote sea.

5. **The Gladiator: The Secret History of Rome's Warrior Slaves** by Alan Baker, 2001 – Well-written if a tad on the sensational side, Baker's page-turning overview of gladiatorial life merits a "thumbs up."

6. **Handbook to Life in Ancient Rome** by Roy A. and Lesley Adkins, 1998 – Illustrated with photographs, line drawings and maps, *A Handbook to Life in Ancient Rome* would make a terrific addition to any home reference library.

7. **Livia: First Lady of Imperial Rome** by Anthony A. Barrett, 2002 – Immortalized in Robert Graves' *I, Claudius* as evil incarnate, the wife of Emperor Augustus was not quite the ruthless, endlessly scheming harpy of lore, according to Barrett, in his persuasively argued biography.

8. **The Rise of Rome: The Making of the World's Greatest Empire** by Anthony Everitt, 2012 – Many an author has deconstructed the demise of the Roman Empire, but in this "riveting" (according to the *Chicago Tribune)* volume, Everitt, a bestselling biographer known for his works on Cicero, Augustus and Hadrian, focuses on how a few villages grouped around seven hills became the superpower of the ancient world. The book brings ancient history to life through its vivid portrayal of a society based on democratic ideals that, of course, ultimately succumbs to its own success, and through perfectly etched characters, including the legendary Alexander the Great and scrupulously ethical Cato.

9. **Route 66 AD: On The Trail of Ancient Roman Tourists** by Tony Perrottet, 2002 – Going off the proverbial beaten path of most travel writers, Perrottet uses a map drawn by ancient Roman warrior Marcus Agrippa to visit the antiquity's favorite vacation getaways. A wryly funny and informative blend of history and personal travelogue.

10. **Roman Sex: 100 BC to AD 250** by John Clarke, 2003 – An art history professor at the University of Texas, Clarke tells readers everything they ever wanted to know

about Roman sex, and then some, in this lavishly illustrated, eye-opening book that's not for prudes.

11. **A Taste of Ancient Rome** by Ilaria Gozzin Giacosa, 1992 – A celebration of ancient Roman cuisine, long before pasta and tomato sauce were staples in the Italian kitchen. Giacosa provides over 200 recipes, both in English and Latin, for such delicacies as roasted thrushes and stuffed dormice.

12. **The Twelve Caesars** by Suetonis, 121 AD – A Roman historian/biographer who briefly served as Hadrian's imperial secretary, Suetonius chronicles the reigns of twelve emperors — from Julius Caesar to Domitian — in unsparing, often lurid detail that makes for highly entertaining reading.

ROMANTIC FICTION
Classic and Contemporary Favorites

Boy meets girl. Boy falls in love with girl. Boy…turns into werewolf? Romantic fiction has definitely changed over the centuries, but its themes remain timeless and intact: unrequited love; forbidden love; love that defies time, fate and nature.

Western culture gave birth to romantic fiction. And it's no wonder. We seem to be ever in love with love. Tracing the roots back to Arthurian legend, tales of heroism and chivalry by French poet Chretien de Troyes helped define courtly love, its pleasures and its consequences. Indeed, passion could help forge a nation — or bring it to its knees. By the early nineteenth century, Jane Austen would bring social realism and a biting wit to the genre, creating the template for contemporary romance.

Though the romance novel has often been dismissed as the purview of female writers and readers, catering to a low sensibility, countless authors — of both genders — have explored the depths and limits of human passion. Listed alphabetically by author, the following books represent the best and most popular romantic fiction, capturing our imaginations and of course, our hearts.

1. **Sense and Sensibility** by Jane Austen, 1811 – Published at Austen's own expense, the well-observed *Sense and Sensibility* tells the parallel stories of the Dashwood sisters: impulsive Marianne and restrained Elinor. As each sister struggles to find the perfect match in a world obsessed with status and wealth, each sister comes to realize that the quest for love indeed requires both sense and sensibility.

2. **Wuthering Heights** by Emily Brontë, 1847 – The tortured, ultimately doomed romance of brooding Heathcliff and his mercurial love Cathy continues to enthrall new generations of readers. Moodily atmospheric and passionately told, Brontë's

185

only published novel has been adapted for the screen several times, most notably the classic 1939 version starring Laurence Olivier and Merle Oberon.

3. **Rebecca** by Daphne du Maurier, 1938 – Written from the point of view of its unnamed protagonist (referred to only as the second Mrs. DeWinter), this beautifully written psychological thriller unravels the mystery behind the English estate of Manderley and its brooding heir, Maxim DeWinter. To escape the long shadow of the past, the timid Mrs. DeWinter will need to uncover some ugly truths about her husband's first marriage, even as her nemesis, housekeeper Mrs. Danvers, clings to her obsessive love for the first Mrs. DeWinter, Rebecca.

EXCERPT: REBECCA:

Last night I dreamt I went to Manderley again. It seemed to me I stood by the iron gate leading to the drive, and for a while I could not enter, for the way was barred to me. There was a padlock and a chain upon the gate. I called in my dream to the lodge-keeper, and had no answer, and peering closer through the rusted spokes of the gate I saw that the lodge was uninhabited.

4. **Outlander** by Diana Gabaldon, 1998 – The first in a bestselling series, *Outlander* propels former combat nurse Claire Randall back in time from 1945 to war-torn Scotland in 1743. There she meets James Fraser, a Scottish warrior, and finds herself leading a double life that spans centuries: wife in the twentieth century, lover in the eighteenth. Gabaldon's first novel succeeds on the strength of both its historical detail and endearing characters.

5. **The Quiet Gentlemen** by Georgette Heyer, 1953 – Dubbed the "Queen of Regency Romance," Georgette Heyer wrote her first novel while still in her teens and became one of the most prolific and well-loved writers of the twentieth century. *The Quiet Gentlemen* introduces the element of mystery to the customary wit and well-drawn characters of her romances. When the Seventh Earl of St. Erth returns home from the Battle of Waterloo to claim his inheritance, the reception from his family is not exactly warm. When he falls for his half-brother's sweetheart, things get downright murderous.

6. **The Thorn Birds** by Colleen McCullough, 1977 – This worldwide bestseller tells the story of three generations of the Cleary family, who emigrate from Ireland to the Australian Outback during World War I. The story's centerpiece is the forbidden love between Meggie Cleary and Catholic priest Ralph de Bricassart. The novel continues to win over fans, more than thirty-five years after it was published.

7. **Twilight** by Stephenie Meyer, 2005 – The first novel in the bestselling series tells the story of a troubled romance between human Bella Swan and vampire Edward Cullen. As their relationship blossoms, Bella finds herself drawn into centuries-old conflicts with other vampires and a resident pack of shape-shifters, one of

whom has also fallen in love with her. Tinged with purple prose, the series still wins devoted fans of all ages for its escapist fantasy.

8. **Gone With the Wind** by Margaret Mitchell, 1936 – The tempestuous romance between the strong-willed Scarlet O'Hara and the roguish Rhett Butler plays out against the backdrop of the American Civil War and Reconstruction. Scarlett matures from spoiled Southern belle to shrewd businesswoman but can't let go of her feelings for the ineffectual Ashley Wilkes, even after she's married Rhett. This sweeping epic remains an insightful, witty —and quotable — portrait of a remarkable young woman surviving war and privation.

9. **The Notebook** by Nicholas Sparks, 1996 – A sentimental, familiar story of two teenagers from opposite sides of the tracks who fall in love in 1932 then go their separate ways, destined to be reunited fourteen years later — after she's already engaged to a well-to-do lawyer. Setting the novel apart is a clever framing device that leaves it up to the reader to decide if the story will be tragic or join the happily-ever-afters.

10. **The Bridges of Madison County** by Robert James Waller, 1992 – When photographer Robert Kincaid travels to Iowa's Madison County to capture its scenic covered bridges, his chance encounter with farm wife Francesca Johnson leads to a passionate affair neither will forget. Having written only essays prior to penning this now beloved classic, Waller treats his story as if it were nonfiction, lending it poignancy and realism.

ROMANCE NOVELS
Contemporary Favorites

Each of the romance writers listed here has secured a substantial fan base by approaching the genre with a unique sense of story and character. What they have in common is the notion that true love trumps all, and despite the perils and pitfalls, it always rewards us in the end. For stories that are heartwarming, daring and exciting, enjoy these popular favorites, listed in alphabetical order.

1. **Foxfire Light** by Janet Dailey, 1982 – Janet Dailey's novels have sold more than 300 million copies in a career spanning four decades, but many readers find her earliest novels to be her most charming, including this story about a pampered California rich girl who finds love in the Kentucky Ozarks.

2. **Infamous** by Suzanne Brockman, 2010 – After a hiatus of almost six years, Suzanne Brockman returned to the *New York Times* bestseller list with this contemporary story of a history professor who becomes consultant to a Hollywood western, only to find that the real drama — both adventure and romance —is happening in her own life.

EXCERPT: INFAMOUS:

"Who is she?" Trace's wife demanded through her tears, her mascara making black streaks down what had once been a ridiculously pretty face. Now she just looked ridiculous, the plastic surgery she'd had leaving her looking perpetually surprised as she confronted her philandering husband. "I want to know – I deserve to know!"

3. **It Had to Be You** by Susan Elizabeth Phillips, 1994 – The first novel in Susan Elizabeth Phillips' Chicago Stars/Bonner Brothers series introduces Phoebe Somerville who inherits a football team — and its sexist, curmudgeonly head coach who, in spite of himself, cannot resist the new owner's charms.

4. **A Knight in Shining Armor** by Jude Deveraux, 2002 –Deveraux's charming bestseller brings together the maiden Dougless Montgomery and her knight Nicholas Stafford, Earl of Thornwyck, for a story driven by swift adventure and smoldering desire.

5. **Low Pressure** by Sandra Brown, 2012 – In Brown's romantic thriller, a woman finds herself in danger when clues and suspects related to her sister's unsolved murder begin to emerge, forcing her to solve the crime before she becomes the killer's next victim.

6. **Morning Glory** by LaVyrle Spencer, 1989 – In this compelling romance set in a small Georgia town in the forties, Spencer's heroine is a young woman, widowed at age twenty-six, who finds a new love — and unexpected drama — after placing an ad in the local paper seeking a mate.

7. **My Lady Notorious** by Jo Beverly, 1993 – Jo Beverly's Mallory novels, set in Georgian England, are among her most popular creations, and the first of five Cyn and Chastity stories is *My Lady Notorious*, an exciting tale in which two lovers find each other amidst a tangle of secrets and deceptions.

8. **The Witness** by Nora Roberts, 2012 – The author of more than 170 *New York Times* bestselling novels, Roberts brings both romance and thrills to *The Witness* — her 200th book — with the story of a woman on the run from the Russian mob after witnessing a murder.

ROMANCE NOVELS

RITA Awards for Best HistoricalRomantic Novels, 2000-2012

Romance Writers of America is a writers association dedicated to advancing the professional interests of romance writers through advocacy and networking. Every year, the organization presents its RITA Awards for the best in the genre, and the following list represents the winners since 2000 in the historical romance category. Loosely defined as any romance tale taking place in a historical period, you'll see below that that the Regency era in England — i.e., the opening decades of the nineteenth century — is a popular choice, as are Victorian and medieval times. But why England? We venture that a nation where the aristocracy was shackled by propriety yet rife with scandal seems the ideal Petri dish for the cultivation of romance. So here are the RITA winners, listed in reverse chronological order.

1. **The Black Hawk** by Joanna Bourne, 2012 - It's 1818, Napoleon is in exile following his disastrous war with Russia, and France has restored the monarchy. In London, French secret agent Justine DeCabrillac is attacked by an unknown assassin with a knife. She drags herself to the home of Sir Adrian Hawkhurst, head of the British Intelligence Service, as well as her archenemy and former lover. Thus begins this fourth book in Bourne's Spymaster series about these two characters who first cross paths during the French Revolution.

2. **His at Night** by Sherry Thomas, 2011 - Within society circles in Victorian London, the unmarried Lord Vere is considered a buffoon; secretly, however, he's a private investigator for the Crown. His latest case brings him in contact with his suspect's niece, Elissande, who, desperate to escape her malevolent uncle, tricks Vere into marrying her. Some clunky complications ensue, but Thomas's clever dialogue and nimble prose more than compensate.

3. **Not Quite a Husband** by Sherry Thomas, 2010 - Sherry Thomas's third book, and her first to win a RITA, transports the reader to late-nineteenth century India, where Dr. Byrony Asquith ministers to patients at a clinic in the northwest. In England three years prior, her marriage to handsome society darling Leo Marsden had fallen apart, but now Leo shows up on the Indian Subcontinent to escort Byrony back to England to see her dying father. The couple's passions reignite as they find themselves caught up in a local uprising.

4. **The Edge of Impropriety** by Pam Rosenthal, 2009 - In 1829 London, Countess Marina Wyatt, a writer of romance novels, scandalously dumps her current lover, Sir Anthony Hedges, in order to generate gossip that will benefit the sales of her latest book. But when she inadvertently becomes involved with art appraiser Jasper James Hedges — Sir Anthony's mature yet abundantly virile "uncle"— a May-December affair blossoms that gives Rosenthal a chance to show off her skill at tastefully erotic prose.

5. **Lessons of Desire** by Madeline Hunter, 2008 - Richard Drury, a member of Parliament, dies and leaves his memoirs to his illegitimate daughter, Phaedra Blair. The memoirs contain damaging tales about some of England's most powerful families, which is why Elliot Rothwell, the scion of one such clan, is sent to keep Phaedra from publishing the dirt. What follows is a steamy love affair, of course, between the socially conscious Elliot and Hunter's fiercely independent heroine.

6. **On the Way to the Wedding** by Julia Quinn, 2007 - A love triangle — or more accurately, a pentagon — brings the author's eight-book Regency-era Bridgerton series to a close. This one concerns Gregory Bridgerton, who, having observed the romantic fortunes of his many siblings, has come to believe in love at first sight. That's why, when he falls for Miss Hermione Watson, he's hardly prepared to fall even harder for her best friend Lucinda Abernathy.

7. **The Devil to Pay** by Liz Carlyle, 2006 - Sidonie Saint-Godard leads a double life. By day, she's a respectable widow who teaches London society girls the importance of good posture; at night, however, she becomes the Black Avenger, a sort of wronged-woman's Robin Hood, punishing the rich roués for whom misogyny is a hobby. But then she tangles with the notorious Marquess of Devellyn, who's out for revenge.

8. **Shadowheart** by Laura Kinsale, 2005 - Kinsale's fans had to wait more than a decade for this sequel to ***For My Lady's Heart***, but the author finally returned to fourteenth century Italy with this tale of the brutal assassin Allegreto and his princess bride Elena. Elena's hardly a fan of her husband's homicidal tendencies, but her moral dilemma seems to incite some rather passionate lovemaking, even when Allegreto goes after his rival and Elena's ex-fiancé, Franco Pietro.

EXCERPT: SHADOWHEART:

He caught the shelf with one hand, turning to her. His blackened eye gave his face a strange asymmetry in the failing light, as if half of a pagan mask had been painted upon his temple. He tilted back his head and opened his arms on the steamy water with a fierce sound of pleasure.

"Heaven," he said, with the vapor rising around him, his voice echoing in the vault. He looked
toward her, unsmiling. "Come join me. This is as close as I will ever come to it."

9. **The Destiny** by Kathleen Givens, 2004 - Givens transports the reader to late-seventeenth Scotland, simmering under the joint reign of William and Mary, where Eileen Ronley has become a virtual prisoner on her father's estate, now run by a former servant. When the latter makes a real prisoner of Neil MacCurrie, a rebel Scottish chief disguised as a French Huguenot, Eileen, smitten with the captive, helps him escape, setting the stage for a romantic adventure brimming with political and emotional drama.

10. **Stealing Heaven** by Madeline Hunter, 2003 - In medieval England, King Edward III, looking to foster peace between his kingdom and Wales, orders his loyal knight Marcus of Anglesmore to marry Genith, the youngest daughter of a Welsh chieftain. Things get dicey when Marcus falls instead for Genith's sister Nesta, who happens to be part of an underground movement

fighting for Welsh independence. Marcus marries her anyway, and soon loyalty and passion are at war.

11. **The Bridal Season** by Connie Brockway, 2002 - With style and wit, Brockway tells the tale of Letty Potts, a music hall performer and small-time conniver ready to go straight. To escape her crooked boyfriend, she flees London by train for the hamlet of Little Bidewell, where she's mistaken for the train ticket's original purchaser, society wedding planner Lady Agatha Whyte. Soon Letty has fallen in love with the impossibly handsome local magistrate, Sir Elliot March, soon to be tasked with prosecuting the imposter he, too, is smitten with.

12. **Devilish** by Jo Beverley, 2001 - The author returns to the eighteenth century London of King George III for her fifth book in the saga of the patrician Malloren family. Bey Malloren, the Marquess of Rothgar, is determined never to marry because of a family secret that forbids him from producing an heir. Diana Westmount, Countess of Arradale, is similarly anti-matrimony, lest the male-chauvinist laws of the era spell an end to control of her own destiny. That said, once the two are brought together by the king, their isolationist tendencies soon fall to the wayside.

13. **Silken Threads** by Patrician Ryan, 2000 - In this story full of engaging plot twists and medieval ambiance, Graeham Fox is on a mission to rescue the daughter of his overlord, Lord Gui, from her abusive mate. In exchange, he will wed Lord Gui's other daughter — a promise weighted with material incentives. But before he can even get started, Graeham is robbed, injured and stranded in London at the home of a pretty young "widow," Joanna Chapman.

RUSSIAN NOVELS

Of the literary classics that comprise Daniel Burt's _The Novel 100: A Ranking of the Greatest Novels of All Time_, eight were penned by Russian writers. Tolstoy and Dostoevsky, those two grand old men of Russian letters, each contribute two titles to Burt's list, which skews heavily towards books written during the nineteenth century, the acknowledged "Golden Age of Russian Literature." In fact, the only twentieth century Russian novel to make Burt's list is Andrey Bely's _Petersburg,_ a symbolist narrative of brewing political unrest in turn-of-the century Russia, which eerily anticipates the Russian Revolution of 1917. Conspicuously missing from Burt's list are such acknowledged masterpieces as Boris Pasternak's _Doctor Zhivago_, Mikhail Bulgakov's _The Master and Margarita_ and Alexander Solzhenitsyn's _One Day in the Life of Ivan Denisovich._ And while Vladimir Nabokov's _Lolita_ came in #47 on Burt's rankings, it takes place primarily in the United States — and therefore does not qualify as a Russian novel per se.

Weighty tomes all — both thematically and literally (the shortest comes in just under 300 pages) — here are Burt's eight greatest Russian novels, listed per his ranking.

1. **War and Peace** by Leo Tolstoy, 1866 – If you only read one Russian epic, make it Tolstoy's *War and Peace*. Yes, it's a HUGE undertaking, but his spellbinding saga of Russian aristocrats during the Napoleonic Era is a monumental achievement.

2. **The Brothers Karamazov** by Fyodor Dostoevsky, 1880 – Brooding, gloom-laden novel from the novelist many consider the father of existentialism. The title characters must wrestle with the profound consequences of killing their hated father.

3. **Anna Karenina** by Leo Tolstoy, 1877 – The novel's legendary first sentence sets the tone of Tolstoy's other masterpiece: "Happy families are all alike; every unhappy family is unhappy in its own way." A mercurial, passionate aristocratic beauty embarks on an ill-fated affair with a handsome nobleman in this tragic, sweeping romance.

EXCERPT: ANNA KARENINA:

Anna, in that first period of her emancipation and rapid return to health, felt herself unpardonably happy and full of the joy of life. The thought of her husband's unhappiness did not poison her happiness. On one side that memory was too awful to be thought of. On the other side her husband's unhappiness had given her too much happiness to be regretted. The memory of all that had happened after her illness: her reconciliation with her husband, its breakdown, the news of Vronsky's wound, his visit, the preparations for divorce, the departure from her husband's house, the parting from her son — all that seemed to her like a delirious dream, from which she had waked up alone with Vronsky abroad.

4. **Crime and Punishment** by Fyodor Dostoevsky, 1866 – Considering himself beyond moral reproach, a poverty-stricken St. Petersburg student murders a despised money-lender and her feeble sister, only to succumb to paranoia and guilt in Dostoevsky's influential novel.

5. **Dead Souls** by Nikolai Gogol, 1842 – Contrary to its morbid title, Gogol's *Dead Souls* is a rollicking, over-the-top satire of Russian provincial life. A rabidly ambitious young man of limited means attempts to scheme and spend his way towards prosperity in a village populated by neurotic, larger-than-life characters.

6. **Fathers and Sons** by Ivan Turgenev, 1862 – An insightful examination of the generation gap, vis-à-vis the philosophical divide between nihilism and

spirituality that arose in mid-nineteenth century Russia. Amid growing political unrest, a political revolutionary plots to assassinate a high ranking Czarist official: his father.

7. **Petersburg** by Andrey Bely, 1913 – First translated into English in 1959, Bely's innovative symbolist novel has been compared to James Joyce's *Ulysses* for its allusive text and dense wordplay.

8. **Oblomov** by Ivan Goncharov, 1859 – Content to daydream his life away, a fallen member of the Russian aristocracy nearly loses everything, including his one true love, due to his paralyzing apathy, in Goncharov's tragicomic classic.

SCANDINAVIAN MYSTERIES
Murder in the Land of the Midnight Sun

The question as to why mysteries set in contemporary Scandinavia are such hot properties in world literature today can be endlessly debated. Is it the very bleakness of those chilly countries that lends such a palpable sense of dread to these novels? Or is the depiction of shockingly lurid and violent crimes in a region known for being tolerant and peace-loving?

Of course, Scandinavian novelists have been writing top-notch mysteries for several years, but it was Stieg Larsson's international phenomenon, *The Girl with the Dragon Tattoo,* that sparked the current fascination with Scandinavian mysteries. Here are ten noteworthy mysteries, listed alphabetically, by writers from the Land of the Midnight Sun.

1. **Borkman's Point** by Håkan Nesser, 2006 – Nesser's frequent protagonist Chief Inspector Van Veeteren may be cynical and temperamental, but he's also a brilliant and methodical detective who's solved every case except one. In *Borkman's Point*, Van Veeteren interrupts his vacation to investigate the horrific ax murders of an ex-con and a wealthy mogul. A riveting and unsettling murder mystery.

2. **The Devil's Star** by Jo Nesbø, 2005 - Nesbø's anti-hero, alcoholic detective Harry Hole, has a brilliant mind and a perpetually upset stomach. In *The Devil's Star*, Hole wrestles with his demons as he pursues a serial killer who leaves a red diamond at the scene of each crime.

3. **Don't Look Back** by Karin Fossum, 2002 - Inspector Sejer, the hero of Fossum's crime novels, is neither flashy nor rumpled. Described as both "patient" and "shrewd," he delves into complex cases, like the murder of a teenaged girl in a Norwegian village that propels the narrative of *Don't Look Back*, which *Publishers Weekly* praised for Fossum's "mastery of psychological suspense."

4. **Faceless Killers** by Henning Mankell, 1997 – The first of the highly popular Kurt Wallander series introduces Mankell's likable hero. Like everyone, Wallander is bothered by a thousand things and tortured by a dozen, but he retains a resolute professionalism throughout his investigation of a grisly double murder at a remote Swedish farmhouse.

5. **The Girl with the Dragon Tattoo** by Stieg Larsson, 2008 – Lisbeth Salander, the title character of Larsson's bestseller, is one of the most fascinating female characters in all of contemporary literature. Sexually and emotionally abused as a child, she possesses a formidable intelligence and a feral instinct for survival. In the first book of Larsson's *Millennium* trilogy, Lisbeth teams with a disgraced journalist to investigate the long-ago disappearance of a young woman from a wealthy Swedish family.

6. **The Hand That Trembles** by Kjell Eriksson, 2011 – Eriksson has been compared to British mystery writer Ruth Rendell and Henning Mankell for his haunting mysteries featuring Inspector Ann Lindell. In *The Hand That Trembles*, a man disappears without a trace from Sweden, only to be spotted twelve years later in India — or is it an imposter?

7. **The Ice Princess** by Camilla Lackberg, 2008 – Camilla Lackberg wrote her first novel when she was four or five-years-old, but she spent her first seven years out of college as an economist. She made the leap from number-crunching to writing with the creepily atmospheric *The Ice Princess*, the first of Lackberg's seven mysteries set in a Swedish coastal town. Lackberg's depth of characterization has led to her being called "the Swedish Agatha Christie."

EXCERPT: THE ICE PRINCESS:

Mercifully, the corpse's eyes were shut, but the lips were a bright blue. A thin film of ice had formed around the torso, hiding the lower half of the body completely. The right arm, streaked with blood, hung limply over the edge of the tub, its fingers dipped in the congealed pool of blood on the floor. There was a razor blade on the edge of the tub. The other arm was visible only above the elbow, with the rest hidden below the ice. The knees also stuck up above the frozen surface. Alex's long blonde hair was spread out like a fan over the edge of the tub but looked brittle and frozen in the cold.

8. **The Laughing Policeman** by Maj Sjöwall and Per Wahlöö, 1971 – The world of Sjöwall and Wahlöö's hard-bitten Stockholm police detective Martin Beck is vitally alive. A classic of the mystery genre, *The Laughing Policeman* finds Beck on the hunt for an assassin who's gunned down nine people on a city bus.

9. **Silence of the Grave** by Arnaldur Indrioason, 2005 – Indrioason's fourth novel featuring his Icelandic detective Erlendur is one of the finest in the popular series. The discovery of a skeleton at a Reykjavík construction site leads Erlendur to

investigate a family with a tortured past. An expert blend of police procedural and wrenching family drama.

10. <u>**Smilla's Sense of Snow**</u> by Peter Høeg, 1996 – At the heart of Høeg's bestseller is his unusual heroine, Miss Smilla, who not only has a special feeling for the different types of snow that fall on northern countries, but sits uneasily between two cultures as the daughter of a female Inuit hunter and a wealthy urban Danish doctor. Her "sense" and her spirit are put to the test investigating the suspicious death of a young boy who, like Smilla, is an outsider in an uncomfortable land.

SCIENCE BOOKS
Science in Unexpected Places

There are lots of science books about black holes, DNA and the like, many of them excellent. But sometimes it's fun to learn about science from an unpredictable angle — to discover how the laws of physics determine what happens in your favorite sport, or how penguins' physiologies allows them to walk "barefoot" across expanses of Antarctic ice without suffering frostbite. Listed alphabetically, these ten books are not only entertaining and illuminate all kinds of little mysteries — they also provide fresh perspectives to spark new questions about ourselves and the world all around us.

1. <u>**The Disappearing Spoon: And Other True Tales of Madness, Love, and the History of the World from the Periodic Table of Elements**</u> by Sam Kean, 2010 - Make a spoon out of gallium (number 31 on the Periodic Table), a solid which liquefies at 84°F, and it will dissolve as your victim stirs his cup of tea. Thus goes the title anecdote of this witty and authoritative book that tells a myriad of amazing and dramatic tales about the elements in the Periodic Table and the scientists who discovered them.

2. <u>**Life at the Extremes: The Science of Survival**</u> by Frances Ashcroft, 2002 – Ashcroft's book explains clearly and precisely how the bodies of humans and animals manage (or fail) to withstand intense heat and cold, high water pressure and low air pressure, and other extreme situations. Astronauts, athletes, whales, birds, and the author herself all illustrate the marvels of biology and the power of conditioning.

3. <u>**Life's Matrix: A Biography of Water**</u> by Philip Ball, 2001 - Dew, clouds, tears, living cells, oceans, snow, steam, glaciers — water in its myriad forms is just about everywhere, and life as we know it would be impossible without it. This book covers the physics and chemistry of this essential substance, as well as the history of our understanding of it, and current ecological issues.

4. **The Physics of Baseball** by Robert K. Adair, 1990 (3rd ed. 2002) - A fun way to learn more about physics *and* to gain a deeper understanding of the game — Adair explains players' neurophysiology, the finer points of wind resistance and much more.

5. **Radar, Hula Hoops, and Playful Pigs: 67 Digestible Commentaries on the Fascinating Chemistry of Everyday Life** by Joe Schwarcz, 1999 - A popular lecturer in chemistry, Schwarcz discusses the uses and misuses of science, the chemical reasons for everyday phenomena, and what the three items in the title all have in common. You'll come away from the book with a bit more insight, wisdom, and savvy.

6. **Uncorked: The Science of Champagne** by Gérard Liger-Belair, 2004 - You can add a whole new dimension to the lovely experience of drinking champagne with this book. Liger-Belair explains the sometimes poetic, sometimes comical history of champagne, the molecular structure of its bubbles (and provides close-up photographs to illustrate their phases), and exactly why connoisseurs prefer flutes to goblets.

7. **Universal Foam: From Cappuccino to the Cosmos** by Sidney Perkowitz, 2000 - Another book by an author passionate about bubbles, *Universal Foam* takes the reader into geometry, chemistry, physics, geology, cosmology and many other fields. There's a dizzying array of types of foam in our world — including sea foam, latte foam, shaving cream, cheese soufflés, pumice from volcanoes, and possibly even "quantum foam," to name just a few. But Perkowitz makes sense of them all in this delightful book.

8. **The Wave: In Pursuit of the Rogues, Freaks, and Giants of the Ocean** by Susan Casey, 2010 - Adroitly mixing science, surfing, tsunamis and more, author Susan Casey, editor-in-chief of *O* magazine, explores in depth the huge waves that prowl our oceans to the chagrin of mariners and the delight of extreme surfers like Laird Hamilton. The *Los Angeles Times* said Casey's book will leave you "with a healthy respect for the power of these waves" as Casey attempts to unravel one of the great mysteries of our oceans.

EXCERPT: THE WAVE:

During the endless trains of massive waves, Discovery itself was collecting data that would lead to a chilling revelation. The ship was ringed with instruments; everything that happened out there was being precisely measured, the sea's fury captured in tight graphs and unassailable numbers. Months later, long after Avery had returned everyone safely to the Southampton docks, when Holliday began to analyze these figures, she would discover that the waves they had experienced were the largest ever scientifically recorded in the open ocean. The significant wave height, an average of the largest 33 percent of the waves, was sixty-one feet, with frequent spikes far beyond that. At the same time, none of the state-of-the-art weather forecasts and wave models—the information upon which all ships, oil rigs, fisheries, and passenger boats rely—had predicted these behemoths. In other words, under this particular set of weather conditions, waves this size should not have existed. And yet they did.

9. **What Einstein Told His Cook: Kitchen Science Explained** by Robert L. Wolke, 2002 - A funny and eloquent writer, dedicated gourmand, and professor of chemistry, Wolke explains some of the mysteries of cooking, as well as familiar processes that you might never have thought of in a scientific light before. There are also a few tempting recipes so that you can see and taste how things work for yourself.

10. **Why We Love: The Nature and Chemistry of Romantic Love** by Helen Fisher, 2004 - Why does love make us feel so rapturous? Why do so many couples divorce after just a few years, while others manage to stay together their whole lives? Do animals experience romantic love? Neurochemistry, evolutionary theory, and love poetry all come together in this thought-provoking and appealing book

SCIENCE FICTION NOVELS
Alien Encounters

If only the aliens who invade the Earth in many of the following science fiction novels followed the benign lead of Klaatu, the extraterrestrial emissary of peace in the classic film *The Day the Earth Stood Still*. Whereas Klaatu comes to Earth to save us from ourselves in Robert Wise's still-potent cold war parable, the Martians in H.G. Wells' *War of the Worlds* pursue an intergalactic form of "scorched earth policy" after landing outside London. And then there's the more insidious threat to mankind posed by the interstellar pods in Jack Finney's *Invasion of the Body Snatchers*. They're simply taking over our bodies and minds while we sleep. It's enough to make you welcome chronic insomnia!

Here are ten science fiction novels, listed alphabetically, that depict our first contact with aliens — none of whom even vaguely resemble little green men.

1. **The Alien Years** by Robert Silverberg, 1998 – Silverberg's ambitious melding of family saga and alien invasion story. *The Alien Years* spans fifty years in the lives of the Carmichael family, the leaders in a resistance movement against alien oppressors, known as the "Entities."

2. **Blindsight** by Peter Watts, 2006 – Watts puts a strikingly original and imaginative spin on the "first contact" narrative in *Blindsight*, which depicts an exploration team's rendezvous with a massive alien artifact at the edge of our solar system. A 2007 nominee for a Hugo Award.

3. **Childhood's End** by Arthur C. Clarke, 1953 – An alien race initially brings peace and prosperity to Earth, but over time, reveal its sinister ulterior motive for mankind. An unnerving and provocative classic from the visionary author of _2001: A Space Odyssey_.

EXCERPT: CHILDHOOD'S END:

For a moment that seemed to last forever, Reinhold watched, as all the world was watching, while the great ships descended in their overwhelming majesty — until at last he could hear the faint scream of their passage through the thin air of the stratosphere.

He felt no regrets as the work of a lifetime was swept away. He had labored to take man to the stars, and, in the moment of success, the stars — the aloof, indifferent stars — had come to him. This was the moment when history held its breath, and the present sheared asunder from the past as an iceberg splits from its frozen, parent cliffs, and goes sailing out to sea in lonely pride. All that the past ages had achieved was as nothing now: only one thought echoed and re-echoed through Reinhold's brain: The human race was no longer alone.

4. **The Forge of God** by Greg Bear, 1987 – The arrival of two groups of aliens on Earth is greeted as a sign of the imminent apocalypse. The _Los Angeles Times_ praised Forge's novel as "profound and unusual."

5. **Invasion of the Body Snatchers** by Jack Finney, 1955 – Finney's chilling, oft-filmed story of aliens replacing people with emotionless replicas.

6. **The Mote in God's Eye** by Larry Niven and Jerry Pournelle, 1974 – Two of science fiction's most distinguished writers collaborate on this epic novel, set in 3016, when a probe returns to earth with a dead alien. Scientists follow the probe's course back to the Mote, a huge star that's home to ancient civilization. Robert Heinlein called _The Mote in God's Eye_ "quite possibly the finest science fiction novel I have ever read."

7. **The Puppet Masters** by Robert Heinlein, 1951 – Secret agents in a shadowy, government organization known only as "The Section" face a deadly, seemingly unstoppable foe in the repellant form of mind-controlling, slug-like aliens. Heinlein skillfully plays on cold war-era jitters about the Soviet Union in _The Puppet Masters_.

8. **The Sparrow** by Mary Doria Russell, 1996 – The sole survivor of a doomed first expedition to the planet Rakhat, a Jesuit priest struggles with his faith as he recounts his experiences in Russell's first acclaimed novel, which _Entertainment Weekly_ praised for its "smooth storytelling and gorgeous characterization." An equally fine sequel, _**Children of God**_, followed in 1998.

9. **War of the Worlds** by H. G. Wells, 1898 – The sun nearly sets on the British Empire, and everywhere else for that matter, when Martians unleash hell on mankind in Wells' classic, Victorian-era version of alien Armageddon.

10. **Year Zero** by Robert H. Reid, 2012 – An intergalactic case of copyright violation has bankrupted aliens hooked on pop music, which they've been listening to since "Year Zero," i.e., 1977. Furious about being owned by humans, they're plotting mankind's imminent destruction — unless hapless entertainment lawyer Nick Carter can resolve the biggest case of his career. Fans of Douglas Adams' ***The Hitchhiker's Guide to the Galaxy*** will enjoy this hilarious blend of satire and science fiction by Silicon Valley author and entrepreneur Reid.

SCIENCE FICTION NOVELS
Visionary Classics

One of humanity's earliest questions must have been "What if?" Perhaps extraterrestrials asked that too. And humankind has never stopped asking it! That's how the joys of science fiction came to be. No single genre may be as remarkably rich and splendidly diverse. From the sword-and-sorcery adventures on Mars of Edgar Rice Burroughs to social satire made notable by *Galaxy* magazine to "hard science" and poetical whimsy, science fiction has something for everyone. Sometimes it may be pointedly trying to teach a lesson; other times it may be a clear and simple flight of imagination. Because of its origins in pulp magazines, where pay-by-the-word was minimal, the search for success for the science fiction writer meant creating lots of product. So now there is a vast universe of writing to for the science fiction fan to discover and savor. The following classics are listed alphabetically by author.

1. **The Hitchhiker's Guide to the Galaxy** by Douglas Adams, 1979 – Originally a BBC radio series, the wackiness-in-outer-space adventure of Arthur Dent was an immediate hit. Adams' off-kilter sense of humor spilled over into four more novels, a television series and a major film, but the first book is the most refreshingly silly. Science fiction, which often takes itself much too seriously, is skewered deliciously by Adams in this laugh-out-loud funny novel.

2. **The Foundation Trilogy** by Isaac Asimov, 1951-1953 – The grand sweep of galactic history, told with a bold voice by one of science fiction's most revered writers, the *Foundation* trilogy began as a series of short stories, which Asimov ultimately expanded into seven novels. It received the one-time Hugo Award for Best All-Time Series in 1966.

3. **The Stars My Destination** by Alfred Bester, 1957 – Perhaps no character in any literary genre goes through a transformation as dramatic as Gully Foyle, the

protagonist of Bester's acclaimed novel. Stranded in a demolished spaceship, he finds the fire of revenge enough to lead him to a new dimension of existence. Visionary, challenging, thrilling.

4. **Fahrenheit 451** by Ray Bradbury, 1953 – Bradbury's writing legacy is vast, touching every medium and around a dozen genres. But this novel set in the near future may be his most engaging as well as his most provocative work. In a world where reading books can mean death by fire, how does the sane person behave?

5. **Ender's Game** by Orson Scott Card, 1985 – Winner of both the Hugo and Nebula Awards, *Ender's Game* is a coming-of-age story set in a school for child warriors, where the prodigiously intelligent Ender Wiggin is learning how to fight hostile aliens. Hailed as "a major science fiction novel by any reasonable standards" by *Booklist*, *Ender's Game* has spawned four sequels and developed an ardent following among young readers.

6. **2001: A Space Odyssey** by Arthur C. Clarke, 1968 – Clarke wrote this novel while collaborating on the screenplay for Stanley Kubrick's iconic film of the same name. The discovery of an ancient monolith on the moon sends the crew of the spaceship *Discovery* in search of the extraterrestrials who built it. Their epic journey into the unknown is undercut by the ship's computer system, HAL, which takes command of the ship with disastrous results. Clarke wrote three sequels to this spellbinding and challenging novel: *2010: Odyssey Two*, *2061: Odyssey Three* and *3001: The Final Odyssey*.

7. **Neuromancer** by William Gibson, 1984 – Some science fiction novels are eerily prophetic, predicting a future that becomes a reality. *Neuromancer* does that in spades, anticipating computer hacking and the cyberspace, a word Gibson himself coined. The first-ever winner of the "triple crown" of science fiction (the Hugo, Nebula and Philip K. Dick Awards), the original "cyberpunk novel" is a must-read.

EXCERPT: NEUROMANCER:

A year here and he still dreamed of cyberspace, hope fading nightly. All the speed he took, all the turns he'd taken and the corners he'd cut in Night City, and still he'd see the matrix in his sleep, bright lattices of logic unfolding across that colorless void...The Sprawl was a long strange way home over the Pacific now, and he was no console man, no cyberspace cowboy. Just another hustler, trying to make it through. But the dreams came on in the Japanese night like livewire voodoo, and he'd cry for it, cry in his sleep, and wake alone in the dark, curled in his capsule in some coffin hotel, his hands clawed into the bedslab, temperfoam bunched between his fingers, trying to reach the console that wasn't there.

8. **Stranger in a Strange Land** by Robert A. Heinlein, 1961 – "The most famous science fiction novel ever written" is the blurb on several editions of this book, and it's a point that's hard to argue. The story of Valentine Michael Smith, a human born and raised on Mars, *Stranger in a Strange Land* was an immediate hit and a Hugo Award winner, but Heinlein's masterpiece found its greatest success when it became a baby-boomer cult classic.

9. **Dune** by Frank Herbert, 1965 – When you combine the words "science fiction" and "saga," you naturally think of *Dune*. Epic in scale, rich in philosophy, and fascinating in science, this is a big book in every way, as Herbert expertly draws you into the strange and mystical world of the desert planet Arrakis. *Dune* inspired five sequels by Herbert himself, and more by his son and Kevin J. Anderson. It also spawned a big movie, several TV miniseries, board games, computer games, and even songs.

10. **The Left Hand of Darkness** by Ursula K. LeGuin, 1969 – A high school classmate of fellow science fiction visionary Philip K. Dick, LeGuin (***The Dispossessed***) is one of the masters of the genre. She's received multiple Hugo and Nebula Awards, won the National Book Award for her children's book ***The Farthest Shore*** and was a Pulitzer Prize finalist for her short story collection, ***Unlocking the Air and Other Stories***. In *The Left Hand of Darkness*, a human emissary to the planet Winter struggles with the aliens' gender fluidity, which upends his perceptions of society and self.

SELF-HELP BOOKS
Stress Relief

Ordinary life in our society has become a bit crazy. Each day, we're confronted with a whirlwind of information both important and trivial, and many of us have more responsibilities than we can easily handle. All too often our attention is fragmented, our bodies are tense, and our lives feel out of control. There are lots of quick fixes available (fast food to solve the eating problem, mindless television to relax, sleeping pills for insomnia) but in the long run these don't give us the vitality and joy we wish for in our lives.

Are there straightforward solutions to these problems? Sometimes there are, even if you can't spend the rest of your life at a spa. The books that follow provide alternative perspectives on contemporary life. They offer a wealth of practical ways to cut down on stress and respond better to the stressful circumstances that remain, giving you more time and energy for the things (and people) you value most. Listed in alphabetical order.

1. **Clear Your Clutter With Feng Shui** by Karen Kingston, 1999 — Even if you're skeptical about some of the esoteric aspects of feng shui — the traditional Chinese practice of arranging objects and buildings to optimize energy flow — this lovely book can inspire you to let go of the clutter in your home (and mind and body) that may be "clogging" your life.

2. **Conscious Breathing: Breathwork for Health, Stress Release, and Personal Mastery** by Gay Hendricks, 1995 — One of the most profound influences on our mental and emotional states is hidden right under our noses (or flowing right through them, to be more precise). This book explains the physiology of breathing and provides illustrated exercises to help you experience the difference that conscious breathing can make.

3. **Finding Flow: The Psychology of Engagement With Everyday Life** by Mihaly Csikszentmihalyi, 1997 — Written by a cutting-edge researcher, this book teaches us how we can have "peak experiences" of consciousness more often and how to live richly at work, in our leisure time, and even when doing our least favorite chores.

4. **How to Stop Worrying and Start Living** by Dale Carnegie, 1944 — With his talent for getting at the heart of a matter, the author of ***How to Win Friends and Influence People*** offers timeless wisdom about prioritizing, effectiveness, and authenticity.

5. **Life Is Not a Stress Rehearsal: Bringing Yesterday's Sane Wisdom Into Today's Insane World** by Loretta LaRoche, 2001 — LaRoche presents a clear-headed look at the excesses, misplaced values, and unnecessary complications that are rampant in our culture — all with a healthy dose of humor.

6. **The Simple Living Guide: A Sourcebook for Less Stressful, More Joyful Living** by Janet Luhrs, 1997 — The editor of *Simple Living* magazine shares realistic ideas and useful resources for enjoying a well-planned, relaxed, and vibrant lifestyle. The book includes inspiring examples of people who've radically changed their lives in the direction of simplicity.

EXCERPT: THE SIMPLE LIVING GUIDE:

When you live deeply, consciously, sucking the marrow out of life, you will live a full, robust, honest, and intimate life. When you skim over the surface, never stopping to really, deeply feel or think about what you are doing, or when you simply react to one event after another, you will discover, as Thoreau laments, that you have not lived. This is the essence of simplicity . . . to live with full awareness and with passion.

7. **The Simple Truth: Meditation and Mindfulness for the Modern World** by Jeff Cannon, 2011 – Combining Eastern philosophical traditions with Western medical perspectives, this book occupies a unique niche between the humanities and hard sciences. Cannon was running a host of successful businesses when he discovered he had seven brain tumors, a consequence, according to him, of all the stress he was under. Healthy now, he espouses a message of meditation and breathing techniques. Smoothly written and compelling in its life details, *The Simple Truth* is a convincing read for those seeking greater balance in their lives.

8. **Sustainable Wellness: An Integrative Approach to Transform Your Mind, Body, and Spirit** by Dr. Matt Mumber and Heather Reed, 2012 – Mumber, a radiation oncologist, is a seasoned speaker on the topic of integrative approaches to health, while co-author Reed has been teaching yoga — especially to those with cancer and chronic illnesses — since 1996. This easily accessible book promotes a three-legged approach — physical activity, good nutrition, and stress management — to living well, and contains simple exercises and mnemonic devices for assisting readers in conceptualizing and achieving their health goals.

9. **The Wellness Book: The Comprehensive Guide to Maintaining Health and Treating Stress-Related Illness** by Herbert Benson and Eileen M. Stuart, 1992 – Benson is the renowned author of ***The Relaxation Response***; here, he and co-author Stuart discuss that topic and many others, covering both physical and psychological aspects of health.

10. **Wherever You Go, There You Are: Mindfulness Meditation in Everyday Life** by Jon Kabat-Zinn, 1994 – This is a clear, friendly introduction to different types of meditation and their benefits from the founder of the Stress Reduction Clinic at the University of Massachusetts Medical Center. It even shows you how parenting (often one of the most stressful experiences as well as one of the most rewarding) can be a route to mindfulness.

SHORT STORY COLLECTIONS
Masters of the Short Story, Past and Present

Short story writers can create a world in just a few pages. Although they can be read in a brief period of time, the best works of short fiction give you things to think about for long afterward.

Here are twelve collections, listed alphabetically, from masterful practitioners of the form, past and present.

1. **Binocular Vision: New and Selected Stories** by Edith Pearlman, 2011 - The winner of the 2011 National Book Critics Circle Award for Fiction, Pearlman's

latest collection of short stories depict the frailties and foibles of characters of all ages, as well as the themes of accommodation and dislocation, in prose that is emotionally lucid and often poetic.

2. **The Complete Stories** by Flannery O'Connor, 1971 – The ailing young woman from Georgia who kept peacocks on her lawn wrote some of America's most haunting and strange religious fiction. There are always unexpected moral dimensions to the portraits she drew of a wide range of people in her native South.

3. **The Essential Tales of Chekhov** by Anton Chekhov, translated by Constance Garnett and edited by Richard Ford, 1998 – Chekhov, who lived in the second half of the nineteenth century, had a life cut short by illness. The Russian playwright was also a master of the short story, revealing the internal dramas in his characters' lives with both humor and gravity.

4. **High Lonesome: Stories 1966–2006** by Joyce Carol Oates, 2006 – The stories in this collection were chosen by the author herself from four decades of work. Oates has a distinct vision of contemporary American life that's often expressed in tightly wound tales of dysfunctional families and individuals. As edgy and dark as they can be, her stories achieve a believability that makes them compelling.

5. **Interpreter of Maladies** by Jhumpa Lahiri, 1999 – Set in India and the United States, these stories offer a gentler look at contemporary life and its often perplexing, unmoored experiences. They explore the nuances of marriages and other relationships, including the relationships between different cultures.

6. **Nine Stories b**y J.D. Salinger, 1953 – Published two years after *The Catcher in the Rye*, Salinger's short story collection features such classics as "A Perfect Day for Bananafish," "Uncle Wiggily in Connecticut" and "For Esmé — with Love and Squalor."

7. **Paris Stories** by Mavis Gallant, 2002 – Gallant is a Canadian writer who has spent many years living in Paris, the setting for some of her best fiction. Her sharp powers of observation join forces with a strong awareness of the past, which often seems to haunt the people and places she writes about in these compelling short stories.

8. **Runaway** by Alice Munro, 2004 – Called "our Chekhov" by writer Cynthia Ozick, Munro received the 2009 Man Booker International Prize for her body of work. Her astutely drawn portraits of complex women experiencing quiet epiphanies are the focus of the eight stories in *Runaway*, which received Canada's prestigious Giller Prize in 2004.

9. **The Short Stories** by Ernest Hemingway, 1938 – Hemingway's famous prose style — spare and understated yet vivid, tough yet moving—has stood up well through the years and continues to inspire other writers. This collection contains classics such as "The Snows of Kilimanjaro," which is about a writer's encounter

with death while he is on safari, and "Hills Like White Elephants," a brief story of a couple conversing over drinks that manages to be fraught with realistic tension.

10. **Sorry Please Thank You** by Charles Yu, 2012 – Mixing deadpan humor, surreal, science fiction-inspired conceits, satirical flourishes and genuine pathos, Yu's often fantastical short stories have prompted critics to mention him in the same breath as Ray Bradbury, Philip K. Dick and Kurt Vonnegut.

11. **The Stories of John Cheever** by John Cheever, 1978 – Cheever writes about troubled characters trapped in normal suburban life. His narratives describe ominous, sometimes surreal events and reveal buried inner struggles. You'll find favorites such as "The Enormous Radio" and "The Swimmer" in this collection, which won both the Pulitzer Prize and the National Book Critics Circle Award.

EXCERPT: THE STORIES OF JOHN CHEEVER: "THE SWIMMER":

He dove in and swam the pool, but when he tried to haul himself up onto the curb he found that the strength in his arms and shoulders had gone, and he paddled to the ladder and climbed out. Looking over his shoulder he saw, in the lighted bathhouse, a young man. Going out onto the dark lawn he smelled chrysanthemums or marigolds — some stubborn autumnal fragrance — on the night air, strong as gas. Looking overhead he saw that the stars had come out, but why should he seem to see Andromeda, Cepheus, and Cassiopeia? What had become of the constellations of midsummer? He began to cry.

12. **Where I'm Calling From: Selected Stories** by Raymond Carver, 1988 – In contrast to Cheever's portrayals of middle-class America, Carver's home terrain is working-class America. His writing is spare but sophisticated, and wonderfully heartfelt as well.

SLAVE STORIES
The Age of Slavery in American Literature

When Abraham Lincoln met Harriet Beecher Stowe in 1862, he reportedly said, only half in jest, "So you're the little woman who wrote the book that started this great war!"

The "book" was Stowe's classic novel *Uncle Tom's Cabin*, which had first appeared in serialized form in the abolitionist newspaper *The National Era,* in 1851. Later published in book form, Stowe's harrowing tale of slaves enduring brutal abuse and abject cruelty at the hands of their masters was an immediate cause célèbre that polarized readers and became a huge bestseller. While its melodramatic plot and egregious racial stereotypes don't hold up very well, *Uncle Tom's Cabin* nonetheless remains one of the most influential novels ever written for its galvanizing effect on the abolition movement. It therefore rates a place on the following, alphabetical list of twelve novels about the age of slavery in the United States.

1. **The Autobiography of Miss Jane Pittman** by Ernest J. Gaines, 1971 – Gaines' wonderful and intensely moving novel about a 110-year-old former slave telling her life story to a young writer was later turned into a classic, made-for-television film starring Cicely Tyson in the title role.

2. **The Bondwoman's Narrative** by Hannah Crafts, 1850s – Discovered by Harvard historian Henry Louis Gates Jr. at an auction, *The Bondwoman's Narrative* may be the first novel written by an African-American woman. Melodramatic and stilted, this story about a young slave woman escaping to freedom nevertheless holds your interest.

3. **Clotel; Or The President's Daughter** by William Wells Brown, 1853 – One of the first novels written by an African-American writer, *Clotel* tackles a controversial subject head-on: the rumored mulatto offspring of Thomas Jefferson and his slave mistress. In Brown's compelling, swiftly-paced narrative, the heroine escapes slavery, only to risk capture when she attempts to rescue her daughter from Jefferson's home.

4. **The Confessions of Nat Turner** by William Styron, 1967 – Based on the actual jail house confession of Turner, who led a slave revolt in Virginia in 1831, Styron's Pulitzer Prize- winning classic has polarized African-American critics over its portrait of the title character, an educated slave whose long-simmering rage explodes in bloody violence.

5. **Jubilee b**y Margaret Walker, 1966 – Inspired by her grandmother's stories, Walker transforms the true story of a Mississippi slave woman born to her master and his slave mistress into a riveting and sensitively wrought piece of historical fiction.

6. **The Known World** by Edwin P. Jones, 2003 – Jones' superb, Pulitzer Prize- winning novel addresses a subject that's rarely discussed about the age of slavery: freed slaves who became slaveholders themselves. Set in antebellum Virginia, this mesmerizing and brilliantly nuanced novel depicts the social and psychological repercussions of black-on-black ownership from multiple points of view.

EXCERPT: THE KNOWN WORLD:

It took Moses more than two weeks to understand that someone one wasn't fiddling with him and that indeed a black man, two shades darker than himself, owned him and any shadow he made. Sleeping in a cabin beside Henry in the first weeks after the sale, Moses had thought that it was already a strange world that made him a slave to a white man, but God had indeed set it twirling and twisting every which way when he put black people to owning their own kind. Was God even up there attending to business anymore?

7. **Middle Passage** by Charles Johnson, 1990 – On the run from creditors and a lovelorn schoolteacher, a freed slave stows away aboard a ship, unaware that he's boarded an illegal slave trader bound for Africa under the erratic command of a sadistic taskmaster. The winner of the National Book Award, *Middle Passage* has the sweep and emotional heft of the seafaring novels of Conrad and Melville.

8. **Property: A Novel** by Valerie Martin, 2002 – The author of ***Mary Reilly*** ventures into Southern Gothic territory with this atmospheric novel about the tense relationship between a wealthy Louisiana woman and her husband's beautiful slave mistress.

9. **Song of Slaves in the Desert** by Alan Cheuse, 2011 – Cheuse, who has reviewed books on National Public Radio for two decades, captures the horrors of slavery and the moral anguish they engender in this historical novel about Nathaniel Pereira, a New York Jew who travels to the antebellum South to resurrect his uncle's plantation. Two parallel stories — that of Pereira and his infatuation with a beautiful slave, and another that follows a family's 200-year journey from Timbuktu in Mali to enslavement in America— eventually tie powerfully together.

10. **Uncle Tom's Cabin** by Harriet Beecher Stowe, 1851 – Yes, it is clichéd and painfully overwrought, but *Uncle Tom's Cabin* has an undeniably raw power and sincerity that nearly compensates for Stowe's problematic depiction of the slave characters.

11. **Walk Through Darkness** by David Anthony Durham, 2002 – Durham beat the sophomore slump with this terrific follow-up to his well-received debut novel, ***Gabriel's Story***. He skillfully balances the parallel story lines of two men in the antebellum South: a runaway slave and the old Scottish immigrant tracking him down.

12. **Wench** by Dolen Perkins-Valdez, 2010 – In her debut novel, Perkins-Valdez takes us to a mid-1850s Ohio resort where Southern slave owners vacation with their black mistresses. Based on extensive research (the resort actually existed and ultimately became the nation's first black college), the book tells the story of four slave women who are tempted to flee to freedom in the North, but tormented over the prospect of abandoning their children.

SOUTHERN LITERATURE
Top Ten of the Twentieth Century

Few regions in the United States exert a more enduring hold on the popular imagination than the American South. Alternately romanticized and reviled, the South remains haunted by a tumultuous, often terrible past that continues to shape and inform the culture of the region to this day, nearly 150 years after the Civil War ended with Lee's surrender to Grant at Appomattox.

One of the legacies of the South's unique culture has been a rich literary tradition that's produced many of America' greatest writers: William Faulkner, Zora Neale Hurston, Flannery O'Connor, Eudora Welty and Thomas Wolfe immediately spring to mind. Along with scores of other Southern writers, they cast a light on this misunderstood and often maligned region that's lent itself to caricature and egregious stereotyping.

In 2000, while researching his three-part documentary series on twentieth century Southern literature, *Tell Us About the South: Voices in Black and White*, filmmaker Ross Spears polled book editors, publishers, scholars and reviewers regarding their selections for "the most remarkable works of modern Southern literature." Here are the top ten vote-getters in fiction, ranked in descending order.

1. **Invisible Man** by Ralph Ellison, 1953 – Winner of the 1953 National Book Award, Ellison's magisterial novel follows the unnamed African-American narrator on his journey of self-discovery from the South to Harlem, where he becomes involved with a black nationalist group called The Brotherhood. A startling, provocative novel that burns itself in your memory.

2. **The Sound and the Fury** by William Faulkner, 1929 – Arguably *the* greatest of all the Southern novelists, Faulkner immerses you in the tumultuous lives of the Compson family in this demanding, stream-of-consciousness novel divided into four sections. Set in Yoknapatawpha County, Mississippi, the fictional setting for many of Faulkner's novels, *The Sound and the Fury* was selected the sixth greatest English-language novel of the twentieth century by Modern Library.

3. **Look Homeward, Angel** by Thomas Wolfe, 1929 – Although some critics now regard it as overwrought and hyperbolic, Wolfe's first, unabashedly autobiographical novel remains a pivotal work of modern Southern literature. His sprawling, coming-of-age narrative follows Eugene Gant as he flees his North Carolina hometown for the sophisticated world of Harvard University.

4. **To Kill a Mockingbird** by Harper Lee, 1960 – A perennial favorite that's brought generations of readers to tears, Lee's elegiac, sensitively written coming-of-age novel is set against the backdrop of a racially-charged rape trial in Depression-era Alabama. Lee's only novel, *To Kill a Mockingbird* won the 1961 Pulitzer Prize.

5. **The Color Purple** by Alice Walker, 1982 – An epistolary novel, *The Color Purple* tells the heartbreaking yet finally uplifting story of Celie, a poor, downtrodden African-American woman trapped in an abusive marriage to a widower with several children. Gradually, through her relationship with a fiery blues singer, Celie finds the strength to take charge of her destiny in Walker's feminist classic, written in the black vernacular of her uneducated heroine.

6. **Their Eyes Were Watching God** by Zora Neale Hurston, 1937 – A key figure of the Harlem Renaissance, novelist/folklorist Hurston achieved her greatest success with this evocative novel about a strong-willed woman chafing under the status quo in the all-black community of Eaton, Florida. Although some of Hurston's fellow Harlem Renaissance writers criticized this novel for reinforcing negative racial stereotypes, *Their Eyes Were Watching God* has influenced such writers as Maya Angelou and Alice Walker.

EXCERPT: THEIR EYES WERE WATCHING GOD:

Oh to be a pear tree   any tree in bloom! With kissing bees singing of the beginning of the world! She was sixteen. She had glossy leaves and bursting buds and she wanted to struggle with life, but it seemed to elude her. Where were the singing bees for her? Nothing on the place nor in her grandma's house answered her. She searched as much of the world as she could from the top of the front steps and leaned over to gaze up and down the road. Looking, waiting, breathing short with impatience. Waiting for the world to be made.

7. **Absalom, Absalom!** by William Faulkner, 1936 – Peripherally connected to *The Sound and the Fury*, *Absalom, Absalom!* is a quintessentially Southern Gothic saga of three Mississippi families before, during and after the Civil War. Told in flashback form, Faulkner's mesmerizing novel paints a disturbing portrait of the American South at its most degenerate.

8. **All the King's Men** by Robert Penn Warren, 1946 – Bearing more than a passing resemblance to Huey P. Long, the polarizing Louisiana governor turned U.S. senator who was assassinated in 1935, Warren's Willie Stark is one of the most unforgettable characters in all of American literature. This Pulitzer Prize-winning classic depicts the rapid rise and sudden fall of the volatile, larger-than-life Stark, who becomes Louisiana's governor in the thirties.

9. **Collected Stories b**y Eudora Welty, 1982 – A strong sense of place and character inform Welty's superb short stories, which effortlessly span multiple genres in this National Book Award-winning collection, which includes such classics as "Petrified Man," "Why I Live at the P. O." and "The Wide Net."

10. **The Moviegoer** by Walker Percy, 1961 – Emotionally isolated and haunted by his combat experiences in the Korean War, a New Orleans stockbroker spends his evenings at local movie theaters, his refuge from reality, as he struggles to find

meaning and purpose in his life. The winner of the National Book Award, *The Moviegoer* is a profound and elegantly written novel that stays with you.

SPORTS BOOKS
Sports Illustrated's Top Ten of All Time

When *The New Yorker* journalist A. J. Liebling quipped, "I can write better than anybody who can write faster, and I can write faster than anybody who can write better," it wasn't just idle boasting on his part. A dazzling writer of pungent wit and brilliant insight who could turn a phrase that made his peers sigh with envy, Liebling could write on everything from Louisiana politics to food to boxing with equal authority. Hailed by no less than Tom Wolfe as one of the pioneers of "new journalism," Liebling is probably best remembered today for *The Sweet Science*, his superb collection of essays on boxing.

In 2002, the editors of *Sports Illustrated* declared Liebling's *The Sweet Science* the all-time best sports book. Here are the *Sports Illustrated* editors' top ten nonfiction sports books, ranked in descending order, plus two more recent titles worth reading.

1. **The Sweet Science** by A. J. Liebling, 1956 – A knockout collection of essays on boxing that *SI*'s editors pronounce "timeless." Pugilists famous (Rocky Marciano) and obscure duke it out, figuratively speaking, in the essays of *The Sweet Science*, which the *SI* editors compare to the novels of Henry James for the extraordinary richness of detail.

2. **The Boys of Summer** by Roger Kahn, 1971 – A monumental portrait of the Brooklyn Dodgers, whose relocation to Los Angeles in 1958 plunged the team's Brooklyn fans into mourning. Kahn's superbly written account of the players' lives on and off the baseball diamond is as dramatic as any novel. According to *SI*'s editors, "No book is better at showing how sports is not just games."

3. **Ball Four** by Jim Bouton, 1970 – Bouton's controversial, hilarious warts-and-all memoir of the 1969 Yankee season spares no one, least of all himself, in airing the players' dirty laundry. According to *SI*'s editors, Bouton's "biting observations" rendered him persona non grata in the Yankee dugout.

4. **Friday Night Lights** by H.G. Bissinger, 1990 – In the flat, dusty towns of West Texas, high school football is practically a religion. Bissinger's masterful and socially acute portrait of an Odessa, Texas high school football team in the late eighties is a "brilliant look at how Friday-night lights can lead a town into darkness," per *SI*'s editors.

5. **A Season on the Brink: A Year with Bobby Knight and the Indiana Hoosiers** by John Feinstein, 1986 – Known as "The General," former Indiana Hoosiers basketball coach Bobby Knight is a textbook polarizing figure. His remarkable

record is frequently overshadowed by his notorious, sometimes violent fits of rage, Knight gave Feinstein unlimited access to watch his every move over the course of a season. Called "unsparing" by *SI*'s editors, Feinstein's book was a huge bestseller.

6. **Paper Lion: Confessions of a Last-String Quarterback** by George Plimpton, 1965 – Not many rank amateurs would test their mettle against professional football players, but that's just what Plimpton did in 1963, when he participated in the Detroit Lions' training camp. Not only did Plimpton survive the bone-crunching experience, he also wrote about it —"brilliantly" — per *SI*'s editors, in *Paper Lion*, his insider account of the NFL.

7. **The Game** by Ken Dryden, 1983 – Now a politician in his native Canada, former Montreal Canadien goalkeeper Dryden sheds light on the rough-and-tumble world of professional hockey in *The Game*, his perceptive memoir about the Canadiens' 1979 Stanley Cup-winning season that *SI*'s editors call "well-crafted."

8. **Seabiscuit: An American Legend** by Laura Hillenbrand, 2001 – Hillenbrand's exhilarating, prize-winning book about the knobby-kneed Depression-era racehorse who dominated the nation's headlines is a modern day classic. "Irresistible," according to *SI*'s editors.

9. **Loose Balls: The Short, Wild Life of the American Basketball Association** by Terry Pluto, 1990 – Julius "Doctor J" Erving, Rick Barry and Mel Daniels are just some of the basketball greats reminiscing about the long-gone American Basketball Association in this oral history teeming with anecdotes *SI*'s editors call "almost too-good-to-be-true."

10. **Heaven is a Playground b**y Rick Telander, 1976 – Telander's "intriguing account of inner-city hoops" will appeal to anyone who loved the 1994 documentary, *Hoop Dreams*.

CONTEMPORARY TITLES

11. ***A Terrible Splendor: Three Extraordinary Men, a World Poised for War, and the Greatest Tennis Match Ever Played*** by Marshall Jon Fisher, 2009 – The winner of the 2010 PEN/ESPN Award for Literary Sports Writing, Fisher's account of the marathon 1937 Davis Cup final between American hero Don Budge and the aristocratic German champion Baron Gottfried von Cramm is as riveting as any novel. Mentored by the controversial former champion Bill Tilden, von Cramm plays for the "glory" of Nazi Germany — even as he tries to keep his homosexuality secret from the Gestapo.

EXCERPT: A TERRIBLE SPLENDOR:

July the twentieth, 1937, and Baron Gottfried von Cramm tosses a new white Slazenger tennis ball three feet above his head. It seems to hang there suspended for the slightest of moments, a distant frozen moon, before his wooden racket plucks it out of the electrified air of Wimbledon's Centre Court, rocketing a

211

service winner past J. Donald Budge. The deciding match of the Davis Cup competition between the United States and Germany has begun, a contest that will long be called "the greatest tennis match ever." Fourteen thousand onlookers — aristocrats out to be seen, sportswriters, any tennis fans who could take off work on a Tuesday; Queen Mary, her entourage, several members of Parliament, and foreign diplomats in the Royal Box — shift in their seats as von Cramm's serve finally splits the fine membrane between anticipation and fulfillment. The thud of tight "catgut" strings against ball marks the moment: it is 4:57 p.m.

12. **Those Guys Have All The Fun: Inside the World of ESPN** by James Andrew Miller and Tom Shales, 2011 – The rise of the phenomenally successful television sports network makes for addictive reading in this immensely entertaining oral history, compiled from more than five hundred interviews with everyone from ESPN network honchos to athletes to broadcast journalists.

TERRORISM STUDIES
Making Sense of the Senseless

It's hard to believe that human beings would choose to air their grievances by deliberately targeting civilians for slaughter. But the ideologies that celebrate this behavior are followed by enough people to make this a pressing international issue. We need to understand the whys and hows of fanaticism and terror in order to fight it — and not make the same mistakes that fuel terrorist attacks. Here are ten insightful books, listed alphabetically, about this baffling global scourge.

1. **500 Days: Secrets and Lies in the Terror Wars** by Kurt Eichenwald, 2012 – In the devastating aftermath of 9/11, President George W. Bush declared a "War on Terror." Yet the campaign against terrorists and the states that support them was impeded by what Eichenwald calls the "decisions, deceptions, and delusions" of the first eighteen months after 9/11. Exhaustively researched and paced like an espionage thriller, *500 Days: Secrets and Lies in the Terror Wars* is an eye-opening — and sometimes shocking — account that sheds much-needed light on this time.

2. **Dying To Kill: The Allure of Suicide Terror** by Mia Bloom, 2005 - Bloom traces the use of suicide attacks throughout history in places as diverse as Japan, Ireland, and the West Bank. Drawing on research in the field as well as historical analysis, she examines the motivations of attackers and the ways their decisions are influenced by attitudes within their communities. She finds that harsh counterattacks often lead to a cycle of violence, and discusses ways to avoid this deadly spiral. The book also includes a chapter on female suicide bombers.

3. **Dying to Win: The Strategic Logic of Suicide Terrorism** by Robert Pape, 2005 - Pape collects information about suicide attacks around the world since the eighties and subjects the data to rigorous analysis, coming up with some surprising conclusions. Far from being ignorant and desperately poor, many suicide bombers are actually well-educated and middle class. Pape shows how the strategic goals of the organized groups that are responsible for most such attacks can both drive them forward and rein them in. He also notes a striking similarity among contemporary suicide terrorist campaigns — all are aimed at expelling the military forces of a democracy from land they consider theirs.

4. **Ghost Wars: The Secret History of the CIA, Afghanistan, and bin Laden, from the Soviet Invasion to September 10, 2001** by Steve Coll, 2004 - During the cold war, the United States supplied arms to Islamists in Afghanistan to fight the Soviets. Unfortunately, this support came back to haunt us in the form of an extremist Taliban that sheltered Osama bin Laden. In his Pulitzer Prize-winning book, Coll recounts this history, along with the experiences and ideas that shaped the Clinton and Bush administrations in their fight against terror.

EXCERPT: GHOST WARS:

Ahmed Shah Massoud remained Afghanistan's most formidable military leader. A sinewy man with a wispy beard and penetrating dark eyes, he had become a charismatic popular leader, especially in northeastern Afghanistan. There he had fought and negotiated with equal imagination during the 1980s, punishing and frustrating Soviet generals. Massoud saw politics and war as intertwined. He was an attentive student of Mao and other successful guerrilla leaders. Some wondered as time passed if he could imagine a life without guerrilla conflict. Yet through various councils and coalitions, he had also proven able to acquire power by sharing it. During the long horror of the Soviet occupation, Massoud had symbolized for many Afghans — especially his own Tajik people — the spirit and potential of their brave resistance.

5. **How Terrorism Ends: Understanding the Decline and Demise of Terrorist Campaigns** by Audrey Kurth Cronin, 2009 – Though the U.S. focus on terrorism is ongoing with no end in sight, Cronin makes the case that terrorist campaigns are not indefinite, and that every one eventually comes to an end. She explains how terrorist movements have historically faded out or been permanently dismantled, what we can learn by studying those conclusions, and how this knowledge can be applied to an anti-al Qaeda strategy.

6. **The Looming Tower: Al-Qaeda and the Road to 9/11** by Lawrence Wright, 2006 – Wright deservedly won the Pulitzer Prize for his powerful, decades-spanning history of the people and events that ultimately led to the deadliest attack on American soil. Based on more than 500 interviews and extensive research, *The*

Looming Towner: Al-Qaeda and the Road to 9/11 explores the origins of Islamist movement, the radicalization of Osama bin Laden and the rise of Al-Qaeda in a book the *New York Times* called "wrenchingly intimate and boldly sweeping in its historical perspective."

7. **Nuclear Terrorism: The Ultimate Preventable Catastrophe** by Graham Allison, 2004 - Nuclear weapons, whether in the form of airborne missiles or "dirty bombs," represent the basis of the most horrifying terror scenarios. Allison outlines the dangers, as well as a strategy for keeping nukes from falling into the wrong hands, including more aggressive action to secure Russian nuclear materials.

8. **Terrorism and Homeland Security** by Jonathan R. White, 7th edition, 2011 – A landmark book, considered by many to be the most informative volume of its kind. White provides a basic framework for understanding terrorism — how it occurs and why — as well as an assessment of the latest theories by analysts from around the world.

9. **Terrorism and U.S. Foreign Policy** by Paul R. Pillar, 2001 - Pillar suggests that successfully fighting terrorism is not only a matter of taking drastic actions, but also of serious dedication to the everyday work of monitoring and preventing terrorist activity. His detailed knowledge of intelligence comes from years with the CIA.

10. **Understanding Terror Networks** by Marc Sageman, 2004 - Sageman explores the psychology of the alienated young men — often living in the West — who form groups of Muslim extremists bent on jihad (holy war). The men who attacked the United States on September 11, 2001, are one example of this type of terrorist cell. According to Sageman, preventing these tight-knit groups from being coached by members of al Qaeda is one of the ways to reduce the threat they pose.

TIME TRAVEL NOVELS
Classic and Contemporary Favorites

Before 1895, most people probably never considered traveling more than fifty miles beyond their home, much less through another dimension. In 1895, however, an English writer who had once supported himself as a draper before committing himself to the study of science would introduce readers to the concept of time travel and coin the term "time machine." Subsequently adapted into movies, television programs, radio dramas and comic books, H. G. Wells' first novel, *The Time Machine*, established science fiction — and time travel — as serious literary genres. Wells' dystopian tale continues to endure because it dwells less on technical or scientific details, using time travel instead to illuminate the human condition, the better angels — and demons — of our nature. *The Time Machine* has made its own journey through the last century as the subject of critical discussion, winner of science fiction's prestigious Hugo and Nebula Awards, and progenitor of a pop culture phenomenon. Wells himself would travel in time — at least in the pages of ***Time After Time***, which transports the Victorian-era author to seventies-era San Francisco in pursuit of another time traveler: Jack the Ripper!

The following books, listed alphabetically, bring wit, insight — and sometimes romance — to this now familiar literary trope.

1. **11/22/63** by Stephen King, 2011 – King's tour de force marks a departure for the master of horror, hurtling its protagonist, Jacob Epping, back to 1958 to prevent the assassination of J.F.K. — and meet the love of his life along the way. *11/22/63* was selected as one of the *New York Times'* top five fiction books of the 2011.

2. **Enchantment** by Orson Scott Card, 1999 – Card here brings a wry sense of humor to his engaging reimagining of an ancient fairy tale. Ukraine-born graduate student Ivan finds himself transported back to the ninth century to enact the Russian version of *Sleeping Beauty*, noting that while the English and French versions of the story always end happily ever after, "only a fool would want to live through the Russian version of any fairy tale."

3. **The End of Eternity** by Isaac Asimov, 1955 – One of the masters of the science fiction genre, Asimov won raves for *The End of Eternity*, which many regard as his greatest novel. Existing outside of time and space in the future, the members of a mysterious organization travel back in time to make "Reality Changes:" subtle alterations to the course of events for the greater good of mankind, albeit with repercussions. When an "Eternal" falls in love with a woman living in real time, he risks everything to be with her — even if means upsetting the space-time continuum.

4. **How to Live Safely in a Science Fictional Universe** by Charles Yu, 2011 – Wildly imaginative and witty "metafiction" that's heady but never loses its sense of fun. In Yu's debut novel, a lonely and isolated time travel repairman living in "Minor Universe 31" goes in search of his MIA father, who invented time travel. Reminiscent of the work of Italo Calvino, Philip K. Dick and Douglas Adams, *How to Life Safely in a Science Fictional Universe* was called "compulsively rereadable" by the *Los Angeles Times*.

5. **Slaughterhouse Five** by Kurt Vonnegut, 1969 – Vonnegut's experiences as a World War II P.O.W. who witnessed the firebombing of Dresden inform this classic absurdist novel, which Modern Library ranked one of the greatest English-language novels of the twentieth century. Vonnegut's protagonist, Billy Pilgrim, has become "unstuck in time" after aliens kidnap him. Careening pell-mell between World War II and the future, where Billy lives on the planet Tralfamadore with porn star Montana Wildhack, *Slaughterhouse Five* envisions a world where fate trumps free will.

6. **Somewhere In Time** by Richard Matheson, 1975 – Originally published as *Bid Time Return*, *Somewhere in Time* tells the story of a modern man who finds his soul mate in a nineteenth century actress and travels back through time to be with her. Or so he thinks. The 1979 film version starring Christopher Reeve and Jane Seymour is a cult classic, but fans of the book prefer to curl up with Matheson's beautifully rendered prose.

7. **Time and Again** by Jack Finney, 1970 – Called "mind-boggling, imagination-stretching, exciting, romantic entertainment" by the *San Francisco Examiner*, Finney's charming illustrated novel opens in 1970, when an advertising sketch artist agrees to travel back in time to New York, circa 1882, to determine if the past and present co-exist. Complications ensue when he falls in a love with a spirited young woman. A sequel ***From Time to Time*** was published posthumously in 1995.

8. **The Time Machine** by H. G. Wells, 1895 – Wells' classic takes the unnamed Time Traveller into the year 802,701 AD, where the world is divided into two races: the childlike Eloi and the subterranean, predatory Morlocks. The Time Traveller rescues an Eloi woman named Weena and plans to take her back to his own time. But the Morlocks have their own plans to ensnare the scientist.

EXCERPT: THE TIME MACHINE:

There was a minute's pause perhaps. The Psychologist seemed about to speak to me, but changed his mind. Then the Time Traveller put forth his finger toward the lever. "No," he said suddenly. "Lend me your hand." And turning to the Psychologist, he took that individual's hand in his own and told him to put out his forefinger. So that it was the Psychologist himself who sent forth the model Time Machine on its interminable voyage. We all saw the lever turn. I am absolutely certain there was no trickery. There was a breath of wind, and the lamp flame jumped. One of the candles on the mantel was blown out, and the little machine suddenly swung round, became indistinct, was seen as a ghost for a second perhaps, as an eddy of faintly glittering brass and ivory; and it was gone — vanished!

9. **The Time Traveler's Wife** by Audrey Niffenegger, 2004 – This inventive bestseller traces the asynchronous relationship between artist Clare and her husband Henry, a librarian suffering "Chrono Displacement" disorder, which dooms him to be whisked involuntarily back and forth in time. As far as he's concerned, the couple first met when they were in their twenties. According to Clare, however, she first met Henry when he was dropped naked into her parents' meadow when she was just six. The story itself shifts back and forth in time, and Henry and Clare take

turns narrating. Fans and critics alike call *The Time Traveler's Wife* "powerful" and "original." **ONLINE DETAILS**

10. **To Say Nothing of the Dog by** Connie Willis, 1998 – Willis may not have the name recognition of Isaac Asimov, Ray Bradbury or Arthur C. Clarke, but she's a major talent who's won the coveted Hugo Award eleven times — including one for this dazzling novel that's a slyly witty amalgam of science fiction and English comedy of manners. Jumping back and forth between the future and the twentieth century, an exhausted time traveler wants nothing more than to stay put for a while. There's no rest for the weary, however, when a fellow time traveler brings something back from Victorian-era England that threatens to change the course of history.

TINY THINGS
Books About The Microscopic World

In the daily rush of life, it's all too easy to forget how *magical* everything is. There are marvels both visible and invisible all around us, and even inside us. You may not have looked through a microscope since high school biology, but the ten books in this alphabetical list will remind you just how amazing little things can be — helping you "see a world in a grain of sand," as William Blake put it.

1. **The Ants** by Bert Hölldobler and Edward O. Wilson, 1990 – Ants — so much more than picnic pests! This book, which won a Pulitzer Prize, will show you why. It explores ants' altruistic behavior, how they divide labor, their communication by the aromatic chemicals known as pheromones, and many other aspects of their society. There are special chapters on such interesting varieties as army ants, ants that cultivate fungus, and weaver ants. It's also a lovely book with captivating photos and illustrations.

2. **Atom: Journey Across the Subatomic Cosmos** by Isaac Asimov, 1992 – Getting tinier still, as tiny, in fact, as it's possible to get — how far can you divide matter? The great science fiction writer addresses this question, explaining the world of the infinitesimal with such clarity that you won't need to be a physics whiz to understand such mysteries as fission, fusion, leptons, antiparticles, and the beginning and end of the universe.

3. **Nanofuture: What's Next For Nanotechnology** by J. Storrs Hall, 2005 – This fascinating book offers both a realistic and an imaginative assessment of the prospects for nanotechnology — tiny machines engineered at the molecular level. The field is still at an early stage, but it holds great potential for future advances in medicine and other areas.

4. **The Nature of Diamonds** edited by George E. Harlow, 1998 – Get your science and your social history together in this book about the little rocks that mean so

much. Enticingly illustrated, it will teach you how diamonds form in nature, why they come in different colors, how we cut them, the role they've played in the history of fashion and romance, and much more.

5. <u>**The Private Life of Spiders**</u> by Paul Hillyard, 2008 – A former curator at the Natural History Museum in London, Hillyard is an arachnid fan who wants to spread that love to the reader. Lavishly illustrated, this entertaining book provides an intimate glimpse into the world of the creatures, from their web spinning techniques to their courtship rituals. Hillyard even includes a section on overcoming arachnophobia, so determined is he that the world share his enthusiasm for the 40,000 spider species that populate every nook and cranny of the earth.

6. <u>**The Secret Life of Germs: What They Are, Why We Need Them, and How We Can Protect Ourselves Against Them**</u> by Philip M. Tierno Jr., 2001 – Moving on to a somewhat less pleasant but no less fascinating subject than diamonds, germs — they're all over. (Yes, even at the engagement-ring counter at Tiffany's — the author takes a sampling there.) The author explains how normally "friendly" germs can cause disease, the prospects for bioterrorism, and other unsettling matters, but mostly it is a comforting book. However, you *should* wash your hands.

EXCERPT: THE SECRET LIFE OF GERMS:

The air we breathe, the water we drink, the food we eat, the ground we walk on, the surfaces we touch, all of it is a teemingly populous, roiling sea of germs. Germs inhabit every inch of our skin, and every channel of our bodies. In fact, some germs and some exposure to germs throughout life are vital to human health and immunity. There are more germs in our intestines than there are stars in the sky, some thousand billion germs per gram of matter. The number of germ cells in a human body actually exceeds the number of body cells by a factor of ten. And the combined weight of microscopic germs exceeds the combined weight of all living animals and plants.

7. <u>**Secrets of Saffron: The Vagabond History of the World's Most Seductive Spice**</u> by Pat Willard, 2001 – Back to little things that are actually visible to the naked eye, saffron is a colorful and richly perfumed spice made from the stigma of a purple crocus. Unlike less precious spices that are sold by the jar, you'll find saffron sold in vials containing just a pinch of the wee (but powerful) threads. Enjoy the legends and history of saffron, along with the author's own experiences with the spice and lots of recipes.

8. <u>**The Social Amoebae: The Biology of Cellular Slime Molds**</u> by John Tyler Bonner, 2008 – A biologist who has advanced the theory of evolution in his work with

slime molds, Tyler has studied the subject for more than six decades, and his enthusiasm and his intimate knowledge are on ample display in this lively tome. In clear language accessible to the layman, Tyler explains how slime molds operate on molecular, cell, and multicellular levels and places the amoebae in context with biology in general. "An enlightening and enjoyable read," wrote Randy Wayne in *Bioscience*.

9. **The Tipping Point: How Little Things Can Make a Big Difference** by Malcolm Gladwell, 2000 – This is a more abstract discussion of the importance of tiny things — subtle nonverbal signals that people make during conversations, for example, and small numbers of people with particular skills that make them influential — and how they can create social change on a grand scale.

10. **The World of the Hummingbird** by Robert Burton, 2001 – Learn about the unusual flying skills, nectar-sipping ways, and social lives of the world's smallest birds. In addition to all the fascinating facts, this volume is appealing for its stunning photos of the beautiful little creatures.

TRUE CRIME CLASSICS
Ripped from the Headlines

When Truman Capote unveiled his self-proclaimed "nonfiction novel" *In Cold Blood* in 1966, critics and readers were astonished. Although he'd won wide acclaim for ***Breakfast at Tiffany's*** and ***Other Voices, Other Rooms***, nothing in Capote's literary oeuvre suggested that he was capable of pulling off such an ambitious project as this mesmerizing, fact-based account of a mass murder in rural Kansas. But the elfin, much-imitated Southern-born writer with the instantly recognizable voice confounded skeptics with this brilliantly textured and piercingly observed book. With remarkable insight, Capote delves into the hearts and minds of the two drifters who slaughtered four members of a family in 1959. An instant classic, *In Cold Blood* effectively set the literary template for all true crime sagas that followed. Fascinating, lurid and deeply disturbing, the following true crime books, listed alphabetically, are not the faint-hearted.

1. **Blind Eye: The Terrifying Story of a Doctor Who Got Away with Murder** by James B. Stewart, 1999 – Winner of the Mystery Writers of America Edgar Allan Poe Award, *Blind Eye* tells the chilling story of Dr. Michael Swango, who left a conspicuous trail of dead patients in his wake as he moved from one hospital job to the next.

2. **A Cold Case** by Philip Gourevitch, 2001 – Twenty-seven years after his friend was gunned down by a mobster who subsequently vanished, a tenacious New York police detective reopens the case in Gourevitch's tautly drawn character study.

3. **The Devil in the White City: Murder, Magic and Madness at the Fair that Changed America** by Erik Larson, 2003 – Set against the backdrop of Chicago's 1893 World's Fair, Larson's bestseller reveals the nightmarish underside to this celebration of progress. As architect Daniel Burnham supervised construction on the fairgrounds, serial killer H.H. Holmes preyed upon tourists staying in his World Fair's Hotel, which contained a gas chamber and crematorium.

EXCERPT: THE DEVIL IN THE WHITE CITY:

Darker forces marshaled in the smoke. Somewhere in the heart of the city a young Irish immigrant sank still more deeply into madness, the preamble to an act that would shock the nation and destroy what Burnham dreamed would be the single greatest moment of his life.

Closer at hand a far stranger creature raised his head in equally intent anticipation. "I was born with the devil in me," he wrote. "I could not help the fact that I was a murderer, no more than the poet can help the inspiration to sing."

4. **The Executioner's Song** by Norman Mailer, 1979 – Often compared to *In Cold Blood*, Mailer's epic "nonfiction novel" examines the tragic, violent life, and controversial execution of Utah inmate Gary Gilmore, who rejected his lawyers' attempts to appeal his death sentence — and sparked intense debate over capital punishment. A mammoth accomplishment, *The Executioner's Song* won Mailer his second Pulitzer Prize.

5. **Fatal Vision** by Joe McGinnis, 1983 – In 1970, Dr. Jeffrey MacDonald's pregnant wife and two young daughters were viciously murdered by hippies strung out on acid — or so MacDonald loudly maintains. And for a while, McGinnis believed him — until he began poring over the evidence and interviewing the charming yet ice-cold doctor. Although some balk at McGinnis' theory that MacDonald killed his family in an amphetamine-fueled rage, *Fatal Vision* remains a haunting book.

6. **Helter Skelter: The True Story of the Manson Murders** by Vincent Bugliosi with Curt Gentry, 1974 – Few crimes ever gripped the American public like the Tate-LaBianca murders in Los Angeles, circa 1969. The definitive book on horrific mass murder remains *Helter Skelter* by Bugliosi, the Los Angeles assistant district attorney who successfully prosecuted the killers, Charles Manson and four members of his hippie "family."

7. **In Cold Blood** by Truman Capote, 1966 – Capote's masterpiece, *In Cold Blood* would sadly turn out to be the writer's swan song. He would never write another book of comparable scope and artistry. **The Onion Field** by Joseph Wambaugh, 1973 – A former LAPD sergeant, Wambaugh became a bestselling novelist in the

seventies, with such hard-hitting crime dramas as **_The New Centurions_** and **_The Blue Knight_**. He took a detour into true crime with *The Onion Field*, about the 1963 kidnapping/murder of a Los Angeles police officer by two robbers, pulled over on a routine traffic stop.

8. **People Who Eat Darkness: The True Story of a Young Woman Who Vanished from the Streets of Tokyo — And the Evil That Swallowed Her Up** by Richard Lloyd Parry, 2012 – To say that Parry's account of a young British woman's murder in Tokyo is chilling would be an understatement. Yet what could have been just a lurid page-turner in a lesser writer's hands turns out to be a fascinating examination of contemporary Japanese society, thanks to Parry's insightful and detailed writing. And while Parry paints a disturbing portrait of the killer, whom the judge described as "unprecedented and extremely evil," he also writes sensitively about the devastating impact of the murder on the victim's family in *People Who Eat Darkness: The True Story of a Young Woman Who Vanished from the Streets of Tokyo —and the Evil That Swallowed Her Up*, which *Publishers Weekly* named one of the best books of 2012.

9. **The Stranger Beside Me: The Twentieth Anniversary Edition** by Ann Rule, 2000 – The doyenne of true crime writing, Rule first burst onto the scene in 1980 with this riveting book about the notorious serial killer Ted Bundy — whom Rule knew as fellow volunteer at a Seattle suicide hotline. Gruesomely detailed but never exploitative, this updated version of *The Stranger Beside Me* packs a real wallop, thanks to Rule's firsthand experience with the sexual psychopath, thought to have killed upwards of thirty-five women.

10. **Under the Banner of Heaven: A Story of Violent Faith** by Jon Krakauer, 2003 – The Mormon Church lambasted Krakauer for this study of religious extremism taken to homicidal lengths in contemporary Utah. Although the primary focus is on the religiously motivated slaying of a woman and her toddler by her Mormon fundamentalist brothers-in-law, *Under the Banner of Heaven* also explores the rise and spread of Mormonism in America.

11. **We Have Your Husband: One Woman's Terrifying Story of a Kidnapping in Mexico** by Jayne Garcia Valseca and Mark Ebner, 2011 – The son of a renowned Mexican newspaper publisher is kidnapped from a quaint tourist spot in the mountains of Guanajuato, Mexico, the victim of a profitable and ever-growing criminal enterprise. Enduring physical and emotional torture, he's held in a dark box for seven months, subsisting on food scraps, while his American-born wife engages in a ransom stand-off with his abductors. Written with exacting detail in a way that slowly ratchets up the tension, this book is a testament to the human ability to draw on hidden reserves of strength when everything seems hopeless.

TRUE-LIFE ADVENTURES
Recommended Reading for Armchair Explorers

Ever since legendary explorer Marco Polo dictated his memoirs to a fellow prisoner in thirteenth-century Genoa, the true-life adventure has been one of the most enduring genres in nonfiction. By turns triumphant and tragic, these incredible, often first-person accounts of men and women pushing the limits take readers to the farthest reaches of the planet — without ever leaving their armchairs.

To select twelve "must-reads" from the scores of gripping true-life adventures, we turned to no less an authority than the National Geographic Society for guidance. In the July/August 2001 issue of *National Geographic Adventure*, a panel of experts chose the "100 All-Time Best Adventure Books." The following list reflects the panel's top ten picks, listed alphabetically, plus two more recent titles worth reading.

1. **Annapurna** by Maurice Herzog, 1997 – Three years before Sir Edmund Hillary and Tenzing Norgay reached the summit of Mount Everest, mountain climber Maurice Herzog joined the French Alpine Club in an attempt to climb the 26,493-foot Himalayan mountain Annapurna. With only a rough map of the mountain and no clear route to the summit, Herzog and teammate Louis Lachenal somehow reached the top of Annapurna. But as he recounts in this riveting account of the 1950 expedition, they nearly died on their hellish descent to the base camp.

2. **Arabian Sands** by Wilfred Thesiger, 1959 – A romantic, larger-than-life figure cut from the same mold as "Lawrence of Arabia," Sir Wilfred Thesiger spent five years exploring the Empty Quarter of Saudi Arabia, where he lived among the Bedouins and twice crossed the Rub-al-Kahli deserts. In *Arabian Sands*, the Oxford-educated Englishman describes how he was often forced to wear disguises to find acceptance among the suspicious and hostile tribes, who have lived in this bleak and unforgiving region for thousands of years.

3. **Desert Solitaire: A Season in the Wilderness** by Edmund Abbey, 1968 – One of the most colorful and paradoxical figures in the environmentalist movement, Edmund Abbey was a beer-swilling, gun-toting naturalist who opposed what he called "industrial tourism" in America's national parks. *Desert Solitaire* is an irreverent, passionate memoir of Abbey's tenure as a park ranger in Utah's Arches National Monument.

4. **The Exploration of the Colorado River And Its Canyons** by John Wesley Powell, 1875 – In 1869, John Wesley Powell headed a 1,000-mile expedition down the Colorado River and into the Grand Canyon. Neither Powell nor his men knew the terrain or how they would be received by the Native Americans. The lack of supplies, the punishing heat, and the Colorado's dangerous rapids took their toll on some of Powell's men, who eventually turned on their commander. Powell survived and turned his field writings into a dramatic account of the expedition that has lost none of its punch for contemporary readers.

222

5. **Into Thin Air: A Personal Account of the Mount Everest Disaster** by Jon Krakauer, 1997 – A fixture on the nonfiction bestseller list in the late nineties, Krakauer's first-person account of a disastrous 1996 Mount Everest expedition is a compelling tale of fatal hubris at the highest place on Earth. In addition to the graphic and suspenseful account of the climb, Krakauer also sheds much needed-light on what drives people to risk their lives by climbing Mount Everest.

6. **The Journals of Lewis and Clark,** by Meriwether Lewis and William Clark, 1814 – From 1804 to 1806, explorers Meriwether Lewis and William Clark led an expedition into the vast uncharted territory of the Louisiana Purchase. In addition to mapping rivers and staking claim to the Idaho, Washington, and Oregon territories, Lewis and Clark collaborated on a meticulous journal of their "Voyage of Discovery" from the banks of the Missouri River to the Pacific Northwest. Both a fascinating travel narrative and invaluable source of data on the plants, animals and terrain of the frontier, *Journals* continues to enthrall new generations of readers.

7. **The Travels of Marco Polo** by Marco Polo, 2006 edition – The book that started it all, Marco Polo's *Travels* remains a fascinating and fantastic account of the merchant-traveler's thirteenth-century trek from Venice across Asia. Although some historians initially dismissed Polo's *Travels* as fictitious, time has proven that many of his observations of Asian life and customs are grounded in fact.

8. **West With the Night** by Beryl Markham, 1982 – No less a writer than Ernest Hemingway hailed Markham's memoir of her life as aviatrix as "bloody wonderful." A glamorous blonde who grew up on a Kenyan farm, Markham was the first woman in Africa to hold a pilot's license. In 1936, she made history by becoming the first pilot to fly solo across the Atlantic Ocean from east to west. *West With the Night* is an entertaining account of Markham's remarkable African upbringing and aviation career.

9. **Wind, Sand & Stars** by Antoine de Saint-Exupery, 1939 – Best known in the United States as the author of ***The Little Prince,*** French aviator, novelist and bon vivant Antoine de Saint-Exupery thrived on adventure. His memoir *Wind, Sand & Stars* is widely regarded as Saint-Exupery's finest work, an epic and thrilling account of his experiences flying solo over the Andes and crash-landing in the Sahara Desert.

10. **The Worst Journey in the World** by Apsley Cherry-Garrard, 1922 – Cherry-Garrard's harrowing account of Robert Falcon Scott's ill-fated 1911 expedition to the South Pole plunges the reader into the frozen landscape of the Antarctic, where perpetual darkness reigns and temperatures regularly drop seventy degrees *below* zero. The sole survivor of the expedition, Cherry-Garrard vividly describes the extreme hardship and emotional anguish he and other members of Scott's team endured during this nightmarish trek into the unknown.

CONTEMPORARY TITLES

11. <u>**Lost in Shangri-La: A True Story of Survival, Adventure, and the Most Incredible Rescue Mission of World War II**</u> by Mitchell Zuckoff, 2011 – The "Shangri-La" of Zuckoff's enthralling bestseller is a remote valley in Dutch New Guinea, where an American transport plane crashed in 1945, killing everyone on board except for two servicemen and a WAC. Severely injured, the trio encounters a multitude of perils, including tribesmen and warriors rumored to be cannibals, while paratroopers plan a daring rescue operation.

EXCERPT: LOST IN SHANGRI-LA:

When the plane burrowed through the trees, John McCollom flew across the center aisle, from the left side of the plane to the right. He lurched forward by momentum, turning somersaults as he fell. He momentarily blacked out. When he came to, he found himself on his hands and knees halfway up the cabin toward the cockpit, surrounded by flames. Driven by instinct, he searched for an escape route. He saw a flash of white light where the tail had been. The roof of the cabin had flattened down like a stepped-on tin can, so he couldn't stand. He crawled toward the light, landing on the scorched earth of the mountain jungle, disoriented but with barely a scratch.

McCollom began to comprehend the horror of what had happened. He thought about his twin brother and the twenty-two others on board — all trapped inside and dead, he believed. As he rose to his feet outside the broken plane, he told himself: "This is a heck of a place to be, 165 miles from civilization, all by myself on a Sunday afternoon."

12. <u>**Space Probes: 50 Years of Exploration from Luna 1 to New Horizons**</u> by Philippe Seguela, 2011 – The fully illustrated *Space Probes* is the first comprehensive history of space exploration, from the first tests of the early sixties to the New Horizons mission, scheduled to touch down on Pluto in 2015. Every U.S. space probe is examined, as well as those launched by Japan, China, India, and other countries, including the purposes behind each launch, the technology employed, and the information gained.

URBAN HISTORIES
Books about Cities

Every great city has its own history, flavor, and way of life — sometimes developed in relative seclusion, like Tokyo, and sometimes a composite of several cultures melded together, like New York City. Whether you live in a great city or love to visit them, there are some fascinating books written by people who know the cities well and love them passionately. Here are twelve portraits of cities, listed alphabetically by city, which will illuminate your travels and your daydreams.

1. **Alexandria: Alexandria: A History and a Guide** by E. M. Forster, 1922 – The ancient and mysterious city in northern Egypt comes to life in Forster's account. Founded by and named after Alexander the Great, the city was important in Jewish, Hellenistic, and early Christian culture, and was restored to importance in the nineteenth century by Muhammad Ali.

2. **Barcelona: Barcelona** by Robert Hughes, 1992 – Hughes is an enthusiastic chronicler of this independent-minded city in Spain's northeastern region of Catalunya. Discover its long and lively history from Roman times to the creation of the fanciful, undulating buildings of the modern architect Gaudí and beyond.

3. **Chicago: Chicago: A Biography** by Dominic A. Pacyga, 2009 – This expansive history of Chicago succeeds in highlighting its most famous citizens — from Al Capone to Barack Obama — while also paying respect to the brick homes and corner taverns so essential to the windy city character. A former stockyard worker, the author digs deep into the industrial history of the city, and brings the story up to the present, where former printing factories now serve as condos, overlooking public sculpture gardens and museums.

4. **London: London: A History** by A.N. Wilson, 2004 - The author, also a novelist and biographer, traces two thousand years of London's history, encompassing royal intrigues, plague, extraordinary literary productions, brave resistance to the Nazis, and the contemporary scene.

5. **Los Angeles: L.A. Noir: The Struggle gor The Soul of America's Most Seductive City** by John Buntin, 2009 – In the fifties, while Hollywood promoted Los Angeles as a sunny, prosperous playground, two men waged battle for control of the city. One was former boxer Mickey Cohen, who made his leap to the rackets when he became the enforcer for Benjamin "Bugsy" Siegel. The other was William H. Parker, a police chief determined to clean up crime in all its forms. Buntin recounts the standoff in this exciting portrait of one of America's greatest cities.

6. **Mexico City: La Capital: The Biography of Mexico City** by Jonathan Kandell, 1988 – Once the capital of the Aztecs, now one of the most populous cities of Latin America, Mexico City has a rich but violent history. Learn about its notable inhabitants from Montezuma to the great muralist Diego Rivera and events from colonial times to independence to modern politics and culture.

7. **New Orleans: New Orleans: A Cultural History** by Louise McKinney, 2006 – For much of its history, the Big Easy, home of wild Fat Tuesday celebrations, jazz, and beautiful architecture, has seemed exotic and alluring to the rest of America. McKinney's compelling book is an excellent overview of the city's remarkable

melting-pot history, which both sets it apart from other cities and makes it distinctively American.

8.**New York City: <u>Empire City: New York Through the Centuries</u>** edited by Kenneth T. Jackson and David S. Dunbar, 2002 – The Big Apple is a cacophony of voices. This is not a conventional history book, but an anthology of writings about the city, starting in the early seventeenth century and ending in the fateful year of 2001. The incredible diversity and grandeur of the city are reflected in this collection of works by writers both famous and obscure.

9. **Paris: <u>Seven Ages of Paris</u>** by Alistair Horne, 2002 – This is a delightful narrative of a delightful city that has nurtured culture, philosophy, high art, and the arts of living for centuries — though its history has been tumultuous at times. The Calvinist Henry IV became Catholic for the city, calling it "well worth a Mass." Horne describes the conquerors, dreamers, and remakers of the city over the course of "seven ages."

10. **Rome: <u>Rome: A Cultural, Visual and Personal History</u>** by Robert Hughes, 2011 – You couldn't ask for a more erudite or engaging tour guide to one of the world's great cities than the late critic/historian and essayist Hughes. The Eternal City comes to vivid life in the pages of *Rome: A Cultural, Visual and Personal History*, which the *New York Times* called "engrossing, passionately written."

EXCERPT: ROME:

Although nobody can say when Rome *began, at least there is reasonable certainty of where it did. It was in Italy, on the bank of the river Tiber, about twenty-two kilometers inland from its mouth, a delta which was to become the seaport of Ostia.*

The reason no one can pinpoint when the foundation took place is that it never ascertainably did. There was no primal moment when a loose scatter of Iron and Bronze Age villages perched on hills agreed to coalesce and call itself a city. The older a city is, the more doubt about its origins, and Rome *is certainly old. This did not prevent the Romans from the second century b.c.e. onward coming up with implausibly exact-looking dates for its origins:* Rome, *it used to be asserted, began not just in the eighth century but precisely in 753 b.c.e., and its founder was Romulus, twin brother of Remus. Here a tangled story begins, with many variants, which tend to circle back to the same themes we will see again and again throughout* Rome's *long history: ambition, parricide, fratricide, betrayal, and obsessive ambition. Especially the last. No more ambitious city than* Rome *had ever existed, or conceivably ever will, although New York offers it competition. No city has ever been more steeped in ferocity from its beginnings than* Rome. *These wind back to the story of the city's mythic infancy.*

11. **Tokyo***: Low City, High City: Tokyo from Edo to the Earthquake** by Edward Seidensticker, 1983 - Sophisticated but long insulated from foreigners, Tokyo has become a cosmopolitan world financial and cultural capital. Seidensticker covers the history of the city from the seventeenth century Edo period through the earthquake of 1923.

12. **Venice: The World of Venice** by Jan Morris, 1988 - Past and present flow together in the city of great artists and craftsmen, commerce and theater in this charming book. Morris shares her profound appreciation of the city's dazzling history and its unique way of life.

VERSE ANTHOLOGIES
Ten Essential Collections

A good anthology of poetry is a delight in itself and can also be the starting point for a well-chosen collection of books by individual poets. Maybe you'll fall in love with the work of Li Po, Pablo Neruda or Mary Oliver — who knows what will speak to you? Here are some outstanding anthologies for every mood and interest, covering an enormous range of history, languages, and emotions. Have fun looking through these treasure chests of verse, which are listed alphabetically by title.

1. **The 100 Best Love Poems of All Times** edited by Leslie Pockell, 2003 – Throughout the history of literature, from Catullus to Cisneros, love has inspired some of the most intense and beautiful poetry. This book is wonderful whether you find yourself looking for something to read at a wedding, an eloquent way to communicate with someone near your heart, or just a way to meditate on one of mankind's greatest sources of sorrow and joy.

2. **Americans' Favorite Poems: The Favorite Poem Project Anthology** edited by Robert Pinsky and Maggie Dietz, 1999 – During his term as U.S. Poet Laureate, Robert Pinsky invited Americans to write in with their favorite poems and why they love them. From thousands of responses, he culled 200 favorites from people of many different backgrounds, collected here along with impassioned testimonials of what they mean to their readers.

3. **A Book of Women Poets from Antiquity to Now: Selections from the World Over** edited by Aliki Barnstone and Willis Barnstone, 1992 – Beginning with a Sumerian priestess who lived and composed four thousand years ago, this collection brings us the voices of women from all over the world. It includes work by writers both familiar and obscure and places them all in historical context.

4. **The Enlightened Heart: An Anthology of Sacred Poetry** edited by Stephen Mitchell, 1989 – An inspiring collection of religious and mystical verse from several

different traditions, both Eastern and Western — Lao Tzu, selections from the Book of Psalms, Rumi, and Whitman are all here.

5. **The Norton Book of Light Verse** edited by Russell Baker, 1986 – A charming book with more than 400 pages of amusing nursery rhymes, satirical verses, limericks, nonsense, witty song lyrics, and more. It is organized into such categories as "Twentieth Century Blues," "Some Fun with the Mother Tongue," and "Words to Live By."

6. **The Oxford Book of English Verse** edited by Christopher Ricks, 1999 – Ah, the English poets! In the pages of this anthology you'll find anonymous poems from the distant past ("Sumer is icumen in") and some of the most enduring verses by Shakespeare, Tennyson, Hardy, and many more.

7. **Twentieth-Century Latin American Poetry: A Bilingual Anthology** edited by Stephen Tapscott, 1996 – This anthology offers excellent translations from more than seventy-five of Latin America's best modern poets. The Spanish-language versions on the facing pages enrich the collection even for readers who don't speak Spanish — try reciting a few lines aloud to hear the music of the originals.

8. **The Vintage Book of African American Poetry** edited by Michael S. Harper and Anthony Walton, 2000 – The variety of approaches to language and the search for authentic identity and self-expression make this anthology a fascinating and important book. Spanning American history from the eighteenth century to the present day, it brings together the work of African American poets ranging from self-taught slaves to Robert Hayden, Langston Hughes, Sterling Brown and other twentieth-century greats.

EXCERPT: THE VINTAGE BOOK OF AFRICAN AMERICAN POETRY:

"The Bean Eaters"
They eat beans mostly, this old yellow pair.
Dinner is a casual affair.
Plain chipware on a plain and creaking wood,
Tin flatware.
Two who are Mostly Good.
Two who have lived their day,
But keep on putting on their clothes
And putting things away.
And remembering...
Remembering, with twinklings and twinges,
As they lean over the beans in their rented back room that is full of beads and receipts and dolls and cloths, tobacco crumbs, vases and fringes.
– Gwendolyn Brooks

9. **The Vintage Book of Contemporary World Poetry** edited by J.D. McClatchy, 1996 – How often do we get to read the work of a Swedish poet, or a Korean? This anthology is a window into the lives and hearts of eighty noteworthy poets of our time — voices from Senegal, Ireland, Japan and all over the globe.

10. **World Poetry: An Anthology of Verse from Antiquity to Our Time** edited by Katharine Washburn, John S. Major, and Clifton Fadiman, 1998 – This is a heftier anthology of world poetry than the previous one — heftier because it goes back thousands of years. Lively translations of verse from all the world's great traditions that have become part of our common heritage will surprise you every time you browse through it exhaustive collection.

VIETNAM WAR NONFICTION
Dispatches from the Quagmire

Hired to be *Esquire Magazine's* Vietnam bureau chief, journalist Michael Herr arrived in the war-torn country just before the Tet Offensive — and went right into the field to cover the firefights and night attacks that American soldiers faced daily. When he wasn't dodging enemy fire or joining the fight against the Viet Cong in the Mekong Delta, Herr jotted down his impressions of battle and snatches of soldiers' conversation in his notebook. Years later, after he'd returned to the United States, Herr shaped his notes into a book that became an instant classic of war reportage: *Dispatches*. Novelist John Le Carré praised *Dispatches* as "the best book I have ever read on men and war in our time." Herr would go on to work with Francis Ford Coppola and Stanley Kubrick on their respective Vietnam War films, *Apocalypse Now* and *Full Metal Jacket*. Although he continues to write, albeit sporadically, Herr remains best known for his acid trip of a book, one of twelve justly acclaimed nonfiction books about the Vietnam War.

1. **The Best and the Brightest** by David Halberstam, 1972 – A masterful and thorough account of the foreign policy decisions and other factors that led to the U. S. involvement in the Vietnam War.

2. **Born on the Fourth of July** by Ron Kovic, 1976 – A gung-ho, patriotic soldier becomes an antiwar activist after combat injuries leave him paralyzed from the chest down.

3. **A Bright Shining Lie: John Paul Vann and America in Vietnam** by Neil Sheehan, 1988 – Pulitzer Prize-winning, warts-and-all biography of the highly controversial, larger-than-life Vann, an army field adviser who dared to speak openly to the press about U.S. military setbacks in Vietnam.

4. **Chickenhawk** by Robert C. Mason, 1983 – Powerful memoir by an army helicopter pilot who flew more than 1,000 missions in Vietnam between 1964 and 1968.

5. **Dispatches** by Michael Herr, 1977 – Herr's electrifying, mind-bending prose plunges you headlong into the insanity of Vietnam War.

EXCERPT: DISPATCHES:

After enough time passed a memory receded and settled, the name itself became a prayer, coded like a prayer to go past the extremes of petition and gratitude: Vietnam Vietnam Vietnam, say again until the word lost all its old loads of pain, pleasure, horror, guilt, nostalgia. Then and there, everyone was just trying to get through it, existential crunch, no atheists in a foxhole like you wouldn't believe. Even bitter refracted faith was better than none at all, like the black marine I'd heard about during heavy shelling at Con Thien who'd said "Don't worry, baby, God'll think of something."

6. **Embers of War: The Fall of an Empire and the Making of America's Vietnam** by Fredrik Logevall, 2012 – Vietnam became a quagmire for the United States — and an unsolvable puzzle for five successive presidents — after France had tried and failed to stabilize the region in the fifties. Why two major powers were so roundly defeated has been a source of study ever since, and Logevall sheds light on this conundrum with *Embers of War*, a look at the politics of Vietnam in the decades leading up to American involvement, from the 1919 Versailles Peace Conference to the first American deaths in 1959.

7. **Fire in the Lake: The Vietnamese and the Americans in Vietnam** by Frances Fitzgerald, 1972 – Fitzgerald examines the war from a sociological perspective in this study of two cultures on a deadly collision course. Winner of both the Pulitzer Prize and the National Book Award.

8. **A Rumor of War** by Philip Caputo, 1977 – The *New York Times* called Caputo's harrowing memoir of his six-month tour of duty as a platoon leader in Da Nang "a marvelous and singular work."

9. **Steinbeck in Vietnam: Dispatches from the War** by John Steinbeck, edited by Thomas E. Barden, 2012 – Best-known for his Depression-era novels and stories, John Steinbeck was also a war correspondent, starting with Pearl Harbor and continuing into the Vietnam War, when the acclaimed author was well into his sixties. This volume is the first complete collection of Vietnam dispatches Steinbeck wrote for *Newsday*, including his reports from combat areas in South Vietnam and Laos. Editor Thomas E. Barden puts these writings in context with an introduction explaining Steinbeck's political views, and the reasons he chose to immerse himself in the conflict.

10. **Street Without Joy** by Bernard B. Fall, 1961 – Invaluable account of the French Indochina War (1946-1954) that led to the U.S. involvement in the conflict. Pessimistic about the U.S. military's chances for victory in Vietnam, Fall would be killed by a North Vietnamese landmine in 1967.

11. **Vietnam: A History** by Stanley Karnow, 1983 – The Pulitzer Prize-winning journalist examines the Vietnam War within the wider context of Vietnam's French colonial past. A comprehensive and enormously readable book from a journalist who covered the Vietnam War in its entirety.

12. **We Were Soldiers Once...And Young: Ia Drang—The Battle That Changed the War in Vietnam** by Lt. General H.G. Moore and Joseph L. Galloway, 1992 – A compelling story of uncommon valor and self-sacrifice in the first major battle between the United States and the North Vietnamese.

WESTERN LITERATURE
W. Somerset Maugham's Top Ten Picks

Over the course of a prolific, genre-hopping literary career that spanned more than sixty years, English novelist/playwright/essayist and short story writer W. Somerset Maugham established himself as one of the twentieth century's great men of letters. Revered for such classic novels as *The Razor's Edge* and the semi-autobiographical *Of Human Bondage*, the latter widely considered his masterpiece, Maugham defied the starving artist stereotype to lead a wildly glamorous life in a sumptuous French Riviera villa, until World War II turned him into a jet-setting refugee.

During the twenties and thirties, however, Maugham's wealth and celebrity provoked the scorn of many critics and fellow writers, who unfairly — perhaps jealously — dismissed him as a literary dandy. Yet Maugham was intensely passionate about literature, which should "be read with enjoyment. If it does not give that it is worthless." Or so he writes in the introduction to his 1948 collection of essays, *Great Novelists and Their Novels*. With those criteria in mind, Maugham chose the following ten novels as the all-time best, which are listed per his ranking.

1. **War and Peace** by Leo Tolstoy, 1866 – A perennial fixture on critics' lists of the world's great novels, Tolstoy's massive yet intimate epic depicts the interwoven lives of three aristocratic families during Napoleon's invasion of Russia, circa 1805-1813. Both a sweeping epic and a polemic — Tolstoy interrupts the narrative to discourse on politics and history — *War and Peace* is a demanding yet utterly enthralling novel. ONLINE details

2. **Pere Goriot** by Honore de Balzac, 1834 – Balzac casts a jaundiced eye on nineteenth century Paris in this realistic novel about a poor but ambitious young

231

man determined to make his mark in high society. Remarkable for its vivid evocation of nineteenth century Paris, which registers as strongly as any of the flesh and blood characters, *Pere Goriot* has been cited as a major influence on such writers as Emile Zola and Marcel Proust. ONLINE details

3. **The History of Tom Jones, A Foundling** by Henry Fielding, 1749 – A rollicking comic picaresque teeming with bawdy good humor, *Tom Jones* chronicles the misadventures of the title character, a cheerfully unrepentant womanizer looking for his parents in eighteenth century England. ONLINE details

4. **Pride and Prejudice** by Jane Austen, 1813 – Austen's brilliant comedy of manners is one of the most beloved novels of all time. Two hundred years after its publication, the tempestuous love story of Elizabeth Bennett and Fitzwilliam Darcy continues to enchant readers with its sparkling mixture of droll wit, heartfelt romance and astute class observations in Regency-era England.

5. **The Red and the Black** by Stendhal, 1831 – Along with Balzac, nineteenth century French novelist Stendhal is regarded as one of the founders of realistic literature. *The Red and the Black* is undeniably his masterwork — a dense, psychologically acute rendering of an amoral, self-deluding young man whose hunger for society's approval ultimately seals his downfall. Laden with allusions to the work of Shakespeare and Voltaire, among many others, *The Red and the Black* is unsparing in its criticism of French high society.

6. **Wuthering Heights** by Emily Brontë, 1847 – Has there ever been a more swoon-worthy love story than *Wuthering Heights*? Brontë's only novel, published the year of her death from tuberculosis, is a brooding, mood-drenched tale of the volatile romance of Heathcliff and Cathy, set in the dreary Yorkshire moors where Brontë grew up, the younger sister of *Jane Eyre* novelist Charlotte Brontë.

7. **Madame Bovary** by Gustave Flaubert, 1857 – Considered scandalous when published, *Madame Bovary* depicts the gradual downward spiral of the title character, a vain and restless bourgeois woman who deserts her husband and child to embark on a brazen love affair. A bold and frankly realistic novel, *Madame Bovary* sent a shock wave through nineteenth century literary circles.

EXCERPT: MADAME BOVARY:

Then the lusts of the flesh, the longing for money, and the melancholy of passion all blended themselves into one suffering, and instead of turning her thoughts from it, she clave to it the more, urging herself to pain, and seeking everywhere occasion for it. She was irritated by an ill-served dish or by a half-open door; bewailed the velvets she had not, the happiness she had missed, her too exalted dreams, her narrow home.

14. **David Copperfield** by Charles Dickens, 1850 – Reportedly the most autobiographical of Dickens' novels, this wonderfully engaging character study follows the title character through triumph and tragedy from birth to middle age. Filled with some of the memorable characters in all of English literature — Micawber, Uriah Heep and the title character/narrator — David Copperfield was the author's "favorite child" of all his novels.

15. **The Brothers Karamazov** by Fyodor Dostoevsky, 1880 – Hailed by Sigmund Freud as "the most magnificent novel ever written," Dostoevsky's final novel is a towering achievement of psychological depth and philosophical complexity. The murder of the drunken, n'er-do-well Karamazov patriarch draws us into the lives of the title characters, who struggle with the moral and spiritual repercussions of parricide in nineteenth century Russia.

8. **Moby Dick** by Herman Melville, 1851 – The sole American novel on Maugham's list, *Moby Dick* is much more than simply a seagoing yarn about Captain Ahab's obsessive pursuit of the legendary white whale. While contemporary readers may find Melville's huge, sprawling allegorical novel a bit unwieldy, due to Melville's tendency to go off on nonfiction tangents, *Moby Dick* is nonetheless a stunning, one-of-a kind novel that occupies an almost mythic place in American literature.

WORLD WAR I NONFICTION
Histories of the Great War

On June 28, 1914, the assassination of Archduke Franz Ferdinand of Austria provoked one of the world's largest and deadliest wars. Before its end, the conflict would involve all the major economic powers, mobilize seventy million military personnel, and witness technological advances that contributed to some of the greatest numbers of casualties in history.

World War I redrew the map of Europe as the German, Russian, Austro-Hungarian and Ottoman empires fell. The United States did not declare war on Germany, and thus formally enter the war, until 1917. With the passage of the Selective Service Act, the United States subsequently drafted thousands of men each month, helping the Allied forces defeat the Germans.

Since the 1918 Armistice, the Great War has inspired numerous books, films and nonfiction accounts. First published in 1929, Erich Maria Remarque's ***All Quiet on the Western Front*** told the story from the perspective of the German soldiers. In 1962, Barbara Tuchman's *The Guns of August* would shed new light on the catalysts for the war and win the Pulitzer Prize. Most recently, the BBC series *Downton Abbey* has helped spark new interest in this period of history, depicting its casualties on the home front.

Presented alphabetically, the following books examine in depth — and often through first-person accounts — the complexities and tragedy of the war meant to end all wars.

1. **The Beauty and The Sorrow: An Intimate History of the First World War** by Peter Englund, 2011 — The story of the Great War as told through the voices of the people who lived it — and some who would die in it. Letters and journals from twenty different people around the world, from Britain to Mesopotamia, create a heartrending mosaic of the hopes, fears and reversals of fortune at home and in battle.

2. **Desert Hell: The British Invasion of Mesopotamia** by Charles Townshend, 2011— Described by the publisher as a "cautionary tale for makers of national policy," Townshend's work examines the British invasion of Mesopotamia between 1914 and 1924, which established the country of Iraq and had devastating repercussions for the British Empire — and the rest of the world. Townsend balances the personalities against military and civil history to craft this excellent narrative.

3. **The First World War** by John Keegan, 2000 – Regarded as one of the greatest military historians, Keegan (*A History of Warfare*) brilliantly chronicles the Great War in gripping, sometimes disturbing detail.   Provocative, incisively written and illustrated with twenty-four photographs and fifteen maps, *The First World War* was hailed as a "miracle of concision" by the *Weekly Standard*.

4. **The Guns of August** by Barbara W. Tuchman, 1962 — A sweeping, extensively researched account of the people and events leading up to the war, and of the first month of the war itself, *The Guns of August* won the Pulitzer Prize in 1963.

EXCERPT: THE GUNS OF AUGUST:

So gorgeous was the spectacle on the May morning of 1910 when nine kings rode in the funeral of Edward VII of England that the crowd, waiting in hushed and black-clad awe, could not keep back gasps of admiration. In scarlet and blue and green and purple, three by three the sovereigns rode through the palace gates, with plumed helmets, gold braid, crimson sashes, and jeweled orders flashing in the sun. After them came five heirs apparent, forty more imperial or royal highnesses, seven queens—four dowager and three regnant—and a scattering of special ambassadors from uncrowned countries. Together they represented seventy nations in the greatest assemblage of royalty and rank ever gathered in one place and, of its kind, the last. The muffled tongue of Big Ben tolled nine by the clock as the cortege left the palace, but on history's clock it was sunset, and the sun of the old world was setting in a dying blaze of splendor never to be seen again.

5. **The Somme: The Darkest Hour on the Western Front** by Peter Hart, 2005 — In 1916, the Big Push was intended to end the stalemate between British, French and German forces on the Western Front. Instead, British forces suffered 20,000 losses on the first day of a battle that would drag on for more four months. Hart serves as oral historian for Britain's Imperial War Museum, and his access to extensive resources allows him to combine first-person accounts with detailed narrative and analysis, creating a balanced portrait of an unimaginable tragedy.

6. **Tommy: The British Soldier on the Western Front 1914-1918** by Richard Holmes, 2004 — Twenty-two percent of the adult male population in Britain fought in World War I. Men who would die in battle, leave wives and sweethearts behind, or find their minds and bodies ravaged by shell shock, starvation, disease and injury. This marks the first time their story has been told from their perspective, through their letters, diaries, memoirs and poetry. Historian and television presenter Richard Holmes uses these sources to create the character of Tommy, a British sergeant who helps give voice to this lost generation of soldiers.

7. **To End All Wars: A Story of Loyalty and Rebellion, 1914-1918** by Adam Hochschild, 2011 — This original, absorbing work views the Great War from the perspective of its critics — writers, journalists, even family members of key military officials — who were often jailed for their dissent and saw their families torn asunder by the conflict. Hochschild previously won the Los Angeles Times Book Award for ***Bury the Chains: Prophets and Rebels in the Fight to Free an Empire's Slaves***.

8. **The White War: Life and Death on the Italian Front 1915-1919** by Mark Thompson, 2009 — This "masterful and moving" chronicle renders in unflinching detail a conflict largely overlooked by historians — even by Allied strategists of the time. What starts in nationalist fervor as a territorial dispute between Italy and Austria turns to devastation and massive loss of life. Thompson joins Ernest Hemingway as one of the few writers to consider this forgotten bit of history.

WORLD WAR II NONFICTION
The War in Europe

The Second World War was a *world* war, of course, but for the most part, Europe, along with the South Pacific and East Asia, bore the brunt of the conflict. The eleven books listed alphabetically below were selected with the goal of covering all the major aspects of the war in Europe: the epic battles of Stalingrad, the Bulge and D-Day; the rise of Nazism in Germany and the European response; the three principal European leaders (Churchill, Hitler and Stalin) locked in their live-or-die struggle (the list includes Churchill's own six-volume, Nobel Prize-winning account of the war); and the Holocaust, one of history's darkest episodes. In addition, we've included

Lynn Nicholas's book, *The Rape of Europa,* with its fascinating story of how Europe's treasured works of art were saved, stolen or lost as the world went up in flames around them. Be warned, though, lest you're tempted to believe that these eleven works will tell it all — the Nazis, the society they created and the horrors they unleashed on mankind will continue to be the subject of books for decades, if not centuries, to come.

1. **Battle: The Story of the Bulge** by John Toland, 1959 - The Battle of the Bulge — named for the "bulge" the Germans created in the Allies' front line — could just as well have been the Battle of the Breakthrough, had the outnumbered and outgunned Allied troops not stopped the German advance in the bitterly cold and snowy Ardennes forest of Belgium in January 1945. Through meticulous research that illuminates the viewpoints of generals and infantrymen alike, Toland transports the reader to the vortex of this crucial battle in which more than 20,000 allied troops, mostly Americans, lost their lives.

2. **Bloodlands: Europe between Hitler and Stalin** by Timothy Snyder, 2010 - This study of the Second World War in Europe reminds us of an unpleasant fact — our "ally" Josef Stalin was a mass murderer on par with Hitler. In focusing on the similarities between these two archenemies, Snyder uncovers truths long hidden by, first, the Iron Curtain, and second, time itself. *The New Republic* praised Snyder for "[wresting] back some human dignity for those who died, without treating them solely as victims."

3. **The Coming of the Third Reich** by Richard Evans, 2003 – How did a civilized country like Germany come to embrace Nazism? A British historian at Cambridge, Evans takes readers step by step through the Nazi rise to power, illuminating along the way such factors as Germany's humiliation by the Allies after World War I; the Germans' inability to tolerate the imperfections of the fledgling Weimar democracy; and the presence of the perfect scapegoat in their midst — the Jews — around whom Hitler and his cohorts cultivated a murderous, genocidal and unifying hatred.

4. **The Destruction of the European Jews** by Raul Hilberg, 1961 - No list of books about the Second World War in Europe would be complete without this one: the definitive account of the Nazi campaign to exterminate the Jews. Covering the years 1933-1945, and encompassing the scope of the genocide across the entire continent of Europe, this three-volume masterpiece represents the late author's lifelong obsession with exposing one of the Holocaust's saddest aspects — that what happened to the Jews was not just the work of a relatively small coterie of Nazi murderers, but that, in reality, to borrow a contemporary phrase, "it took a village."

5. **The Duel: The Eighty-Day Struggle between Churchill and Hitler** by John Lukacs, 1990 – The eighty days in question here roughly cover early May through the end of July, 1940. During this time Churchill became England's prime minister; Hitler

launched his assault on Western Europe; and decided not to invade Britain. In between, almost through Churchill's sheer force of will, England, standing alone, refuses to negotiate with the Nazis and valiantly endures the terror of the Blitz. We all know Hitler's disregard for the Russian winter was his gravest mistake, but this book makes his underestimation of Churchill seem equally foolish.

6. **The Longest Day** by Cornelius Ryan, 1959 - The day referenced by the title is, of course, June 6, 1944 — D-Day — when Allied forces stormed the beaches of Normandy, France, as part of their overall plan to liberate Europe from the Nazis. Ryan, a journalist by trade, recreates the invasion from the perspective of its individual participants, i.e., American, British, French and German troops whom he interviewed in the fifties when their memories of that heroic and horrific day were still vivid in their minds.

EXCERPT: THE LONGEST DAY:

In a few short months Rommel's ruthless drive had changed the whole picture. On every beach where he considered a landing possible he had ordered his soldiers, working with local conscripted labor battalions, to erect barriers of crude anti-invasion obstacles. These obstacles — jagged triangles of steel, saw-toothed gatelike structures of iron, metal-tipped wooden stakes and concrete cones — were planted just below high- and low-tide water marks. Strapped to them were deadly mines. Where there were not enough mines, shells had been used, their noses pointing ominously out to sea. A touch would cause them to explode instantly.

Rommel's strange inventions (he had designed most of them himself) were both simple and deadly. Their object was to impale and destroy troop-filled landing craft or to obstruct them long enough for shore batteries to zero in. Either way, he reasoned, the enemy soldiers would be decimated long before they reached the beaches. More than half a million of these lethal underwater obstacles now stretched along the coastline.

7. **No Simple Victory: World War II in Europe, 1939-1945** by Norman Davies, 2007 - This controversial reappraisal of World War II in Europe questions the notion of the war being a titanic struggle between freedom and fascism; in fact, Davies argues, it was a titanic struggle between one dictatorship and another, i.e., Hitler's regime vs. Stalin's, with America and England playing but a secondary role. Whether you agree or not, this provocative work, with its point of view centered on Eastern Europe, rests on a foundation of solid scholarship.

8. **The Rape of Europa: The Fate of Europe's Treasures in the Third Reich and the Second World War** by Lynn H. Nicholas, 1994 – World War II was not only fought on the battlefield, but in museums, galleries and private art collections across war-torn Europe. This National Book Critics Circle Award-winning book

is an indispensable work on the Nazi's systematic plundering of European art and efforts by the Allies to hide it during the war and get it back afterwards. While Hitler dreamed of his "Fuehrermuseum" in Linz (Austria) that would exhibit only works "worthy" of the master race, his henchmen, Goering in particular, were busy making as much money as possible off the stolen masterpieces the Fuehrer had declared "degenerate."

9. **The Rise and Fall of the Third Reich: A History of Nazi Germany** by William L. Shirer, 1959 - Of late criticized in some quarters for its lack of objectivity, this extraordinary book on the Hitler era nevertheless deserves its vaunted status. Shirer, a CBS correspondent and an eyewitness to much of the history he writes about, has left us with a 1,500+-page tome based on personal observation, interviews and bushels of documents, most from the Nazis themselves, chronicling one of the most heinous regimes humanity has ever produced.

10. **The Second World War** by Winston S. Churchill, 1948-53 - Who better than perhaps the greatest Allied leader of World War II to bring us six, Nobel Prize-winning volumes that cover the war in Europe from Hitler's earliest stirrings to the advent of the Atomic Age? Start with the first volume, *The Gathering Storm,* and even if you're put off by some of the former Prime Minister's opinions about his empire's non-English subjects, you'll be astounded by how accurately he gauged Hitler's intentions so many years before the invasion of Poland.

11. **Stalingrad: The Fateful Siege: 1942-1943** by Antony Beevor, 1998 - In August 1942, Hitler's 6th Army reached Stalingrad, perhaps the last obstacle to Germany's complete domination of all of Europe. For five months, in a ferociously brutal battle that many believe ushered in the age of modern warfare, the Russian army stood its ground and eventually beat the Nazis back. Beevor interviewed survivors and pored over German and Russian archives in creating this acclaimed account of the battle that destroyed Hitler's dream of a thousand-year Reich.

WORLD WAR II NONFICTION
The War in the Pacific

The Pacific Ocean theatre in World War II was unlike any battleground in history, an archipelago of thousands of tropical islands populated with villagers whose first exposure to the outside world was the arrival of soldiers equipped for modern warfare. The human experience is central to every book highlighted here, along with essential details about the historic battles now regarded as turning points in the war. Pushing the boundaries of traditional historical and journalistic writing, these authors provide a variety of fresh perspectives in the following books, listed in alphabetical order.

1. **At Dawn We Slept : The Untold Story of Pearl Harbor** by Gordon W. Prange, 1981 – Decades of research went into Prange's definitive study of Pearl Harbor, and the result is a layered account of the attack and its aftermath from multiple points of view. Americans reacted with patriotism and belligerence, he writes, but another strong reaction is illuminated here: Many Americans saw Pearl Harbor is a failure of Roosevelt and the military intelligence community.

2. **The Battle of Midway** by Craig L. Symonds, 2011 – Retired Naval Academy history professor Craig L. Symonds chronicles the famous battle that changed the course of the war in mere minutes in June of 1942. He reveals how that fateful morning, when U.S. Navy dive bombers attacked Japanese aircraft carriers, was possible only through sophisticated code-breaking and a detailed to-the-minute plan of execution.

3. **Flags of Our Fathers** by James Bradley with Ron Powers, 2000 – The moving photograph of six U.S. soldiers planting the flag at Iwo Jima stirred emotions around the world — and continues to inspire today. But beyond the symbolic document is the true story of the G.I.s' battle on Suribachi Mountain, an experience far more difficult and tragic than the legend built around it.

4. **Ghost Soldiers: The Epic Account of World War II's Greatest Rescue Mission** by Hampton Sides, 2001 – Close to 500 American soldiers survived the Bataan death march, only to be held in dismal conditions at the Japanese POW camp on the Philippine island of Luzon. By interviewing survivors, Sides has crafted a riveting narrative of their experiences, and the heroic rescue mission that ended their ordeal.

EXCERPT: GHOST SOLIDERS:

The planes not only dropped bombs, they dropped words. As the battle dragged on, propaganda sheets had fluttered down from the skies. One leaflet depicted a voluptuous woman beckoning soldiers to bed down with her. "Before the terror comes, let me walk beside you . . . deep in petaled sleep. Let me, while there is still a time and place. Feel soft against me and . . . rest your warm hand on my breast." More recently the propaganda had turned from a tone of clumsy prurience to one of dark ultimatum.

Bataan is about to be swept away. Hopes for the arrival of reinforcements are quite in vain. If you continue to resist, the Japanese forces will by every possible means destroy and annihilate your forces relentlessly to the last man. Further resistance is completely useless. You, dear soldiers, give up your arms and stop resistance at once.

5. **Iwo Jima: World War II Veterans Remember the Greatest Battle of the Pacific** by Larry Smith, 2008 – The most personal account of this turning point in the war is

Larry Smith's *Iwo Jima*, a collection of interviews with twenty-two American soldiers who share recollections and feelings about an experience that shaped their lives.

6. **The Pacific** by Hugh Ambrose, 2010 – Ambrose's comprehensive history of the Pacific war is highly personalized and deeply affecting. By focusing on five individuals engaged in the war's most pivotal battles, he provides a moving, intimate narrative on the drama of battle, and the true experiences of G.I.s inside a Japanese prisoner-of-war camp.

7. **Pacific Crucible: War at Sea in the Pacific, 1941-1942** by Ian W. Toll, 2011 – This history of the first seven months of the Pacific war is both expansive and detailed, outlining broad U.S. naval strategy and the history of Japanese expansionism. Central to Toll's study are profiles of the individual analysts laboring to crack the Japanese wartime code in the months immediately after the Pearl Harbor invasion.

8. **The Rising Sun: The Decline and Fall of the Japanese Empire, 1936-1945** by John Toland, 1970 – Toland's Pulitzer Prize-winning history tells the story of the Japanese empire in World War II, and the culminating battles in the Pacific, from the Japanese perspective. It's a story both political and personal that the author describes as "a factual saga of people caught up in the flood of the most overwhelming war of mankind."

WORLD WAR II NOVELS
Stories of G. I. Joe

Ten years after he witnessed the Japanese attack on Pearl Harbor, 27th U.S. Infantry Regiment veteran James Jones burst onto the literary scene with *From Here to Eternity*, his gripping portrait of U.S. soldiers stationed in Honolulu in the days prior and immediately after the attack. Shocking in its day for Jones' frank portrayal of sex and liberal use of profanity, *From Here to Eternity* was an immediate critical and commercial sensation hailed for its authenticity. Jones would later draw upon his combat experiences in The Battle of Guadalcanal for *The Thin Red Line,* the second book in his World War II trilogy of novels. The last novel in the trilogy, *Whistle,* would be published in 1978 — a year after Jones' death. All three rank among the great World War II novels about the American soldiers' experiences in Europe and the Pacific — twelve of which are listed below, in alphabetical order.

1. **Articles of War** by Nick Arvin, 2005 – Drawing upon the wartime experiences of his grandfathers, Arvin makes an auspicious literary debut with this minimalist

prose account of a naïve, eighteen-year-old soldier's hellish combat experiences in the forests of northern France, circa 1944.

2. **A Bell for Adano** by John Hersey, 1944 – Two years before he wrote his classic piece of war reportage, ***Hiroshima,*** Hersey won the Pulitzer Prize for this novel, which depicts an Italian-American U.S. Army Major's life-changing experiences in a Sicilian village during the war.

3. **The Caine Mutiny** by Herman Wouk, 1951 – A petty dictator of the first rank, Captain Queeg of the *U.S.S. Caine* so alienates his crew that they overthrow him in Wouk's spellbinding novel, set in the Pacific theater.

4. **Catch-22** by Joseph Heller, 1961 – Heller's classic anti-war novel is a scathingly funny and audacious critique of military life. Based on a Mediterranean island off Italy, U.S. Army Air Force bombardier Captain John Yossarian runs up against the impossible paradox of "Catch-22" in his efforts to get out of duty.

5. **The Final Storm: A Novel of the War in the Pacific** by Jeff Shaara, 2011 – The son of the late Pulitzer Prize-winning novelist Michael Shaara (***The Killer Angels***), Jeff Shaara has written several critically acclaimed novels set against the backdrop of war (***Gods and Generals***, ***To the Last Man***). *The Final Storm* depicts the punishing battle for Okinawa with great verisimilitude and a strong feel for the psychological and physical toll the battle took on both the American and Japanese troops.

6. **From Here to Eternity** by James Jones, 1951 – The first novel in Jones' World War II trilogy essentially depicts the proverbial calm before the storm, i.e., the attack on Pearl Harbor. With unvarnished honesty, Jones portray the culture of military life —its rigid emphasis on hierarchy and order —and how it profoundly alters the fate of Jones' tragic hero, Private Robert E. Lee Prewitt.

EXCERPT: FROM HERE TO ETERNITY:

And as the last note quivered to prideful silence, and the bugler swung the megaphone for the traditional repeat, figures appeared in the lighted sallyport from inside of Choy's. "I told you it was Prewitt," a voice carried faintly across the quadrangle in the tone of a man who has won a bet. And then the repeat rose to join her quivering tearful sister. The clear proud notes reverberating back and forth across the silent quad. Men had come from the Dayrooms to the porches to listen in the darkness, feeling the sudden choking kinship bred of fear that supersedes all personal tastes. They stood in the darkness of the porches, listening, feeling suddenly very near the man beside them, who also was a soldier, who also must die.

7. **The Girl in the Blue Beret** by Bobbie Ann Mason, 2011 – Forty-four years after he was shot down over Occupied Europe, World War II pilot Marshall Stone returns

to find the people who helped him escape the Germans; he especially wants to find the title character, a beautiful teenager who's haunted his memories for decades. Inspired by the World War II experiences of her father-in-law, Mason's emotionally powerful novel was called "a near-perfect war story" by *USA Today.*

8. **Liberation Road** by David L. Robbins, 2004 – Dubbed the "Homer of World War II" by *Kirkus Reviews*, Robbins tackles the issue of racism in the armed forces with this powerful novel about the famed Red Ball Express: the U.S. Army supply trucks. *Liberation Road* chronicles the experiences of an African-American Red Ball Express truck driver and a Rabbi in the battlefields of Europe.

9. **The Naked and the Dead** by Norman Mailer, 1948 – Mailer established himself as one of the leading post-war novelists with *The Naked and the Dead*, a pulverizing and profane epic inspired by his own combat experiences in the South Pacific.

10. **The Thin Red Line** by James Jones, 1962 – Astonishing and disturbing evocation of the physical and psychological toll of combat on U.S. soldiers in the Battle of Guadalcanal.

11. **Whistle** by James Jones, 1978 – Jones died from congestive heart failure before he could finish *Whistle*, which was completed by writer Willie Morris, using Jones' notes. If *Whistle* pales somewhat in comparison to Jones' earlier books, it's still an intense, viscerally charged narrative about four casualties of Guadalcanal, returning home to a U.S. Army hospital.

12. **The Young Lions** by Irwin Shaw, 1948 – Published the same year as *The Naked and the Dead*, Shaw's unjustly neglected novel portrays the wartime experiences of three soldiers, two Americans and a German, whose paths will ultimately cross.

WORLD WARS I & II NONFICTION
Eyewitness Accounts

Why the war memoir? That's easy. Because history has a way of speaking in dates and occurrences that often omit the human side of things. It's up to those who actually lived through the period or battle described to fill in those gaps, to tell the story of what it was like to lie in a trench while under enemy bombardment, or to liberate a coral atoll from a foe determined to fight to the death. The lists below are far from definitive — the world wars were just that, *world* wars, meaning there were eyewitnesses to many battles and events in just as many countries and continents. But here are some of the most unforgettable memoirs that cover as wide a range of perspectives as possible. No matter which one(s) you choose to read, if the stamp of truth is evident, you'll have graduated from history major to student of the human condition. Listed alphabetically by title.

WORLD WAR I

1. **Goodbye to All That** by Robert Graves, 1929 - Poet Graves wrote this memoir when he was thirty-four-years-old, having survived not only the blood-soaked trenches of the Great War, but also his quintessentially English upbringing and education. Graves does not mince (nor waste) words, either in his caustic descriptions of war and death (as seen through the eyes of a twenty-one-year-old captain in the Royal Welsh Fusiliers), or in his vicious portrayal of England's stratified society and its "educational" system based, in his mind, on petty tyranny and ignorance. Wounded in the war, and submerged in its senseless butchery, Graves could not brook the patriotic platitudes of his fellow citizens back home. Perhaps he should have added "...and Good Riddance!" to the title of this classic remembrance.

EXCERPT: GOODBYE TO ALL THAT:

We were issued with a new gas-helmet, popularly known as "the goggle-eyed booger with the tit." It differed from the previous models. One breathed in through the nose from inside the helmet, and breathed out through a special valve held in the mouth; but I could not manage this. Boxing with an already broken nose had recently displaced the septum, which forced me to breathe through my mouth. In a gas-attack, I would be unable to use the helmet--the only type claimed to be proof against the newest German gas. The Battalion doctor advised a nose-operation as soon as possible.

I took his advice, and missed being with the First Battalion when the expected offensive started. Sixty per cent of my fellow-officers were killed in it. Scatter's dream of open warfare failed to materialize. He himself got very badly wounded. Of "A" Company choir, there is one survivor besides myself: C.D. Morgan, who had his thigh smashed, and was still in hospital some months after the War ended.

2. **Memoirs of an Infantry Officer** by Siegfried Sassoon, 1930 - Although this memoir masquerades as the tale of one George Sherston, it is without doubt the author's own story of life in the trenches and the shell shock that followed. Sassoon, who in his lifetime acquired renown as a poet, was, like many of his contemporaries, transformed from a patriot to a pacifist by the meaningless carnage and inept leadership he witnessed. Though contemptuous of the war, he could never abandon his fellow soldiers, whom he called "citizens of death's grey land, drawing no dividend from time's tomorrows."

3. **Old Soldiers Never Die** by Frank Richards, 1933 - This compelling memoir might have never seen the light of day had Richards not served alongside Robert Graves in the Royal Welsh Fusiliers. Graves was instrumental in the book's publication (with many even claiming he rewrote it), but such quibbles are secondary to the

impact of what Richards witnessed. Somehow, through sheer luck, he survived the war in one piece, at times escaping death by a fraction of a second; those fascinated by the Great War should be glad he did.

4. **Storm of Steel** by Ernst Jünger, 1920 - The French writer Andre Gide claimed Jünger's book was "without question the finest book on war that I know: utterly honest, truthful, in good faith." Gide did not gush alone; the book, written by a German who couldn't wait to enlist, was an international bestseller. Jünger seemed to revel in the war — conducting raids, protecting the trenches from British and French assaults, ready to keep fighting even as his fellow soldiers were blown to pieces. For him, war was not just the business of nations, but a barometer of his own worth.

5. **Testament of Youth** by Vera Brittain, 1933 - Vera Brittain was a twenty-one-year-old Englishwoman in 1914, ready to attend Oxford. The outbreak of World War I nearly ended her plans, but it was her engagement to a young soldier that altered them forever. As a testament to her love, she volunteered as a nurse, only to learn soon after that her fiancé had perished at the front. Given duty in Malta and then France, she witnessed the war's carnage firsthand; by the time it was over, she had also lost a brother and many friends. Her book is a memorial to a generation wiped out by war and a society irrevocably changed by it.

WORLD WAR II

6. **Farewell to Manzanar** by Jeanne Wakatsuki Houston and James D. Houston, 1973 - This World War II memoir is not about a battle but a disgrace. Jeanne Wakatsuki was a child in America when the Japanese attacked Pearl Harbor — a few months later, she and her family were being carted off to an internment camp in the California desert. They were stripped of their civil, legal and economic rights; forced to survive harsh conditions; left to come to terms with one another and the society that had wronged them; and perhaps most painfully of all, asked to pick their fractured lives back up again once the war was over.

7. **Goodbye, Darkness: A Memoir of the Pacific War** by William Manchester, 1980 – Manchester fought with the Marines in Okinawa and was haunted by the experience long after the war had come to an end. He eventually returned to Japan, to the places he had visited — and fought over — as a young soldier, only to discover that much of his discomfiture toward the Japanese had not abated. "A gripping, haunting book," according to William L. Shirer.

8. **Inside the Third Reich** by Albert Speer, 1969 - Languishing in Spandau prison for twenty years, Albert Speer, who had served Hitler as both an architect and arms minister, decided to write about his past. It was to become a riveting look at the inner workings of the Hitler government and the Fuehrer himself. Speer begins with his childhood, but the memoir deals mostly with the fourteen years that

Speer served his Nazi master. He portrays himself as having practiced "Nazism-lite," suggesting that he fell helplessly under Hitler's spell, and that he had no knowledge of the regime's appalling atrocities. The verdict may never come in, but how many Nazi inner-circle eyewitnesses lived to tell about it?

9. **No Surrender: A World War II Memoir** by James Sheeran, 2011 - Written toward the end of his life and published posthumously, Sheeran's book tells the remarkable story of an American paratrooper who was part of the D-Day invasion of Nazi-occupied France. Sheeran survived the landing but was later captured by the Germans who starved him, made him march through gunfire during American attacks, and then put him in a jammed boxcar bound for Germany. He and some comrades escaped the train and found their way to a French village where they ended up fighting with the French Resistance. It's a story that hauntingly demonstrates the limits of human endurance.

10. **With the Old Breed: At Peleliu and Okinawa** by Eugene B. Sledge, 1981 – As the title reveals, the Alabama-born Sledge, as a PFC in the famed 1st Marine Division-3rd Battalion, 5th Marines, fought in two of the most hellishly deadly battles of the war in the Pacific — campaigns that brought forth the full gamut of barbarity and heroism co-existing in the hearts of men. Sledge's powerful memoir provided source material for both Ken Burns' documentary *The War* and the Emmy Award-winning HBO miniseries, *The Pacific*.

11. **Unbroken: A World War II Story of Survival, Resilience and Redemption** by Laura Hillenbrand, 2010 - Louis Zamperini competed in the 1936 Berlin Olympics, got shot down over the Pacific during World War II, and then survived forty-seven harrowing days in a life raft and two years in a Japanese prison camp run by a pitiless monster. In 2003, he told his story in ***Devil at My Heels: A Heroic Olympian's Astonishing Story of Survival as a Japanese POW in World War II***, but Hillenbrand, best-selling author of ***Seabiscuit***, has told it better, turning it into a page-turner worthy of the incredible saga it is. Read Hillenbrand's book and you'll hardly believe that Zamperini could have survived, let alone still be alive well into his nineties.

WRITER'S GUIDES
Books for Aspiring Authors

Becoming a writer doesn't absolutely require formal training in the way that, say, becoming a concert pianist does. But there are times when a good book by an experienced writer or teacher can provide the inspiration, insights, and motivation that you need to get to work and find your own voice. Here are twelve books, listed alphabetically, to inspire and instruct you on the craft of writing.

1. **Bird by Bird: Some Instructions on Writing and Life** by Annie Lamott, 1994 – A funny, wise, and practical book on overcoming writer's block and other challenges to experience the joy of writing for its own sake.

EXCERPT: BIRD BY BIRD:

You are going to love some of your characters, because they are you or some facet of you, and you are going to hate some of your characters for the same reason. But no matter what, you are probably going to have to let bad things happen to some of the characters you love or you won't have much of a story. Bad things happen to good characters, because our actions have consequences, and we do not all behave perfectly all the time. As soon as you start protecting your characters from the ramifications of their less-than-lofty behavior, your story will start to feel flat and pointless, just like in real life.

2. **The Elements of Style** by William Strunk, Jr., and E.B. White, 1959 – The all-time classic on writing good prose in English, with advice like "Prefer the specific to the general, the definite to the vague, the concrete to the abstract" and the pithy "Omit needless words."

3. **The Elephants of Style: A Trunkload of Tips on the Big Issues and Gray Areas of Contemporary American English** by Bill Walsh, 2004 – The author, a witty and alert copy editor for the *Washington Post*, shares his well-reasoned, up-to-date views on some of the nuts and bolts of using the English language.

4. **The Emotion Thesaurus: A Writer's Guide To Character Expression** by Angela Ackerman and Becca Puglisi, 2012 – For the writer who struggles to convey their characters' emotions, *The Emotion Thesaurus* provides a list of seventy-five emotions and the physical cues that go with each. Emphasizing the "show, not tell" school of character development, the authors stress the use of body language, so readers can sense the emotion in play on a deeper, visceral level.

5. **On Becoming a Novelist** by John Gardner, 1983 –. An uncompromising look at what it takes to write serious fiction, as well as the benefits and dangers of workshops. Gardner also shares advice on how to deal with editors and the frustration of rejections and the use of self-hypnosis to prepare for a good writing session.

6. **On Writing** by Eudora Welty, 2002 – One of the greatest Southern writers shares her advice and insights on the "mystery" of fiction writing in seven essays that address the importance of place, voice and language in narrative.

7. **On Writing: A Memoir of the Craft** by Stephen King, 2000 – The hugely successful horror writer discusses how his wife salvaged an early draft of ***Carrie*** from the trash, the importance of wide-ranging reading, how to revise, and the elements of a good story.

8. **The Spooky Art: Some Thoughts on Writing** by Norman Mailer, 2003 – Mailer describes the process of writing *The Naked and the Dead*, offers insights into both technical and philosophical aspects of fiction, and exhorts writers to be courageous artists.

9. **Spunk and Bite: A Writer's Guide to Punchier, More Engaging Language & Style** by Arthur Plotnik, 2005 – While no book is likely to topple Strunk and White's *Elements of Style* from the literary pantheon, *Spunk and Bite* is an exhilaratingly different approach to writing. Using excerpts from masters of vivid prose to illustrate his points, Plotnik reminds us of the value of invention, rule-breaking, and even wildness in literature.

10. **Storycraft: The Complete Guide to Writing Narrative Nonfiction** by Jack Hart, 2011 – From his experience as a managing editor at *The Oregonian* newspaper, Hart shares his knowledge of narrative nonfiction, a style that emerged in the sixties. Hart focuses on story theory and point of view as basic elements of the style, and provides guidance on how aspiring writers can edit their stories for publication.

11. **Writing Down the Bones: Freeing the Writer Within** by Natalie Goldberg, 1986 – Drawing on her experiences as a Zen Buddhist, Goldberg offers stories and exercises to help you "lose control" of your writing and reach new levels of creativity.

12. **The Writing Life** by Annie Dillard, 1989 – This is less a how-to book than an exploration of the hardships, joys, and mystery of the writing life. The author of *Pilgrim at Tinker Creek*, Dillard is an ideal person to accompany on the search for meaning and beauty.

YOUNG ADULT NOVELS
Michael L. Printz Award Winners, 2000-2012

Sponsored by *Booklist*, a magazine published by the American Library Association, the Michael L. Printz Award is given yearly to a book that "exemplifies literary excellence in young adult literature." (Printz was a school librarian involved with YALSA, the Young Adult Library Services Association, a division of the ALA; he had a knack for discovering compelling new books.) Here are the winners since the prize was first given in 2000, listed in chronological order.

1. **2000 Winner: Monster** by Walter Dean Myers, 1999 – This is the story of sixteen-year-old Steve, who is charged with involvement in a robbery that turns murderous. It's told through Steve's own eyes via journal entries and the unusual device of a screenplay that he writes about his experience.

2. **2001 Winner: Kit's Wilderness** by David Almond, 1999 – Thirteen-year-old Kit moves with his parents to an old coal-mining town in Northern England where his family has roots and where a death-haunted past seems quite alive. A thirteen-year-old relative with his own full name, Christopher Watson, in fact, perished in a mining disaster in 1821, bringing Kit even closer to the dark local history.

3. **2002 winner: A Step From Heaven** by An Na, 2001 – Young Jug, a Korean girl who moves to California at the age of four, grows up caught between her family's traditional values and the life of an American schoolgirl. She eventually finds her way, even as her family struggles and eventually dissolves. **ONLINE DETAIL**

4. **2003 Winner: Postcards From No Man's Land** by Aidan Chambers, 2002 – This novel is set in nineties-era Amsterdam, where a seventeen-year-old boy visits the woman who nursed his grandfather long ago during World War II, and the Amsterdam of a half-century earlier, seen through this woman's eyes. The boy's time in the city is marked by revelations both confusing and enlightening.

5. **2004 Winner: The First Part Last** by Angela Johnson, 2003 – A teenage boy becomes a father in this moving and serious story. Bobby's girlfriend Nina, for reasons that don't become clear until late in the book, has no part in taking care of their child. He makes the decision on his own to raise little Feather, accepting the burdens and rewards of parenthood.

6. **2005 Winner: How I Live Now** by Meg Roof, 2004 - Fifteen-year-old Daisy leaves her home in New York and goes to England to stay in the country with her aunt and cousins. Her life there is emotionally intense, but outwardly tranquil — until terrorists invade England and everything changes in this engrossing story of love, war, and growth.

7. **2006 Winner: Looking for Alaska** by John Green, 2005 – Miles Halter flees his lackluster life at home to look for the "Great Perhaps" at boarding school. For the first time he makes what he considers real friends, connecting with his roommate Chip and the beautiful but troubled Alaska on a level he's never experienced. But his new life offers grief as well as joy.

8. **2007 Winner: American Born Chinese** by Gene Lune Yang, 2007 – A National Book Award finalist, Yang's imaginative and insightfully written graphic novel tackles the issues of cultural identity and self-acceptance in three interwoven storylines: a lonely middle school student struggling to fit in with his classmates; a popular teen embarrassed by his visiting Chinese cousin; and the mythic character of the Monkey King, who feels snubbed by the gods.

9. **2008 Winner: The White Darkness** by Geraldine McCaughrean, 2007 – Obsessed with the Antarctic, fourteen-year-old Sym seeks refuge from her loneliness

through an imaginary friendship with Titus Oates, a real-life member of Robert Scott's doomed 1912 expedition to the South Pole. When her uncle invites her to join him on a trip to Antarctica, Sym is thrilled — until she realizes that her uncle has an ulterior motive for exploring "The Ice."

10. **2009 Winner: Jellicoe Road** by Melina Marchetta, 2008 – Although its complex back story demands your complete attention, the dramatic pay-off is well worth it in Marchetta's absorbing young adult mystery, set in the author's native Australia. Abandoned by her mother years ago, a seventeen-year-old boarding school student gradually discovers clues about her past while reading the manuscript of a dorm proctor, who's recently disappeared under mysterious circumstances.

11. **2010 Winner: Going Bovine** by Libba Bray, 2009 – A witty and surreal riff on ***Don Quixote***, Bray's narrative chronicles the experiences of a sixteen year-old slacker diagnosed with mad cow disease. Determined to escape the hospital and find a cure, he embarks on what may be a hallucinatory quest in the spirit of Cervantes' hero, accompanied by a Mexican-American dwarf hypochondriac.

12. **2011 Winner: Ship Breaker** by Paolo Bacigalupi, 2010 – Acclaimed science fiction writer Bacigalupi tries his hand at young adult fiction and succeeds with this gripping, post-apocalyptic saga, set on the Gulf Coast. Scavenging copper wire from grounded oil tankers to survive, a teenage boy discovers a girl trapped on a clipper ship. Torn between his desire to plunder the ship or help her, he struggles with his decision in this fast-paced, darkly realized novel.

EXCERPT: SHIP BREAKER:

Bright tropic sunlight and ocean salt breezes bathed him. All around, sledgehammers rang against iron as swarms of men and women clambered over the ancient oil tanker, tearing it apart. Heavy crews peeled away iron panels with acetylene torches and sent them wafting off the sides like palm leaves, crashing to the beach sands below, where more crews dragged the scavenge above high tide. Light crews like Nailer's tore at the ship's small fittings, stripping copper, brass, nickel, aluminum, and stainless steel. Others hunted for hidden petrol and ship oil pockets, bucketing out the valuable fluid. An ant's nest of activity, all dedicated to rendering this extinct ship's bones into something usable for a new world.

13. **2012 Winner: Where Things Come Back** by John Corey Whaley, 2011 – In 2011, Whaley became the first young adult novelist to be named one of the "Top 5 Under 35" writers by the National Book Foundation. Calling it a "novel about second chances," Whaley depicts the tumultuous summer of a high school

student, desperate to escape his small Arkansas hometown, where a long-thought extinct woodpecker has suddenly reappeared.

ZOMBIES
The Walking Dead in Fiction

Unlike the literature of their supernatural counterparts — ghosts, vampires, werewolves and other creatures of the night — zombie fiction is a relatively new subgenre. Zombies have traditionally been more of a subject for films (and now television, with the smash cable adaptation of the graphic novel ***The Walking Dead***) — but not anymore. The undead are now prowling bookshelves in unprecedented numbers. In fact, Amazon currently lists more than 12,000 zombie titles, which run the gamut from the stomach-churning horror to sly parody; there's even ***The Zombie Cookbook***! Here are eight of the most noteworthy titles in zombie literature, listed alphabetically by author.

1. **Pride and Prejudice and Zombies** by Jane Austen and Seth Grahame-Smith, 2009 – What sounds like a one-joke gimmick turns out to be surprisingly clever and entertaining mash-up of Austen's romantic classic and zombie fiction. Between attending fancy dress balls and trading barbs with the handsome zombie hunter Mr. Darcy, Elizabeth Bennett deftly fends off the undead with her martial arts skills and weapon training in Regency-era England.

2. **World War Z: An Oral History of the Zombie War** by Max Brooks, 2006 – Firsthand accounts from the survivors of the zombie war that nearly wiped out humanity. Written in the style of the great oral historian Studs Terkel, *World War Z: An Oral History of the Zombie War* was hailed as a "milestone in the zombie mythology" by *Booklist*.

EXCERPT: WORLD WAR Z:

You said they didn't call for a doctor, that they were afraid they'd be sent back, but why try to find a cure in the west?

You really don't understand a refugee's heart, do you? These people were desperate. They were trapped between their infections and being rounded up and "treated" by their own government. If you had a loved one, a family member, a child, who was infected, and you thought there was a shred of hope in some other country, wouldn't you do everything in your power to get there? Wouldn't you want to believe there was hope?

3. **The Zombie Survival Guide: Complete Protection from the Living Dead** by Max Brooks, 2003 – Here's what you'll wish you knew when the flesh-eating undead

come chomping at your door. There are sections devoted to the relative merits of different pieces of weaponry, zombie psychology, strategic and tactical maneuvers, and the zombies' relative success in previous undead invasions (!).

4. **The Rising** by Brian Keene, 2003 – A scientist tries to reach his son after a supercollider experiment brings the dead back to life. *The Rising* did much to jumpstart the current fad of zombie fiction, and was followed by ***City of the Dead*** and several others in the genre.

5. **Cell** by Stephen King, 2006 – The modern master of horror fiction pays terrifying homage to the zombie genre with *Cell*, which pits "normies" like hero Clayton Riddell against raging hordes of mindless, soulless zombies. What precipitated this nightmare? Cell phone usage. Turn yours off while reading *Cell*, which King dedicated to Richard Matheson and *Night of the Living Dead* filmmaker George Romero.

6. **Death Has Come Up Into Our Windows (The Zombie Bible)** by Stant Litore, 2011– How would ancient Hebrews — particularly the prophet Jeremiah — have responded to a zombie invasion? Litore's book is no one-joke stunt, but a thought-provoking read that doesn't stint on the gore zombie fiction fans expect from the genre.

7. **Monster Island: A Zombie Novel** by David Wellington, 2004 – Manhattan is overrun by zombies, but one of them, Gary Fleck, retains traces of his former humanity. When a team of East African child soldiers arrives to look for a serum to combat the zombie plague, they run up against Gary and the undead in Wellington's satisfying thriller. The first in a trilogy, *Monster Island* was followed by ***Monster Nation*** and ***Monster Planet***.

8. **Zone One** by Colson Whitehead, 2011 – Best known for his acclaimed novels ***John Henry Days*** and ***Sag Harbor,*** Whitehead dives into zombie fiction with this dark-humored and chilling novel, set in a post-zombie apocalypse New York City, that *Esquire* called "one of the best books of the year."

16466395R00143

Made in the USA
Middletown, DE
17 December 2014